Communards

The story of the Paris Commune of 1871,
As told by those who fought for it

Texts selected, edited, and translated by
Mitchell Abidor
and published by the Marxists Internet Archive, 2010

Marxists Internet Archive
P.O. Box 1541; Pacifica, CA 94044; USA.

CC-SA (Creative Commons Attribution-Share Alike 3.0)
2010 by Marxists Internet Archive
Second Edition, 2018
Printed by Bookmasters, Inc., Ohio.
Cover design by Joan Levinson.
Distributed exclusively by Erythrós Press and Media.

Blanqui, Louis-Auguste; Rochefort, Henri; Reclus, Élie; Marancourt, Léon Massenet de; Malon, Benoît; Da Costa, Gaston; Vermersch, Eugène; Pottier, Eugène.
Abidor, Mitchell
        Communards.
ISBN: 978-0-9805428-9-9

For Joan

Contents

Introduction 1
Timeline of the Civil War in France 6
Prologue 13
Ephemera of the Siege and the Commune 15
The End of the Commune 37
Louis-Auguste Blanqui: "La Patrie en Danger" 38
Inquiry on the Commune 50
Élie Reclus: The Paris Commune Day by Day 87
Men and Things from the Time of the Commune 124
Benoît Malon: The Third Defeat of the French Working Class 153
Gaston Da Costa: The Commune Lived 165
Debate on the Hostages and the Committee of Public Safety 183
The Sessions of the International in Paris During the Commune 204
Eugène Vermersch: The Incendiaries 266
A Word to the Public 281
Epilogue 285
Biographical Index of Names of Communards Mentioned in Texts 287

Introduction

Commune member and National Guard general Antoine Brunel said that the revolution that began on March 18, 1871 was "provoked by a patriotic sentiment," and he was right. For Benoît Malon, member of the Commune and the International Workingmen's Association, the Commune was essentially a socialist undertaking, and he too was right. Gaston Da Costa, a follower of the great revolutionary conspirator Louis-Auguste Blanqui and deputy procurator of the Commune, saw the Commune as continuation of the Jacobin tradition of the first great French Revolution, and he too was right. The journalist and poet Maxime Vermersch saw in the flames set by the dying Commune a foretaste of the purifying revolution that was still to come, and he also was right. Massenet de Marancour, leader of a National Guard battalion and participant in the Commune's battles, saw the entire event as the working class falling into a trap set by the bourgeoisie so the latter could have done with any threat to their rule, and he was right as well.

The Commune, the first instance of a working class seizure of power, of, as Engels later said, the dictatorship of the proletariat, was noble, heroic, and doomed from the start. It was also, as these pages will show, gloriously polyphonic. No one voice dominated the Commune, nor was there any attempt by any of the factions that participated in it to impose one viewpoint. Everything that had been stifled by nearly twenty years of Bonapartist dictatorship exploded and was given free rein during the two and a half months the Commune lived. Every current of opinion had seats on the Commune, all of them had newspapers, and all of them distributed posters expressing their views. It is this multiplicity of voices will be recalled here.

The currents that fed into and led to the Commune had struggled to survive under the repression of the Second Empire, when neo-Jacobins, followers of Blanqui, radical republicans, neo-Babouvist communists, and socialists of all stripes published newspapers that were, as Maxime Vuillaume recounts in these pages, quickly banned. They published pamphlets that were seized, held meetings that were broken up, and went into exile, prison, or were assassinated. This multitude of viewpoints, united only in the drive to overthrow Napoleon III and establish a republic—social or otherwise—carried over to the legislative body they formed in March 1871, the Commune, and the society they attempted to construct within the walls of Paris. As these pages will reveal, both at the time and in the post-mortems that followed its defeat, there was much disagreement as to what the priorities of that that legislature and that society should be. No one involved in the Commune denied that mistakes were made, but just what these mistakes were remains an open question. The debates were lively, the disagreements strong, and they are all presented here.

If the writings included here, in their occasional hints at the futility of the events, resemble the analyses that appear on every ten-year anniversary of May 1968, they more nearly resemble those writings produced in the aftermath of two far more consequential events: the Spanish Civil War of 1936-1939 and Allende's Popular Unity government in Chile of 1970-1973. In these two events the stakes were infinitely higher than those in 1968.

Did the Parisians of the Commune go too far in proclaiming their own government in opposition to the established state? Did they go too far in declaring its socialist measures, in the tearing down of the Vendôme column, in the execution of the hostages? Or did they not go far enough? Should they have seized the money in the Bank of France, been more repressive, executed hostages early on, as their Versaillais enemies did?

Similarly, in Spain, who was right: those in the Republican camp who believed that revolutionary measures should be taken immediately in order to ensure working class and peasant support for the Republic, or those—particularly the Communists—who believed that victory over the fascists was the primary goal and that only once that was achieved should radical steps be taken? And in Chile, those who survived the military coup of September 11, 1973 continue to debate the wisdom of Allende's having maintained his policies, or even remaining in power, once it became clear that a military solution was a real threat. Others, however, feel that the coup's success was owed in large part to Allende's failure to arm the working class and take advantage of the sentiment behind the popular chant: "Allende, Allende, el pueblo te defiende," Allende, Allende, the people defend you!

Such debates are unavoidable after a failed revolution—even in the case of successful ones—and are irresolvable, as is any historical counter-factual. And so a reading of the accounts of the Commune, of its ephemera, of the minutes from its political meetings and governmental body, serve as a veritable type for the analysis of revolutionary events everywhere. In the Commune one can see a foreshadowing of all the revolutionary history that was to follow.

The Communal revolution was fought at the barricades, but also within the Commune itself, at rallies, in the newspapers, on the streets, on the walls, and at the meetings of the Parisian sections of International Workingmen's Association, and all of them have a voice here.

What we will not hear are the voices of supporters, critical and otherwise, from afar, or neutral or partisan historians working from documents. The Commune was in a fight for its life from the moment of its birth, and the members of the Commune, the officers and soldiers of the National Guard, the Commune's administrators, and the people who took up arms in its defense behind the barricades didn't have the leisure to reflect calmly on events. Across the border, across the Channel, across an ocean, it is relatively easy to make considered decisions. In these pages only those who were there at the time describe and judge the days in Paris between March 18 and May 28, 1871, for only they paid the consequences of these decisions.

The writers who figure here were not the literary lights of France. This class, the Flauberts and the Zolas and their fellow *gens de lettres*, detested the Commune, and in their private and public writings didn't attempt to disguise their hatred. Théophile Gautier spoke of "the gorillas of the Commune," Flaubert's friend Maxime Du Camp described them as "obtuse brutes," and Emile Zola, who distinguished himself as the voice of republican reason in the last decades of the nineteenth century, praised the massacres of the Bloody Week as "a horrible necessity to calm certain of [the people's] fevers." Some writers, such as Rimbaud, Verlaine, and Victor Hugo supported the Commune, and Jules Vallès, revolutionary journalist and member of the Commune, produced the sole great novel of the revolution, *L'Insurgé* (*The Rebel*), the final volume of his autobiographical trilogy. The writers found here were revolutionaries first and writers second.

There is another important conclusion to be drawn from this anthology. In 1891 Engels wrote in his preface to the twentieth anniversary edition of Marx's analysis of the Commune, *The Civil War in France,* "Look at the Commune. That was the dictatorship of the proletariat." Engels's opinion, was correct as well. As co-inventor of the term "dictatorship of the proletariat," he could not be wrong, since the dictatorship of the proletariat was whatever he said it was. And so if we view the Commune through the writings that follow, we get a different view of the meaning and destiny of the term "dictatorship of the proletariat."

For Engels (and Marx), aside from the fact that it was a government made up of workers, the most important characteristic was that "it filled all posts—administrative, judicial, and educational—by election on the basis of universal suffrage of all concerned, subject to the right of recall at any time by the electors. And, in the second place, all officials, high or low, were paid only the same wages received by other workers."

If this Paris Commune, with its flaws and errors, with its countless political currents, with its furious disagreements, with its polyphony of voices was

Engels's dictatorship of the proletariat, then none of its heirs can claim that title.

Repression played no part in this dictatorship, and though pro-Versailles newspapers were ultimately banned, this ban met strong opposition, not least from as uncompromising a revolutionary as Jules Vallès. No school of thought was silenced, and even bourgeois candidates were elected to the Commune, though they immediately resigned, feeling they had no place on that body.

The Commune's experience puts the lie to those who would later defend revolutionary regimes' explanation that they must crush dissent because they were under siege. From the moment of its foundation the Commune was under literal state of siege, yet it remained a democratic body. Perhaps as later critics maintained, most violently Leon Trotsky in his *Terrorism and Communism*, this played a part in its fall; perhaps, as many of the contributors here say, it should have spent more time fighting and organizing defense and less time legislating. But it is of more than passing interest that when in its final two weeks the Commune formed a body with near-dictatorial powers, the Committee of Public Safety, it was those in the Commune closest to Marx, the "minority" made up of members of the Parisian sections of the International Workingmen's Association, who announced they could no longer sit on the Commune because it had abdicated its powers.

The Commune, with its memory of universal suffrage, the right to recall, a free press, and working-class power, lived only seventy-two days, yet it can still serve as an inspiration, it can still touch all whose hearts are on the left. These pages will serve as a reminder that another path was, and is, possible for those who hope for revolutionary change.

*

A note on the selections. The guiding principle here was to not only represent all the points of view within the pro-Commune camp, but also to provide translations of texts previously unknown in English. P.O. Lissagaray's history is readily available, both in book form and online, so his masterpiece isn't excerpted here. Jules Vallès's autobiographical novel covering the Commune, *The Rebel*, has also been translated into English. Most of the writers here are all but unknown to an Anglophone readership, yet they provide vital insights into the life of the Paris Commune.

Louis-Auguste Blanqui, *La Patrie en Danger*. Poulet-Malassis, Paris, 1862.

La Revue Blanche, 1897.

INTRODUCTION

Élie Reclus, *La Commune de Paris au Jour le Jour.* Schleicher, Paris, 1908.

Hommes et Choses du Temps de la Commune. [N.P.], Paris, 1871.

Benoît Malon, *La Troisième Defaite du Prolétariat Français..*, G. Guillaume fils, Neuchatel, 1871.

Gaston Da Costa, *La Commune Vécue*. Librairies-Imprimeries Réunies, Paris, 1903-05.

Les Séances Officielles de l'Internationale à Paris. Lachaud, Paris, 1872.

Eugène Vermersch, *Les Incendiaires*. Temps Nouveaux, Paris, 1910.

Eugène Vermersch, *Mot au Public*. [N.P.], London, 1874.

Réimpression du Journal Officiel de la République Française. Victor Bunel, Paris, 1871.

Eugène Pottier, *Chants Révolutionnaires*. Bureau du Comité Pottier, Paris, 1900.

The author would like to thank the following individuals:

Mike Bessler, for his tireless work as a distributor.

Curtis Price, for providing a copy of Jean Maitron's *Dictionnaire biographique du mouvement ouvrier français*, without which the biographical notes would have been impossible.

Andy Blunden, for his enthusiasm and advice.

And Joan Levinson, for her editing skills, support, and patience while I lived in the Spring of 1871.

> Mitchell Abidor
> Brooklyn, New York
> September 2010

Timeline of the Civil War in France

1870

January 10 Approximately 100,000 people demonstrate against Bonaparte's Second Empire after the death of Victor Noir, a republican journalist killed by the Emperor's cousin, Pierre Bonaparte.

May 8 A national plebiscite votes confidence in the Empire with about 84% of votes in favor. On the eve of the plebiscite, members of the Paris Federation were arrested on a charge of conspiring against Napoleon III. This pretext was further used by the government to launch a campaign of persecution of the members of the International throughout France.

July 19 After a diplomatic struggle over the Prussian attempt for the Spanish throne, Louis Bonaparte declares war on Prussia.

July 23 Marx completes what will become known as his "First Address," rejecting any national antagonism between German and French workers.

July 26 The "First Address" is approved and internationally distributed by the General Council of the International Working Men's Association.

August 4-6 Crown Prince Frederick, commanding one of the three Prussian armies invading France, defeats French Marshal MacMahon at Worth and Weissenburg, pushes him out of Alsace (northeastern France), surrounds Strasbourg, and drives on towards Nancy. The other two Prussian armies isolate Marshal Bazaine's forces in Metz.

August 16-18 French Commander Bazaine's efforts to break his soldiers through the German lines are bloodily defeated at Mars-la-Tour and Gravelotte. The Prussians advance on Chalons.

September 1 Battle of Sedan. MacMahon and Bonaparte, attempting to relieve Bazaine at Metz and finding the road closed, enter battle and are defeated at Sedan.

September 2 Emperor Napoleon III and Marshal MacMahon capitulate at Sedan with more than 83,000 soldiers.

September 4 At news of Sedan, Paris workers invade the Palais Bourbon and force the Legislative Assembly to proclaim the fall of the Empire. By evening, the Third Republic is proclaimed at the Hôtel de Ville (the City Hall) in Paris. The provisional Government of National Defence (GND) is established to continue the war effort to remove Germany from France.

September 5 A series of meetings and demonstrations begin in London and other big cities, at which resolutions and petitions are passed demanding that the British Government immediately recognize the French Republic. The General Council of the First International take a direct part in the organization of this movement.

September 6 GND issues statement blaming war on Imperial government. It now wants peace, but "not an inch of our soil, not a stone of our fortresses, will we cede." With Prussia occupying Alsace-Lorraine, the war does not stop.

September 19 Two German armies begin the long siege of Paris. Bismarck figures the "soft and decadent" French workers will quickly surrender. The GND sends a delegation to Tours, soon to be joined by Gambetta (who escapes from Paris in a balloon), to organize resistance in the provinces.

October 27 French army, led by Bazaine with 140,000-180,000 men at Metz, surrenders.

October 30 French National Guard is defeated at Le Bourget.

October 31 Upon the receipt of news that the Government of National Defense had decided to start negotiations with the Prussians, Paris workers and revolutionary sections of the National Guard rise up in revolt, led by Blanqui. They seize the Hôtel de Ville (City Hall) and set up their revolutionary government—the Committee of Public Safety, headed by Blanqui. On October 31, Flourens prevents any members of the Government of National Defense from being shot, as had been demanded by one of the insurrectionists.

November 1 Under pressure from the workers, the Government of National Defense promises to resign and schedule national elections to the Commune—promises it has no intention of keeping. With the workers pacified by their "legal" charade, the government violently seizes the Hôtel de Ville and re-establishes its domination over the besieged city. Paris official Blanqui is arrested for treason.

1871

January 22 The Paris proletariat and the National Guards hold a revolutionary demonstration, initiated by the Blanquists. They demand the overthrow of the government and the establishment of a Commune. By order of the Government of National Defense, the Breton Mobile Guard, which was defending the Hôtel de Ville, opens fire on the demonstrators. After massacring the unarmed workers, the government begins preparations to surrender Paris to the Germans.

January 28 After four long months of workers' struggle, Paris is surrendered to the Prussians. While all regular troops are disarmed, the National Guard is permitted to keep their arms—the population of Paris remains armed and allows the occupying armies only a small section of the city.

February 8 Elections are held in France, unknown to most of the nation's population.

February 12 New National Assembly opens at Bordeaux; two-thirds of members are conservatives and wish the war to end.

February 16 The Assembly elects Adolphe Thiers chief executive.

February 26 The preliminary peace treaty between France and Germany signed at Versailles by Thiers and Jules Favre, on the one hand, and Bismarck, on the other. France surrenders Alsace and East Lorraine to Germany and pays it indemnities to the sum of five billion francs. German army of occupation slowly withdraws as indemnity payments made. The final peace treaty is signed in Frankfort-on-Main on May 10, 1871.

March 1-3 After months of struggle and suffering, Paris workers react angrily to the entry of German troops in the city and the ceaseless capitulation of the government. The National Guard defects and organizes a Central Committee.

March 10 The National Assembly passes a law on the deferred payment of overdue bills; under this law the payment of debts on obligations concluded between August 13 and November 12, 1870 could be deferred. Thus, the law leads to the bankruptcy of many petty bourgeoisie.

March 11 National Assembly adjourns. With trouble in Paris, it establishes its government at Versailles on March 20.

March 18 Adolphe Thiers attempts to disarm Paris and sends French troops (regular army), but, through fraternization with Paris workers, the troops refuse to carry out their orders. Generals Claude Martin Lecomte and Jacques Leonard Clement Thomas are killed by their own soldiers. Many troops peacefully withdraw; some remain in Paris. With Thiers outraged, the Civil War begins.

March 26 A municipal council—the Paris Commune—is elected by the citizens of Paris. Commune consists of workers, among them members of the First International and followers of Proudhon and Blanqui.

March 28 The Central Committee of the National Guard, which up to then had carried on the government, resigns after it first decrees the permanent abolition of the "Morality Police."

March 30 The Commune abolishes conscription and the standing army; the National Guard, in which all citizens capable of bearing arms are to be enrolled, becomes the sole armed force. The Commune remits all payments of rent for dwelling houses from October 1870 until April 1871. On the same day the foreigners elected to the Commune are confirmed in office, because "the flag of the Commune is the flag of the World Republic."

April 1 The Commune declares that the highest salary received by any member of the Commune does not exceed 6,000 francs

April 2 In order to suppress the Paris Commune, Thiers appeals to Bismarck for permission to supplement the Versailles Army with French prisoners of war, most of whom had been serving in the armies that surrendered at Sedan and Metz. In return for the five billion francs indemnity payment, Bismarck agrees. The French Army begins siege of Paris. Paris is continually bombarded and, moreover, by the very people who had stigmatized as a sacrilege the bombardment of the same city by the Prussians.

The Commune decrees the separation of the Church from the State and the abolition of all state payments for religious purposes as well as the transformation of all Church property into national property. Religion is declared a purely private matter.

April 5 Decree on hostages adopted by the Commune in an attempt to prevent Communards from being shot by the French Government. Under this decree, all persons found guilty of being in contact with the French Government are declared hostages. This decree is never carried out.

April 6 The guillotine is brought out by the 137th battalion of the National Guard and publicly burnt, amid great popular rejoicing.

April 7 On April 7, the French army captures the Seine crossing at Neuilly, on the western front of Paris.

Reacting to French government policy of shooting captured Communards, Commune issues an "eye-for-an-eye" policy statement, threatening retaliation. The bluff is quickly called; Paris workers execute no one.

April 8 A decree excluding all religious symbols from the schools,— pictures, dogmas, prayers, in a word, "all that belongs to the sphere of the individual's conscience". The decree is gradually applied.

April 11 An attack on southern Paris by the French army is repelled with heavy losses by General Eudes's troops of the Commune.

April 12 The Commune decides that the Victory Column on the Place Vendôme, which had been cast from guns captured by Napoleon after the war of 1809, should be demolished as a symbol of chauvinism and incitement to national hatred. This decree is carried out on May 16.

April 16 Commune announces the postponement of all debt obligations for three years and abolition of interest on them.

The Commune orders a statistical tabulation of factories which had been closed down by the manufacturers, and the working out of plans for the carrying on of these factories by workers formerly employed in them, who are to be organized in co-operative societies, and also plans for the organization of these co-operatives in one great union.

April 20 The Commune abolishes night work for bakers, and also abolishes the workers' registration cards, which since the Second Empire had been run as a monopoly by men named by the police —exploiters of the first rank; the issuing of these registration cards is transferred to the mayors of the twenty arrondissements of Paris.

April 23 Thiers breaks off the negotiations for the exchange, proposed by Commune, of the Archbishop of Paris [Georges Darboy] and a number of other priests held hostages in Paris, for only one man, Blanqui, who had twice been elected to the Commune but is a prisoner in Clairvaux.

April 27 In sight of the impending municipal elections of April 30, Thiers enacts one of his great conciliation scenes. He exclaims from the tribune of the Assembly: "There exists no conspiracy against the republic but that of Paris, which compels us to shed French blood. I repeat it again and again...". Out of 700,000 municipal councillors, the united Legitimists, Orleanists, and Bonapartists (Party of Order) carry fewer than 8,000.

April 30 The Commune orders the closing of the pawnshops on the ground that they are a private exploitation of labor, and are in contradiction with the right of the workers to their instruments of labor and to credit.

May 5 The Commune orders the demolition of the Chapel of Atonement, which had been built in expiation of the execution of Louis XVI.

May 9 Fort Issy, which is completely reduced to ruins by gunfire and constant French bombardment, is captured by the French army.

May 10 The peace treaty concluded in February is now signed, known as Treaty of Frankfurt. (endorsed by National Assembly on May 18).

May 16 The Victory Column at Place Vendôme is pulled down.

May 21-28 Versailles troops enter Paris on May 21. The Prussians who held the northern and eastern forts allow the Versailles troops to advance across the land north of the city, which was forbidden ground to them under the armistice—Paris workers held the flank with only weak forces. As a result of this, only a weak resistance was put up in the western half of Paris, in the luxury city; while it grew stronger and more tenacious the nearer the Versailles troops approached the eastern half, the working class city.

The French army spent eight days massacring workers, shooting civilians on sight. The operation was led by Marshal MacMahon, who would later become president of France. Tens of thousands of Communards and workers are summarily executed, as many as 30,000; 38,000 others are imprisoned and 7,000 are forcibly deported.

Prologue

The Government of National Defense Surrenders

The Government of National Defense

Citizens:

The agreement that will put an end to Paris's resistance has not yet been signed, but it is only a matter of hours until this is so.

The foundations remain fixed, just as we announced them yesterday:

The enemy will not enter within the walls of Paris;

The National Guard will preserve its arms and organization;

A division of 12,000 men will remain intact. As for the other troops, they will remain among us in Paris instead of being, as was first proposed, confined to the suburbs. Officers will keep their swords.

We will publish the articles of the agreement as soon as the signatures are exchanged, and we will at the same time make known the state of our supplies.

Paris wants to be assured that resistance continued until the last possible moment.

The figures we will give will be irrefutable proof, and we challenge anyone to contest them.

We will show that there remains to us just enough bread to hold us over until re-supplied, and that we couldn't continue the fight without leading two million men, women, and children to death.

The siege of Paris lasted four months and twelve days, the bombardment a solid month. Since January 15 the bread ration has been reduced to 300 grams; the ration of horse meat has been only 30 grams since December 15. The mortality rate has more than tripled. In the midst of so many disasters there was not a single day of discouragement.

The enemy is the first to render homage to the moral energy and courage of which the entire Parisian populace has just given an example.

Paris has suffered much, but the Republic will profit from its long suffering so nobly borne. We come out of the fight that is ending tempered for the fight to come. We come out of it with our honor, with all our hopes and, despite the sorrows of the present hour, we more than ever have faith in the destiny of the fatherland.

Paris, January 28, 1871

General Trochu, President; Jules Favre, Vice President, Minister of Foreign Affairs; Emmanuel Arago, Eugène Pelletan, Jules Simon, Jules Ferry, Ernest Picard, Garnier-Pagès, Le Flo, Minister of War; Magnin, Minister of Agriculture and Commerce; Dorian, Minister of Public Works

Ephemera of the Siege and the Commune

The National Guard Opposes Prussian Entry into Paris

Central Committee of the National Guard

Citizens:

The general sentiment of the population seems to not oppose the Prussian entry into Paris. The Central Committee, which had issued a contrary opinion, declares that it rallies to the following resolution:

Around all the neighborhoods that the enemy will occupy, a series of barricades will be established capable of completely isolating that part of the city. The residents of the area circumscribed within these limits should immediately evacuate it.

The National Guard, formed in a cordon around this in concert with the army, will ensure that the enemy, thus isolated on land that will no longer be part of our city, cannot in any way communicate with the entrenched parts of Paris.

The Central Committee calls on the entire National Guard to lend its assistance to the execution of the measures needed to arrive at this goal, and to avoid any aggression that would bring about the immediate overthrow of the Republic.

Paris, February 28, 1871

The Members of the Commission:
André Alavoine, A. Bouit, Frontier, Boursier, David, Boisson, Haroud, Gritz, Tessier, Ramel, Badois, Arnold, Piconel, Audoynau, Masson, Webert, Lagarde, Jean Laroque, Jules Bergeret, Pouchain, La Valette, Fleury, Maljournal, Choteau, Cadaze, Gastaud, Dutil, Matte, Mutin.

To the Army

The Delegates of the Paris National Guard

In the provinces odious rumors are being spread.

In Paris there are 300,000 National Guardsmen. Even so, troops are being brought into the city that are being lied to about the spirit of the Parisian populace. The men who organized the defeat, dismembered France, and delivered all our gold want to escape the responsibility they assumed by inspiring civil war. They count on the hope that you will be the docile instruments of the crime they are contemplating.

Citizen soldiers, will you obey the impious order to spill the same blood that flows in your veins? Will you tear out your own entrails? No! You will not agree to become patricides and fratricides.

What do the people of Paris want?

They want to preserve their arms, choose their own chiefs, and revoke them when they no longer have confidence in them.

They want the army to be returned to its homes in order to return hearts to their families and arms to their labor as quickly as possible.

Soldiers, children of the people, let us unite to save the republic. Kings and emperors have done us enough harm. Don't sully your life. Orders don't stand in the way of conscience's responsibilities. Let us embrace in the face of those who want to set us at each other's throats in order to conquer a rank, obtain a position, or return a king.

Eternal life to the republic!

Voted at the session at the Waux-hall, March 10, 1871

At the same session the delegates voted to congratulate the citizens of the Army of the Loire for the pious homage they rendered the martyrs of Liberty by bearing a wreath to the July Column.

To the National Guardsmen of Paris

You charged us with organizing the defense of Paris and the defense of your rights.

We are conscious of having fulfilled this mission: aided by your generous courage and your admirable calm, we have driven out the government that betrayed us.

At this time our mandate has expired, and we yield it, for we don't claim to be taking the place of those whom a revolutionary wind has just overthrown.

So prepare and carry out your communal elections, and as a reward give us the only thing we ever wished for: seeing you establish the true republic.

In the meanwhile, in the name of the people we will remain at the Hôtel de Ville.

Hôtel de Ville, Paris, March 19, 1871

The Central Committee of the National Guard
Assi, Billioray, Ferrat, Babick, Edouard Moreau, C. Dupont, Varlin, Boursier, Mortier, Gouhier, Lavalette, Fr. Jourde, Rousseau, Ch. Lullier, Blanchet, J. Grolard, Barroud, H. Geresme, Fabre, Pougeret

To the People

The people of Paris have shaken off the yoke that the others tried to impose on them.

Calm, impassible in their strength, they awaited without fear or provocation the shameless madmen who wanted to lay hands on the republic.

This time our brothers in the army didn't want to lay hands on the holy arc of our freedoms. We give thanks to everyone, and may Paris and France together lay down the foundation for a republic acclaimed in all ways, the only government that will forever close the era of invasions and civil wars.

The state of siege is lifted.

The people of Paris are convoked in their sections for communal elections.

The security of all citizens is assured by the cooperation of the National Guard.

Hôtel de Ville, Paris, March 19, 1871

The Central Committee of the National Guard
Assi, Billioray, Ferrat, Babick, Edouard Moreau, C. Dupont, Varlin, Boursier, Mortier, Gouhier, Lavalette, Fr. Jourde, Rousseau, Ch. Lullier, Blanchet, J. Grollard, Barroud, H. Geresme, Fabre, Pougeret

Delegations from the Provinces
March 23, 1871

Citizens:

The fugitive government in Versailles has sought to cut you off; the provinces have found themselves suddenly deprived of all news from Paris.

But the isolation in which they wanted to enclose you has not prevented the revolutionary inspiration from making headway, despite all precautions.

Yesterday and today the Central Committee received several delegations from the cities of Lyon, Bordeaux, Marseilles, Rouen, etc, who have come here to learn the nature of our revolution and who left as quickly as possible to give the signal for a similar movement, which has been prepared everywhere.

LONG LIVE FRANCE, LONG LIVE THE REPUBLIC!

Hôtel de Ville , March 23, 1871

The Central Committee of the National Guard:
Ant. Arnaud, Assi, Billioray, Ferrat, Babick, Ed. Moreau, C. Dupont, Varlin, Gouhier, Lavalette, Fr. Jourde, Rousseau, G. Arnold, Viard, Blanchet, J. Grolard, Baroud, H. Geresme, Fabre, Fougeret, Bouit, H. Chouteau, Andignoux, C. Gaudier, Castioni, Prudhomme, Josselin, Maxime Lisbonne, J. Bergeret, Maljournal, Ramvier, Fleury, Avoine fils, Guiller

Your Commune Has Been Constituted

Citizens:

Your Commune has been constituted.

The vote of March 26 sanctioned the victorious revolution.

A cowardly, aggressive power had taken you by the throat. In your legitimate defense you cast from your walls the government that wanted to dishonor you by imposing a king on you.

Today the criminals that you didn't pursue abuse your magnanimity by organizing a center of monarchical activity at the very gates of the city. They invoke civil war; they set in motion all possible corruptions; they accept all possible complicities; they have even gone so far as to beg support from foreigners.

We call down upon these execrable maneuvers the judgment of France and the world.

Citizens:

You have just given yourselves institutions that defy these attacks.

You are masters of your destiny. Strong in your support, the representatives that you have just established will repair the disasters caused by the fallen powers. Compromised industry, suspended labor, paralyzed commercial transactions are all going to receive a vigorous push.

Today the decision will be rendered on rents;

Tomorrow that on the due date of payments;

All public service re-established and simplified;

The National Guard, from now on the only armed force in the city, reorganized without delay;

These will be our first acts.

In order to assure the triumph of the republic, the people's elected representatives only ask that they be supported it with the people's confidence.

As for them, they will do their duty.

Hôtel de Ville of Paris March 29, 1871
The Paris Commune

Decree on the Separation of Church and State

The Paris Commune:

Considering that the first of the principles of the French Republic is freedom;

Considering that freedom of conscience is the first among freedoms;

Considering that the budget of cults is contrary to this principle, since it is imposed on citizens against their own faith;

Considering that, in fact, the clergy was an accomplice in the crimes against freedom of the monarchy,

DECREES:

Article 1. The church is separated from the state.

Article 2. The budget of cults is suppressed.

Article 3. Goods called *mainmorte*, both movable and fixed, belonging to religious congregations, are declared national properties.

Article 4. An inquest will immediately be held concerning these goods in order to establish their nature and to put them at the disposal of the nation.

The Paris Commune
April 3, 1871

Letter from Garibaldi
L'Affranchi, April 5, 1871

Citizens:

Thank you for the honor of my nomination to the command of the National Guard of Paris, which I love, and whose glory and dangers I'd be proud to share.

Nevertheless, I owe you the following considerations:

A commandant of the Paris National Guard, a commandant of the army of Paris, and a leadership committee, whatever they might be, are three powers that cannot be reconciled with France's current situation.

Despotism has an advantage over us in the concentration of power, and it is such a concentration that you should oppose to your enemies.

Choose an honest citizen, something which you don't lack: Victor Hugo, Louis Blanc, Félix Pyat, as well as Edgar Quinet and other doyens of radical democracy can serve you. Generals Cremer and Billot, whom I see have your confidence, can also be counted in this number.

Remember though that only one man should be charged with the supreme post and with full power. This man will choose other honest men to assist him in the difficult task of saving the country. And if you have the honor of finding a Washington, France in a short time will raise itself up from its shipwreck greater than ever.

These conditions aren't an excuse to shirk my obligation to serve Republican France. No! I don't despair at all of fighting myself at the side of these brave men. I am

Yours truly,
G. Garibaldi

Declaration on Reprisals

Citizens:

Every day the bandits of Versailles murder or execute our prisoners, and not a single hour passes without our hearing of one of these killings. And you know that the guilty parties are the gendarmes and *sergents de ville* of the Empire, the royalists of Charrette and Cathelinau, who march on Paris to the cry of "Long live the king!" behind the white flag.

The government of Versailles places itself outside the laws of war and humanity. You will have no choice but to resort to reprisals.

If, continuing to fail to recognize the usual conditions of war between civilized peoples, our enemies massacre yet one more of our soldiers, we will answer with the execution of either the same or double the number of prisoners.

Ever generous and just, even in its anger, the People abhor blood, just as it abhors civil war. But it has the obligation to protect itself against the savage attacks of its enemies and, whatever it might cost, it will take an eye for an eye, a tooth for a tooth.

Paris, April 5, 1871
The Paris Commune

Against the Mania for Braids

To the National Guard

Citizens:

I have observed with sorrow that, forgetting our modest origins, the ridiculous mania for braids, embroidery, and ribbons has begun to make its appearance among us.

Workers, for the first time you have carried out the revolution of labor, by labor, and for labor.

Let us not deny our origins, and especially let us not blush because of them. Workers we were, workers we are, workers we will always be.

Never forget; we triumphed in the name of virtue against vice, duty against abuse, and austerity against corruption.

Let us remain virtuous and men of duty. We will then found the austere republic, the only one that has the right to exist.

Before cracking down I am recalling all my follow citizens to themselves: no more ribbons, no more baubles, no more braids that cost so little to display and are so dear to our responsibility.

In the future any officer who is not justified by right to wear the insignia of his rank, or who adds braids or other vain distinctions to the regulation uniform of the National Guard, shall be subject to disciplinary measures.

I am taking advantage of these circumstances to recall all to the sentiment of hierarchical obedience in the service. In obeying those you elected, you are obeying yourselves.

Paris, April 7, 1871
The Delegate for War
Cluseret

Manifesto of the Freemasons

In the presence of the painful events before which all of France laments; in the presence of the precious blood that flows in torrents, Masonry, which represents the idea of humanity and which has spread it throughout the world, comes again to affirm before you, Government and members of the Assembly, and before you, members of the Commune, those great principles that are the law, and that should be the law of every man with the heart of a man.

Inscribed on the folds of the flag of Masonry is the noble motto:
LIBERTY, EQUALITY, FRATERNITY, SOLIDARITY.

Masonry preaches peace among men, and in the name of humanity proclaims the inviolability of human life.

Masonry curses all wars; it laments all civil wars.

It has the duty and the right to come among you and say: IN THE NAME OF HUMANITY, IN THE NAME OF FRATERNITY, IN THE NAME OF THE DEVASTATED FATHERLAND, stop the spilling of blood. We ask this of you, we beg you to hear our appeal.

We don't come to you to dictate a program, for we rely upon your wisdom; we simply say to you: STOP THE SPILLING OF PRECIOUS BLOOD THAT FLOWS ON BOTH SIDES, and lay down the basis for a definitive peace that will be THE DAWN OF A NEW FUTURE.

This is what we energetically ask of you, and if our voice isn't going to be listened to, we tell you that humanity and the fatherland demand and impose it.

Paris, April 8, 1871

Montanier, Becourt, members of the Council of the Order:
The Venerables: Saugé, Dandre, Baumann. Chanuet, Barré, Limonaire, Motard, Ragaigne, Martin, Marchal, Simon, Hirsch, Vilmotte

Atrocities on Top of Atrocities
L'Affranchi, April 9, 1871

The blood spilled by reaction flows more abundantly every day. Atrocities follow horrors. After Flourens, after Duval, after hundreds of prisoners have fallen before the bullets of the assassins of December, of the Vendéens, Chouans, Orléanists, and left liberals, all of them leagued together against the Republic and conscience; after all the martyrs sacrificed by the madmen, other human hecatombs are now being prepared. The military tribunal of Versailles has just condemned to death those officers and non-commissioned army officers who have refused to fire upon the people and an unexampled act of cruelty has just bloodied the suburbs. Tropmann has been surpassed: Citizen Barrette of Courbevoie had provided hospitality to two wounded National Guardsmen. In order to punish him for his generous act the miserable mercenary thugs of the imperial and royal army executed him, his wife, his two daughters, and the two unfortunate wounded.

The former hired assassins of Pietri, today the valets of the executioner Thiers, surpass in ferocity the hordes of Haynau and Radetzky.

If we don't put a brake to the atrocities of these brigands they will continue to spill blood like water.

We must begin, in an exemplary fashion, by punishing the renegades Jules Favre, Thiers, and Jules Simon who have forgotten that it is thanks to the votes of those Parisians they are massacring that they have come to power.

The houses—the hideouts, we should say—of these bandits must be razed and an ignominious pillory must be built on their ruins, in order to assure these murderous traitors the maledictions of their contemporaries and of posterity.

These brigands who sully prisoners must be terrorized by arresting their wives, their children, their parents, and their accomplices, by imprisoning them as hostages and by holding them responsible with their heads for the blood that the hyenas of Versailles would still like to spill.

Manifesto of the Paris Commune

To the French people:

In the painful and terrible conflict that again threatens Paris with the horrors of a siege and bombardment; that causes French blood to flow, sparing neither our brothers, our wives, nor our children; crushed beneath cannonballs and rifle shots, it is necessary that public opinion not be divided, that the national conscience be troubled.

Paris and the entire nation must know the nature, the reason, and the goal of the revolution that is being carried out. Finally, it is only just that the responsibility for the deaths, the suffering, and the misfortunes of which we are the victims fall on those who, after having betrayed France and delivered Paris to the foreigners, pursue with a blind and cruel obstinacy the ruin of the great city in order to bury, in the disaster of the republic and liberty, the dual testimony to their treason and their crime.

The Commune has the obligation to affirm and determine the aspirations and wishes of the people of Paris, to define the character of the movement of March 18, misunderstood, unknown and slandered by the politicians seated at Versailles.

Once again, Paris works and suffers for all of France, for whom it prepares, through its combats and sacrifices, the intellectual, moral, administrative and economic regeneration, its glory and prosperity.

What does it ask for?

The recognition and consolidation of the Republic, the only form of government compatible with the rights of the people and the normal and free development of society.

The absolute autonomy of the Commune extended to all localities in France and assuring to each one its full rights, and to every Frenchman the full exercise of his faculties and abilities as man, citizen and producer.

The only limit to the autonomy of the Commune should be the equal right to autonomy for all communes adhering to the contract, whose association shall insure French unity.

The inherent rights of the Commune are:

The vote on communal budgets, receipts, and expenses; the fixing and distribution of taxes; the direction of public services; the organization of its magistracy, internal police, and education; the administration of goods belonging to the Commune.

The choice by election or competition of magistrates and communal functionaries of all orders, as well as the permanent right of control and revocation.

The absolute guarantee of individual freedom and freedom of conscience.

The permanent intervention of citizens in communal affairs by the free manifestation of their ideas, the free defense of their interests, with guarantees given for these manifestations by the Commune, which alone is charged with overseeing and assuring the free and fair exercise of the right to assemble and publicize.

The organization of urban defense and the National Guard, which elects its chiefs and alone watches over the maintenance of order in the city.

Paris wants nothing else as a local guarantee, on condition, of course, of finding in the great central administration—the delegation of federated Communes—the realization and the practice of the same principles.

But as an element of its autonomy, and profiting by its freedom of action, within its borders it reserves the right to operate the administrative and economic reforms called for by the populace as it wills; to create the institutions needed to develop and spread instruction, production, exchange and credit; to universalize power and property in keeping with the needs of the moment, the wishes of those concerned and the facts furnished by experience.

Our enemies are fooling themselves or are fooling the country when they accuse Paris of wanting to impose its will or its supremacy over the rest of the nation and to pretend to a dictatorship, which would be a veritable attack on the independence and sovereignty of other communes.

They are fooling themselves or are fooling the country when they accuse Paris of pursuing the destruction of that French unity constituted by the Revolution to the acclaim of our fathers, who hastened to the Fête de la Fédération from all corners of the old France.

Unity, as it has been imposed on us until today by the Empire, the monarchy or parliamentarism is nothing but unintelligent, arbitrary, and onerous centralization.

Political unity, as Paris wants it, is the voluntary association of all local initiatives, the spontaneous and free concourse of all individual energies with a common goal in sight: the well-being, the freedom, and the security of all.

The communal revolution, begun by popular initiative on March 18, begins a new era of experimental, positive, scientific politics.

It's the need of the old governmental and clerical world, of militarism and *fonctionnarisme*, of exploitation, speculation, monopolies, and privileges to which the proletariat owe their servitude and the fatherland its misfortunes and disasters.

Let this beloved and great country—fooled by lies and calumnies—be reassured! The fight between Paris and Versailles is one of those that cannot be ended through illusory compromises. The end cannot be in doubt. Victory, pursued with an indomitable energy by the National Guard, will go to the idea and to right.

We call on France.

Warned that Paris in arms possesses as much calm as bravery; that it supports order with as much energy as enthusiasm, that it sacrifices itself with as much reason as energy, that it only armed itself in devotion to the liberty and glory of all: let France cease this bloody conflict.

It is up to France to disarm Versailles through the solemn manifestation of its irresistible will.

Called upon to benefit by our conquests, let it declare itself in solidarity with our efforts. Let it be our ally in this combat that can only end in the triumph of the communal idea or the ruin of Paris.

As for us, citizens of Paris, our mission is the accomplishing of the modern revolution, the largest and most fecund of all those which have illuminated history.

It is our obligation to fight and to win.

April 19, 1871
The Paris Commune

Masonic Lodge "The Union of Belleville"
Held April 28, 1871 (Common Era)

Considering that questions of universal morality and humanity are the constant concern of Freemasons;

Considering that without straying from the philosophical and non-political sphere that is its place, Freemasonry has the right and the duty to intervene in all questions where the principles of fraternity are misunderstood;

Considering that in the painful period of crisis through which we are passing, which is desolating our fatherland and afflicting humanity, it is the duty of all Masons to affirm the principles that appear to it to conform to universal morality, and those most apt to make the ideas of universal solidarity prevail;

A solidarity that, the day it will exist, will prevent the renewal of all impious struggles among men and will cause the last seed of barbarism to disappear by reuniting all men in one family;

Considering that the proclamation of the Paris Commune, addressed to the French people, contains nothing that is contrary to Masonic principles;

Considering that it is thus the obligation of Freemasonry, which has always been at the head of the march of progress, to employ all the moral force at its disposal to prevail those ideas in conformity with its principles;

Considering that it is the duty of each lodge to indicate, not only to Freemasons, but to all citizens, the path of the just and the true;

The Lodge "The Union of Belleville" declares:

That it desires to stop the spilling of blood, while adhering to the program of the Paris Commune as contained in its proclamation to the French people;

Consequently, and in order to arrive at this result, it invites:

All Freemasons of Paris and the provinces, and all citizens, to join with it to have the government of Versailles and the Paris Commune accept the following arrangement:

Recognition of communal rights for all great cities as well as the smallest towns;

General elections for all Communes and the Constituent Assembly; and

In order to proceed to these elections, which will occur in three months, the establishment of an administrative commission composed in two equal halves of members of the Commune and members of the Assembly of Versailles, named in elections by these two powers.

Such are the basis of an arrangement proposed by the lodge "The Union of Belleville" in order to put an end to the crime we are passing through, and for the success of which it invites all its brothers, Mason or not, to employ all their moral force and all the means placed at their disposal by the Declaration of the Rights of Man.

By order: For the Lodge "The Union of Belleville"
The Tit:.Sec:. The Ven:. Or :.
Voisin H. Fernoux

General Appeal to All Jewelry Workers

At a moment when socialism is being affirmed with a vigor hitherto unknown, it is impossible for us, workers in a profession that suffers in the highest degree from the immoral influence of capital and exploitation, to remain passive before the movement for emancipation that is being undertaken under a government truly and sincerely liberal.

This is why we call on all the workers of the Corporation to examine together what the situation will be for us after the current crisis and to take all necessary measures for facilitating the return to work by all possible means.

It is the obligation of each and every one of us to foresee and combat the hindrances the exploiters will put before our dearest interests in order to discredit any future organization.

We must come together! We must come to agreement! Let us make every effort so that we don't lack for work after the struggle.

The members of the Commission for the Organization of Labor:
Durand, Albouze, Mizeret, Payeur, Guineberteaux, Paul the younger, Marielle, Bibe, Bargeron, Beichlaar, Lamare, Demarcq, Girard, Champy

Meeting of Jewelers
Sunday, May 7 at 2:00,
Salle Larcher, rue du Temple, 79

To France's Major Cities

After two months of constant battle, Paris is neither worn out nor has it been breached.

Paris is still fighting, without pause or rest. Tireless, heroic, undefeated.

Paris has made a pact with death. Behind its forts it has its walls; behind its walls its barricades; behind its barricades its houses that must be taken from it one by one, and these it will blow up if need be, rather than surrender.

Major cities of France, will you be immobile and impassable spectators to this duel of the future with the past, of the Republic against monarchy?

Or will you finally see that Paris is the champion of France and the world, and that failing to aid it would mean betraying it.

You want the republic, or else your votes make no sense. You want the Commune, for rejecting it means abdicating your part of national sovereignty. You want political freedom and social equality, since you write it into your programs. You clearly see that the army of Versailles is the army of Bonapartism, of monarchical centralism, of despotism and privilege, for you know its chiefs and you recall their past.

What then are you waiting for to rise up! What then are you waiting for to chase from among you the infamous agents of this government of capitulation and shame that at this very hour begs and buys from the Prussian army the means to bombard Paris from all sides?

Are you waiting till the last soldier of right has fallen before the poisoned bullets of Versailles?

Are you waiting for Paris to be transformed into a cemetery and each of its houses into a tomb?

Cities of France, you sent it your fraternal solidarity; you said to it: "In our hearts we are with you."

Cities of France, it is no longer the moment for manifestoes. It is the time for acts, when the cannon has the word.

Enough of Platonic sympathy. You have rifles and ammunition: to arms! Arise, cities of France!

Paris looks to you. Paris waits for your circle to surround the cowardly bombers and to prevent them the punishment it holds in reserve for them.

Paris will do its duty up to the bitter end.

But don't forget this, Lyon, Marseilles, Lille, Toulouse, Nantes, Bordeaux, and the others...

If Paris were to succumb fighting for the freedom of the world, avenging history would have the right to say that Paris was slaughtered because you let the murder occur.

Paris, May 15, 1871

Appeal to Working Women
May 17, 1871

The Central Committee of the Union of Women for the Defense of Paris and the Care of the Wounded, charged by the Commune's Labor Commission with the organization of the labor of the women of Paris and with the constituting of federal and union chambers of united working women;

Given the identity of the union and federal chambers of workingmen, of the grouping of workingwomen in professional sections forming free and federated productive associations among themselves,

Consequently, it invites all workingwomen to meet today Wednesday, May 17 at the Bourse at 7:00 p.m. in order to name delegates from each corporation for the constituting of union chambers that will, in turn, each send two delegates for the formation of a federal chamber of workingwomen.

For all information contact the Committee of the Union of Women, instituted and functioning in all arrondissements.

Seat of the Central Committee of the Union: rue du Faubourg-Saint-Martin, at the town hall of the 10th arrondissement.

Seen and approved,

The Delegate for the Department of Labor and Exchange
Leo Frankel

The Executive Committee of the Central Committee
Nathalie le Mel, Aline Jacquier, Leloup, Blanche Lefevre, Collin, Jarry, Elisabeth Dmitrieff

Address of the Third Congress of the Romande Federation of the International Workingmen's Association to the Paris Commune
Geneva, Temple Unique, May 17, 1871

The annual Congress of the Romande Federation cannot close its sessions without casting its gaze at you, BROTHERS OF PARIS, and without proclaiming its adherence to the great labor of political and social reorganization that you are carrying out.

This is the first time that adepts of the INTERNATIONAL have made triumph the political principles of our Association, which is that of National Federations united among themselves across artificial frontiers and having THE COMMUNE as its fundamental basis.

It is also the first time that the international idea of the representation of labor finds its faithful expression in you, our brothers, who are called upon by the people of Paris to the direction of affairs of the great Commune, once again in full possession of itself.

While Paris is blocked by the Chouans of Versailles, it is incumbent upon us to defend you by enlightening those populations still in the dark about the true meaning of the revolution of March 18, accomplished in the name of the economic aspirations of the working classes. Everywhere that human intelligence exists it is up to us to make understood that there is no middle ground between the two irreconcilable parties: social revolution or monarchical reaction.

We can't help but express our profound regret that in the ferocious struggle between these two parties the provinces have not yet understood either their obligations or their interests. They haven't understood that their destiny is intimately tied to that of the Paris Commune, because if Paris were to succumb with it would fall republican freedom, and on the smoking ruins of the cosmopolitan city would once again be installed the "order" of bloody persecution, the transportation of republicans, and the massacre of workers every time they demand their right to live from their labor.

But let reaction know well that we make the solemn commitment to ceaselessly pursue our labor, that of plucking up the courage of the people so that they rise against the reaction of Versailles in order to extend their hands to the combatants of Paris across the gendarmes of Bonaparte and the mercenaries of Thiers, Favre, and Picard.

May this commitment, contracted by the workers of all countries, prove to the forces of reaction that they can't defeat the Commune.

And if reaction has until now prevented you from realizing all the social and political reorganization that the Commune bears within itself; if reaction has forced you to concern yourself for the moment with the suppression of the shadowy attacks of treason and corruption, to consecrate yourselves completely to the fight to the end against the assassination of the republic, thus putting obstacles before the peaceful development of the new social life, the Commune nevertheless remains the only federative form which, through its application extended throughout France, is capable of assuring independence, well-being and equality for all. It alone can create true national unity, that is, the unity of the people through the harmony of all its interests.

It is for this that we proclaim that the principles of the Commune have already triumphed over the debris of the ancien régime and its definitive consolidation cannot be far off, for it is and will remain the object of all the efforts of the workers.

And when the workers are united by an organization as vast as that of the International, the triumph of their cause is assured.

Receive then, Parisian brothers, our warm wishes for your imminent success, and believe that the members of the International of the entire world will join with us to declare that the International should adopt the orphans and the widows of the defenders of the Paris Commune.

Long live the Paris Commune! Long live the International Association!

The Central Committee of the Republican Federation of the National Guard

At a moment when the two camps are reflecting, observing each other and taking up their strategic positions;

At this supreme instant when an entire population, having arrived at a paroxysm of exasperation, has decided to win or die for the maintenance of its rights,

The Central Committee wants its voice to be heard.

We have only fought against one enemy: civil war. Consistent with our beliefs, both when we were a provisional authority and now that we are at a distance from affairs, we have thought, spoken, and acted in this sense;

Today and for the last time, in the presence of the misfortunes that might befall all of us,

We propose to the heroic armed people who elected us, we propose to those who have gone astray and attack us, the only solution capable of stopping the spilling of blood while at the same time safeguarding the legitimate rights conquered by Paris:

The National Assembly, whose role has been terminated, must be dissolved;

The Commune will also be dissolved;

The so-called regular army will quit Paris and will keep itself at a distance of at least 25 kilometers;

An interim power will be named, composed of delegates from cities with 50,000 inhabitants. This power will choose from among its members a provisional government, whose mission will be to proceed to the election of a Constituent Assembly and the Paris Commune;

No reprisals will be taken against either members of the Assembly or members of the Commune for acts subsequent to March 26.

These are the only acceptable conditions.

Let the blood spilled in a fratricidal struggle fall on the heads of those who reject them.

As for us, just as in the past, we will fulfill our obligations up to the end.

4 Prairial, year 79 (May 23, 1871)

The Members of the Central Committee,
Moreau, Pyat, B. Lacorre, Geoffroy, Gouhier, Prudhomme, Gaudier, Fabre, Tiersonnier, Bonnefoy, Lacord, Tournois, Baroud, Rousseau, Laroque, Marèchal, Bisson, Ouzelot, Brin, Marceau, Leveque, Chouteau, Avoine the younger, Navarre, Husson, Lagarde, Audoynaid, Hanser, Soudry, Lavallette, Chateau, Valats, Patris, Fougeret, Millet, Boullenger, Bouit, Grelier, Drevet

To the Citizens of the Twentieth Arrondissement

The moment has come to fight with ferocity an enemy who has made pitiless war on us for two months.

You know what lot is reserved for us if we succumb. To arms then, and don't put them down until after our victory. Be vigilant, especially at night. Be ever ready in order to avoid the ruses of our enemies.

I thus come to you in a common interest, asking in the name of the solidarity that unites all revolutionaries at this moment, that you faithfully execute the orders that will be given to you.

There is a grave danger that I'd like to point out to you, and that's the refusal of the National Guard to go forward under the pretext of guarding the barricades of the neighborhoods that are not threatened. Give your assistance to the 19th arrondissement, help it to repel the enemy. There lies your security, and victory is at this price.

Don't wait for Belleville to be attacked; that would be too late. Forward, and Belleville will have once again triumphed.

Long Live the Republic!

Belleville, May 25, 1871
Member of the Committee of Public Safety
G. Ranvier
The Members of the Commune
Bergeret, Viard, Trinquet

The Revolutionary Federation of Communes

The disastrous situation in which the country finds itself, the impotence of official power, and the indifference of the privileged classes have placed the French nation at the edge of the abyss.

If the people, organized in a revolutionary way, don't hasten to act, its future is lost, the revolution is lost, all is lost. Inspired by the immensity of the danger, and considering that the desperate action of the people cannot be delayed a single instant, the delegates of the Federated Committees of Salvation of France, gathered at the Central Committee, propose the immediate adoption of the following resolutions:

Article 1. Having become powerless, the administrative and governmental machinery of the state is abolished. The people of France return to full possession of themselves.

Article 2. All criminal and civil tribunals are suspended and replaced by the people's justice.

Article 3. The payment of taxes and mortgages is suspended. Taxes are replaced by the contributions of federated communes, levied against the wealthy classes proportional to the needs of the salvation of France.

Article .4. The state, having been deposed, can no longer intervene in the payment of private debts.

Article 5. All existing municipal organizations are annulled and replaced in all the federated communes by Committees for the Salvation of France, which will exercise all powers under the immediate control of the people.

Article 6. Each committee in the capital city of a department will send two delegates to form the Revolutionary Convention for the Salvation of France.

Article 7. This convention will immediately meet at the Lyon town hall, being the second city of France and that most able to energetically provide for the defense of the country.

This convention, supported by the entire people, will save France.

TO ARMS!!!

E-B Saignes, Rivière, Deville, Rajon (of Tarare) Francois Favre, Louis Palix, B. Placet, Blanc (G), Ch. Beauvoir, Albert Richard, J. Bischoff, Doublé, H. Bourron, M. Bakunin, Parraton, A. Guillermet, Coignet the elder, P-J Pulliat, Latour, Guillo, Savigny, J. Germain, F. Charvet, A. Bastelica (of Marseilles), Dupin (of St. Etienne), Narcisse Barret

The End of the Commune

The Chief Executive to Prefects and All Civil, Judicial, and Military Authorities

We are masters of Paris, except for a very small part that will be occupied tomorrow. The Tuileries is in ashes; the Louvre has been saved. That part of the Ministry of Finance that runs along the rue de Rivoli has been set on fire. The palace on the Quai d'Orsay, in which the Council of State and the Cour des Comptes were housed was also set on fire. Such is the state in which Paris has been delivered to us by the scoundrels who oppressed and dishonored it. They left us 12,000 prisoners, and we will certainly have between 18,000 and 20,000. The ground is covered with their corpses. It is hoped that this horrible spectacle will serve as a lesson to the insurgents who dared declare themselves partisans of the Commune. Justice will soon satisfy a human conscience outraged by the monstrous acts that France and the world have just witnessed.

The army was admirable. Even in our misfortune we are happy to be able to announce that, thanks to the wisdom of our generals, it suffered few losses.

Thiers
Versailles, May 23, 1871, 7:25 a.m.

Louis-Auguste Blanqui:
"La Patrie en Danger"

Louis-Auguste Blanqui, the most important of nineteenth century French revolutionaries, began his revolutionary activities as a teenager, activities that never ceased throughout his lifetime. The Commune could be seen as the culmination of his political life, but Blanqui was unable to participate, having been arrested before its outbreak. Nevertheless, he hovers over the seventy-three days of its life as its spiritual leader, and when he was later found guilty by a Versaillais tribunal, one of the charges against him was his role as moral inspiration of the Commune.

Blanqui had participated in the revolutions of 1830 and 1848 and sustained ceaseless conspiratorial activities between these events, before them and after them. With Paris under siege by the Prussians, Blanqui founded his own newspaper, *La Patrie en Danger (The Fatherland in Danger)*, borrowing the rallying cry of the great French Revolution. The selections below are all from this newspaper.

The paper lasted eighty-nine issues, discontinued due to poor circulation on December 8, 1870. In both his newspaper writings and his public activities Blanqui pushed for aggressive defense of Paris and accused commanding general Trochu of working for the crushing of the city.

Blanqui was an officer in the National Guard and participated in the revolutionary uprisings of October 31, 1870 and January 22, 1871, both revolts attempting to replace the bourgeois government with a revolutionary one.

Soundly defeated in the elections of February 1871, Blanqui left Paris to recover his strength at the home of a niece in the provinces, and it was there that he was arrested for his participation in the events of October 31. It was due to this arrest that he missed the Commune. Nevertheless, he was elected to the Commune in absentia and his followers occupied seats on it and in important administrative departments, most prominently in the military and as procurators of the Commune. His importance to the Commune, and the fear he inspired in its enemies, is most glaringly demonstrated by the Commune's proposal that the government in Versailles turn Blanqui over to them in exchange for seventy-four hostages in their hands, and the Versaillais refused; many of the hostages were killed in the final days of the Commune.

After the fall of the Commune Blanqui was tried for his part in the events of October 31 and sentenced to deportation, a sentence which, given his advanced age and the state of his health, was commuted to life in prison.

Blanqui was elected to the Chamber of Deputies in 1879, an election that was invalidated. Released later that year, he continued his political activities until his death in 1881 at the age of 76, a life during which he spent, according to the revolutionary historian Maurice Dommanget, forty-three years, two months in prison.

Iron and Lead
September 22, 1870

The situation is no longer tenable and can't be prolonged without there being a catastrophe.

How can we live in this mortal contradiction: a government of national defense that doesn't want to defend itself?

The country viewed the war with horror, almost with despair. It was only thrown into the war through treason. But if the war was a crime on July 6, on September 20 it is peace that would be a crime.

Can't the Hôtel de Ville understand this?

This is not the moment for recriminations. Nevertheless, one must recall that on July 6 the republicans furiously rejected war as fatal to both France and the republican idea, which is life itself.

The conservative party on the contrary wanted it, as an instrument of counter-revolution.

Today the situation is reversed, but the roles remain the same. The conservatives underhandedly hatch the crime of peace in order to overturn the republic, even if France were to perish from this.

The party of the revolution loudly demands war to the finish, the sole chance for the salvation of the nation.

It will not rise up from the fall that conservatism is preparing for it. Dismemberment and spoliation would be the least of its misfortunes.

To live in disgrace would be a mortal blow.

There are moments in history when a people is crossed off the list of human societies. Its moral life is extinguished; it descends the steps of its sepulcher and will never climb back up.

We are at the edge of this grave dug by Bonaparte. Reaction wants to throw us into it. As it had hoped, it was able to destroy France by exploiting its victory. Now it demands that defeat provide the success of its conspiracies.

It wants to hand France's cadaver over to the monarchy. It doesn't really matter to it whether the prey it hands over is alive or dead.

We demand that all the weapons held in the arsenals of Vincennes and Mont-Valérien be immediately transported to Paris and that this transport be done as quickly as possible through the simultaneous use of a large number of personnel and a great quantity of vehicles.

It was feared yesterday that communications between Mont-Valérien and Paris would be intercepted. The enemy occupies the west of the city with a large force. It is in its interest to deprive us of the considerable quantity of arms contained in the citadel, as well as those stored in Vincennes.

Yesterday's defeat announces that the capital will soon count the National Guard as its sole garrison.

The Mobile Guard have chassepots. The National Guard doesn't. The sixty old battalions are armed with snuffbox rifles, and the new ones, the largest and most energetic, have only piston rifles, incapable of offering serious protection.

Will we, through negligence, deny the countless multitudes of workers of the good weapons of the two citadels, workers who, because of the insufficiency of the bad ones, remain disarmed?

It would constitute a veritable treason not to bring into Paris all the arms found in Vincennes and Mont-Valérien immediately.

Since September 4 the so-called Government of National Defense has only had one idea: peace. Not victorious peace, not even honorable peace, but peace all the same. This is its dream, its *idée fixe*.

It doesn't believe in resistance; it believes in the inevitable triumph of the Prussians. This idea has not ceased to obsess its spirit for a single minute, and in the higher official regions this conviction meets no contradictors.

Are men who are certain of defeat disposed to fight? What is the good of organizing a defense considered useless and powerless in advance?

This fatal preconception can only end in catastrophe. Discouragement and negligence are preparing this, and when it is accomplished they brag of their foresight: "I told you so," shout the authors responsible for the public misfortune.

Thus perish nations.

Are we going to fall into this abyss? Will France, set on fire, bloodied and sacked, also give a tip of several milliards to its destroyers, pay for its own ruin and shame?

Despite so many military errors Paris is still standing. Let us keep our money to purchase iron and lead. A million chassepots would cost us 100,000,000. This is a fifth of what they will demand of us.

No gold for the Prussians! Iron and lead!

The Truth About October 31
November 4, 1871

The newspapers of the reaction have told a completely false tale about the events of the night of October 31.

Slander is habitual to them, and habits can't be changed.

Nevertheless, since public credulity accepts everything offered it, Citizen Blanqui believes he is obliged to tell of his participation in the acts of October 31.

Citizen Blanqui, having no battalion under his orders since he was replaced at the head of the 169th, did not march on the Hôtel de Ville.

He was informed at around 5:30 p.m. that his name figured on the list of the new government proclaimed at the Hôtel de Ville.

At 6:00 he went to the post to which the popular will had called him and was only able to enter the palace with difficulty.

He was received with great satisfaction by the citizens gathered in a room where there was a table covered in papers.

He was immediately invited to assume his function as a member of the new authority. When he asked where Citizen Flourens was, he was told that the members of the former government were under arrest and that Flourens couldn't leave his post.

He tried to go see his colleague to confer with him. Due to the obstinate opposition to his passage by the National Guardsmen of the 106th battalion guarding the entry, he was unable to go to his comrade.

Understanding the danger of the situation, he returned to the room where he was first received and busied himself with seeing to the safety of the Hôtel de Ville and the fortifications.

He wrote and signed only the following orders:

The order to close all the barriers and to prevent any communication that might inform the enemy of dissension inside Paris.

The order to the commanders of the forts to watch for and energetically repel any attacks by the Prussians.

The order to various battalion chiefs, about twenty in all, to gather their soldiers and immediately lead them to the Hôtel de Ville .

The order to the battalions, already gathered on the square, to immediately enter the palace to guard its doors and protect the interior.

The order to have the prefecture of police occupied by a republican battalion currently stationed on the square.

The order to various citizens to install themselves in the place of the present mayors.

There is no need to designate these town halls. There were three or four of them.

Some of these orders were executed. The others weren't able to be.

Citizen Blanqui, warned that hostile battalions inside were acting violently against the popular power, again wanted to reach Citizen Flourens, from whom he remained separated, much to his chagrin.

Blanqui went to him and, returning along with him to the room he had left, had to pass through a room that had just been invaded by the 17th battalion, also composed of National Guardsmen from the faubourg Saint-Germain. These National Guardsmen tussled with the citizens who formed Flourens's entourage.

Recognized by them, Citizen Blanqui at that moment became the special object of their attacks. A violent struggle between the two parties followed. It ended with the removal of Blanqui, who was horribly mistreated and cast half-strangled into a corridor, where there were other Guardsmen of the 17th.

More humane, these men placed him on a bench where he was able to catch his breath. He was next to Tibaldi, who had also been arrested and beaten. They had torn out his abundant hair and beard.

When Blanqui regained his senses, the Guardsmen of the 17th, who had treated him humanely, brought him as a prisoner between two rows of soldiers from the 17th and 15th battalions to a large closed door at the end of a vestibule paved with stones.

Before that door were seven or eight armed citizens who questioned the 17th on the prisoner they were leading. One of the Guardsmen of this battalion, of a colossal stature and herculean vigor, immediately threw himself on the questioner, grabbed him by the throat, and nailed him to the door with irresistible force. Just then a pistol shot was fired in this group.

The National Guardsmen of the 17th precipitously retreated, using all the staircases that ended in the vestibule, raising their rifle stocks in the air. Citizen Blanqui remained alone in the middle of the room between the two parties.

After a few words on the need to avoid spilling blood, he rejoined his liberators. They were Flourens's *tirailleurs*. He owed them his freedom and perhaps his life. It would appear, given the rage that the sacristans of the 17th displayed when they found themselves surrounded and held back by the popular forces, that they would have torn to pieces the object of their hatred if they would have held him far from any peril to themselves.

Blanqui had remained their prisoner for twenty minutes.

Having returned to the room where the deliberations were taking place he found his colleagues Flourens, Delescluze, Millière, and Ranvier seated around the table. Citizen Mottu hadn't sat down. Neither he nor Citizen Delescluze gave their signatures.

No other member of the provisional commission appeared in the room or took part in the labors of the commission from 6:00 until the evacuation of the Hôtel de Ville .

After the total investment of the Hôtel de Ville by General Trochu's forces, deliberations were held on the position to be taken.

Citizen Delescluze proposed the following declaration:

The citizens below, designated in the meetings at the Hôtel de Ville to preside over elections to the Paris Commune and to see to the needs of the moment;

Upon the declaration made by Citizen Dorian that the preliminary formalities for elections to the Commune were already completed; that they will take place tomorrow, Tuesday, under his direction and that of

Citizen Schoelcher; and that the following day there will also be elections to the provisional government;

In the interests of the fatherland in danger and with a view to avoid a conflict that could bloody the baptism of the new republic;

Declare that showing all due respect for the rights of the people, they await the results of the elections that are to take place tomorrow.

In turn, Citizen Blanqui read the following declaration:

> Citizens of Paris,
>
> In the presence of the disastrous news that is arriving from Metz and proposals for an armistice that will hand France over to the Prussians, the population of Paris has judged it necessary to replace the government that so gravely compromised the republic.
>
> It has elected a provisional commission charged with taking the primary measures needed to ensure safety and to summon the electors of Paris to elect a municipal government.
>
> This commission invites all citizens to support these measures taken to preserve order and to await peacefully the results of the vote.
>
> All precautions have been taken to ensure the security of the forts and to protect them and the city's walls from enemy attack.
>
> The provisional commission will resign its powers immediately after the vote.

As this address to Parisians wasn't supported, Blanqui had to rally to Delescluze's proposal.

It was then that the six members of the provisional commission went to Monsieur Dorian's office. Acclaimed by the people and members of the Government of National Defense, Citizen Dorian hadn't left the Hôtel de Ville , but had abstained from taking any part in the deliberations of his recent colleagues.

A pact was concluded between himself and the newly elected representatives on the following bases:

> Elections for the Commune or a municipality on Tuesday, November 1.

Re-election of the members of the Provisional Government on Wednesday, November 2.

Amicable separation of the two authorities sitting at the Hôtel de Ville . No reprisals, no legal measures because of the acts carried out.

To this effect, the members of the National Defense held in the palace and the republicans, followed by their forces, will leave the palace together and will separate after having passed into the ranks of the troops lined up on the square.

This pact, accepted by Messieurs Jules Favre, Garnier-Pagès, Jules Simon, and Tamisier, who were then in the Hôtel de Ville , and M. Jules Ferry who, at that moment, at the head of a battalion of Mobile Guards sought to break down one of the gates of the palace, was only signed after several hours of debate.

A first attempt failed because of the attitude of the Mobile Guards who crossed their bayonets, and the republicans showed themselves to be disposed to stay in the Hôtel de Ville in case the pact were to be violated.

It must be said that during that tumultuous night the members of the provisional commission were not able to confer peacefully among themselves concerning their common situation. They were drowned in a noisy and irritated crowd that made any kind of concerted action impossible.

Flourens was still ignorant of the presence on the square, in the Hôtel de Ville , and at its gates of several republican battalions that had been requested by Blanqui while he was separated from Flourens and alone in one of the deliberation rooms, where he gave numerous orders that were carried outside before the arrival of the troops.

Blanqui, for his part, didn't know that Flourens's *tirailleurs* were on the ground floor and only learned of it when they tore him from the hands of the counter-revolutionary troops.

The stories in the reactionary newspapers are nothing but a tissue of lies and slanders. They don't hesitate before any indignity. We must quote in the first ranks the paper that dared to print the following lines: "The invaders of the Hôtel de Ville first had themselves served dinner. And then, between the pears and the cheese they sent two delegates to the ministry of Finance bearing a bond signed by Blanqui, a bond for 15,000,000 francs!" And later: "They sent a lieutenant to the secretary general (of finance) who presented a requisition signed Blanqui calling on the central cashier to give the bearer 15,000,000."

Citizen Blanqui didn't even take a piece of bread or a glass of water at the Hôtel de Ville , except the two mouthfuls he swallowed at the insistence of a National Guardsman of the 17th after he was beaten.

The comrades of this Guardsman shouldn't be too upset with him for this act of humanity. It didn't prevent him from acting as an escort for the prisoner.

Citizen Blanqui sent no one to the ministry of finance or any other ministry. The demand of 15,000,000 is a miserable fable like those reaction knows how to fabricate. It has never had any other weapons.

The Death Sentence of the Republic on November 3, 1870

November 7, 1870

It's done; the suicide has been carried out. There is no more Paris. All that remains is a decrepit Babylon that, as it fell, didn't know how to maintain the decorum of a fallen woman.

Our rulers could have spared us this shame. It wasn't necessary for their triumph. A final sentiment of modesty, even gratitude, commanded them to treat the old city gently, to not lay bare its secret turpitude, which gave them their victory.

They preferred to hide their own cowardice behind the city's failings and to publicly dishonor it before Europe.

To do this, it sufficed to appeal to the most beastly manifestations of egoism. They didn't hesitate, and 280,000 votes against 52,000 sold the country for a few pounds of meat. They'll give the republic as a deposit.

But make no mistake; the 52,000 votes that protest against this infamy are not alone. Half the voters didn't take part in the vote *intra-muros*, and in a situation where reaction had gathered all its forces the abstentions take on a decisive character.

Admitting there were a fifth who were indifferent or even monarchists, the other abstentionists, together with the 52,000 "no" voters form half the electoral body.

And if, in addition, we take into account the young people of ages 18 to 21 who aren't electors but who still have an opinion and a will, their votes, pure of the filth of egoism, gives the majority to hearts and minds over guts in this struggle.

Despite these reservations, Paris nevertheless stands branded in the eyes of the world. People will only see the votes cast; no one will think of the result's rejection on the part of the silent numbers. Six weeks of resistance had inspired admiration. And then the events of one day brought us universal contempt.

And how disgusting it is when empty palaver is joined to cowardice and we proudly march to capitulation under the big words of heroism. Bismarck no longer has anything to fear or any reason to act with moderation. The government of September 4 had just freed him of his sole sincere enemy: the revolution. The Prussians task is done. All that is left to them is to order the opening of the gates and the ceding of the two provinces of the Rhine. They will be obeyed.

The denouement is not far off. The comedies of preparations and defense are now superfluous. The armistice and its guarantees, and then peace with all its disgrace: this is what the Hôtel de Ville is going to impose on France.

As for the republic, it is dying. The press has today announced its death sentence.

We said in the past: in 1848 the republic's existence was counted in months; in 1870 at best it will be counted in weeks. Making this prediction required no great intelligence. The republicans are now outlawed by the monarchists in the name of the republic.

Tomorrow, the republic will itself be outlawed.

The End of the Drama

December 7, 1870

The final fight has begun and will continue until the denouement. It is now a combat without truce that necessity imposes on us. Famine is hard on our heels and accepts no delays. We are cornered.

It is uncertainty that is causing worry. It's true that the Prussians are losing ground, but the game is complicated. Time is both against them and against us: against us in the form of famine; against them in the rising up of the country. Who will reach the goal first, hunger or the assisting army?

What a coup it would be if hunger had a head start of twenty-four hours. The Parisian forces prisoners, the invasion reconstituted in one mass to crush the army of the provinces, not to mention the fright and the disorganization that would follow the fall of Paris. For whatever people might think, Paris is the soul and palladium of France.

Of course the army, having arrived too late, could continue the war under the direction of a provisional government taking refuge in city after city until it reached Toulon, an impregnable location supplied by our fleet. But this army is doubtless of diverse opinions. Who can say that one of the rival monarchies won't accept the crown from the hands of Wilhelm and that in its despair the country won't bow before the vassal of the German hordes proclaimed in the capitol?

So Paris must count on no one. If the auxiliaries from outside second it in its labor of salvation with their assistance or even by their simple approach, that's fine. If they can't, Paris must free itself on its own.

On November 30 General Trochu attempted to force the Prussian lines. He didn't succeed. On December 2, attacked in the positions he had occupied two days previously, he vigorously repelled the attack. But not thinking himself up to supporting a second attack, he passed over the Marne again. He was right to do so for a failure in this position would have been a disaster, and we can no longer risk a disaster.

This retreat did not resemble those of preceding sorties. It didn't imply a defeat. We retreated after a victorious action because we didn't feel we had sufficient strength for an aggression more powerful than the first. It is probable that prince Frederick Karl was arriving with a part of his army, and it was reckless to expose ourselves to a possible irreparable defeat.

The days of [November] 30 and [December] 2 are thus not a success, since we had to retreat. Even so, they are even less a failure. Paris can be delivered through five or six such failures. Our losses were serious, and it is hard to envision even worse. But the enemy is every bit as damaged, if not more. It lost the battlefield twice, which doesn't usually happen to it. This three-day fight did not discourage the Parisians. On the contrary, but it must certainly have demoralized the Germans.

Their situation is becoming critical. The French armies advance towards Paris and are growing. Prince Frederick Karl, who brazenly marched on Lyon to have done with the centers of resistance, had to retreat quickly in order to cover and perhaps even reinforce the threatened siege army.

Paris unfortunately lacks weapons, and it's impossible to hold back its curses against rulers whose incompetence and banality placed it in its situation of abandonment and deprivation. This lack of weapons paralyzes 300,000 men of the National Guard more than half of our garrison. It's truly distressing.

Suppose we had 300,000 chassepots or Snider rifles and a proportional amount of artillery. The German lines would be broken, dispersed, and the invasion lost. If we had had these 300,000 rifles, Wilhelm would have long since fled.

He persists because the raising of the siege would be a debacle. The situation is as dramatic for the Prussians as it is for us. If they take the city, it perhaps means total victory. If they don't take it, it definitely means total ruin. The game will be decided shortly.

We can still lose it due to famine. Our liberators aren't far away, but their forces have Prince Charles at their head. They came close to us at about November 15, counting on a great sortie in accordance General Trochu's announcement. They had to withdraw, not without having spread terror in Versailles.

Nothing proves that they can win out over the army that blocks their passage. In this state of affairs, with everyone holding everyone else in check and the enemy having everything to gain and us having everything to lose from this immobility that abandons the denouement to famine, it is up to Paris to aid itself.

And so the offensive, the continuous offensive, without pause is our sole resource. We can't count on decisive victories. But seven or eight affairs like those of November 30 and December 2 will force the Prussians to pack their bags. They are in no condition to support such losses. The demoralization of their army will not allow them to carry on that far.

Inquiry on the Commune

In 1897 *La Revue Blanche*, one of France's most important and influential literary journals, ran an "Inquiry on the Commune" in two of its issues asking participants the following three questions:

> What was your role from March 18 to the end of May 1871?
>
> What is your opinion of the insurrectionary movement of the Commune, and what do you think of its parliamentary, military, financial, and administrative organization?
>
> In your opinion, what has been the influence of the Commune, both then and now, on events and ideas?

The following are chosen from among the dozens of participants.

Henri Rochefort

Q: What was your role during the Commune?

A: I simply did my duty as a journalist. I didn't take part in the Commune. But since I clearly published my opinion of Versailles, whose conduct I found odious, I was accused of provoking the rebellion.

Q: On March 18?

A: No, later. On March 18 I was in Arcachon, so ill that my death was announced. In Archachon I received a visit from my children, who were dressed in mourning for their father.

Q: You arrived in Paris?

A: April 2, the day, I think, of Flourens' sortie. *Le Mot d'Ordre*, which I was writing for, was suppressed by Ladmirault, that old, vile, brute.

Q: Can we do without the epithets?

A: No. Ladmirault was an ignoble brute, as were all the professional soldiers. I ignored the prohibition. The government had slipped away to Versailles. I energetically supported Paris's rights. I spoke of Thiers's odious role and his abominable lies. Naturally, all of my sympathies were with the Communal movement, which was both socialist and patriotic.

The Commune was a protest against the peace of Bordeaux, a protest against the clerical and reactionary majority that dishonored us, a protest against the abuse of power of an assembly which, named to negotiate peace, had—without a mandate—declared itself constituent. But the Commune became authoritarian and suppressed the newspapers that weren't devoted to it. Raoul Rigault and Félix Pyat suppressed newspapers; Felix Pyat in particular suppressed newspapers for his own profit. I fought for freedom and good sense, as I did all my life. Raoul Rigault suppressed *Le Mot d'Ordre*. The pretext was my protest against the hostage decree, or rather its execution. We followed the example given by our African generals who, in the name of the government, had taken hostages there and massacred them. Those who had applauded the massacres and razzias in Africa found the Commune's conduct odious. I found it natural, but I didn't want the decree executed. It was this article that later led to me being placed before a military tribunal by the Versaillais. Idiocy! Idiocy! Always the soldiers! All imbeciles. Do you know what they held against me? It's that in the headline the word "hostages" was typed in capital letters. It's idiotic. I approved the decree and I protested against its execution. Raoul Rigault wanted to have me arrested. I was warned of this by a young man, a secretary of Rigault's I think.

Q: Forain?

A: No, not Forain, a member of the Commune's police. I left. I was arrested in Meaux on the 21st.

Q: Was there an order against you from the Versaillais?

A: Not at all; it was from Raoul Rigault. He was an excellent man, quite intelligent. All right. But he was for the fight to the finish. He knew what the Versaillais would do, and he was right. He took no extenuating circumstances into consideration. No quarter! He had participated in my newspaper, but he was a man who would have executed his best friend. If I had been seized by the Commune there was no question what would have happened to me. But in Meaux I was taken by the Versaillais. The commander of the German subdivision wanted to allow me to leave; I remained in prison despite the Prussians. At the court martial those brutes took no account of what I had to say. I was on the point of being executed; it was a near thing. Perhaps what saved me was Rossel's arrest, which occurred at just that moment. He went ahead of me. The court martial had already sentenced members of the Commune to death; it condemned Rossel to death. Perhaps they decided to take it easy on me. I spent five months in prison. After a two-day trial I was sentenced to deportation for life, which in civil matters is equivalent to the death penalty. Even worse, we were dealing with such ignorant judges that they didn't even know that the death penalty in political matters had been abolished since 1848. Officers! I remember that in prison I was Rossel's neighbor. I had won over our guard by sharing with him the victuals that were sent to me; he let us talk. I owe him the few good hours that I passed with the unfortunate Rossel, who they didn't sentence to death, but who they assassinated. Note that before '48 the law punished soldiers who revolted or went over to the enemy with death. Since then the only ones punished with death were traitors: it is by virtue of this law that they killed Rossel. (M. Da Costa, who was present for the interview, observed that of three officers tried and judged by the government of the Third Republic, Rossel, Bazaine, and Dreyfus, only one was sentenced to death: Rossel.)

Rossel was assassinated. I was sentenced to deportation for life to a fortified place as leader of a gang and for inciting to revolt. Jules Simon later told me that Thiers had done all in his power to prevent me from being executed. Cissey the thief, the swindler who poisoned himself, Cissey the general, the minister of war, the supporter of Order and Religion, Cissey demanded that I be executed. In the name of the army he demanded my execution. Thiers defended me. He carried on. He cried. He said that they couldn't put to death a former member of the government. If they executed members of the government... he... But the fact is, it appears he cried in my behalf. He didn't even want me deported. In the end he agreed that I be imprisoned on an island outside of France. There are no islands that aren't outside France. But in the prison prepared for me on Saint-Marguerite, Bazaine was also imprisoned. Edmond Adam showed me a letter from the director of that prison, telling him he wouldn't be a severe host in my regard, but that I would have to do picket duty. You understand that I didn't want any kind of exceptional treatment, and I feared being a prisoner who was, so to speak, on parole. I was already thinking of escaping. In the midst of all this, on May 24 Thiers was overthrown and I was deported. It's pointless, isn't it, to tell you how I escaped, with Jourde, Olivier Pain, Paschal Grousset, Ballière, Granthille; how I lived in London, in Geneva, and finally my return...

Q: Your triumphal return. And your opinion of the Commune?

A: As the Empire had fallen, we believed in the republic. When we ended up with an Assembly even more clerical and reactionary than the preceding ones, we revolted. The majority had exasperated me, and that's why I tendered my resignation in Bordeaux. The Parisians had had enough. The Commune was the explosion of duped and betrayed republican sentiments. Thiers admitted it: the insurrection was produced by the exasperation of disappointed patriotism. Governments rarely change, and they continue to exasperate the governed.

(Going on to talk about Greece, M. Rochefort shows us a statuette that the Greeks just sent him, and ingeniously explains to us what a Tanagra is.)

Q: But the Commune, your opinion?

A: The Commune, quite simply, is the only honest government there has been in France since Pharamond. The rulers earned 15 francs a day. Since then they cost us a bit more. I was with them when I was deported. Not a single one of these men had a sou.

Q: But these honest men, do you think that they were able, were well inspired?

A: It depends. There were moderates and extremists. Naturally, it was the extremists who were right. When you want to act you can't take half measures, or else… Look, the Greeks are hardly anything compared to France, but if they remain boastful up to the bitter end, they'll likely win out over all the powers.

Q: The administration?

A: I know very little about it.

Q: And the influence of the Commune?

A: Enormous. The massacres by the Versaillais have forever discredited bourgeois society. And then the Commune saved the republic.

Q: That we have.

A: I don't want to say anything. Nevertheless, it remains the example.

Paschal Grousset
Member of the Commune, Delegate for External Relations. Currently a Deputy

It's not only a chapter of my life story that you are asking about, it's a whole volume. The volume is written, but will only come out after my death. Let it sleep. In a few words, here are my feelings about March 18.

It's hardly necessary to affirm that 2,000,000 men don't rise up without reason, don't fight for nine weeks and don't leave 35,000 corpses on the streets without having good reasons.

For many, these reasons were the result of the long suffering which is the life of seven-eighths of a so-called civilized nation. For others they were principally born of obsidional angers, of a great effort made sterile through official incompetence, of the shame of the capitulation, and also by an agreement made easier by the coming together of civic forces. For most people the dominant idea, the main idea, was the primordial need to defend the republic, directly attacked by a clerical and royalist Assembly.

The republic of our dreams was assuredly not the one we have. We wanted it to be democratic and social, and not plutocratic. We wanted to make it a precision instrument of economic transformation. For us, republic was synonymous with regeneration. Amid the smoking ruins of the fatherland it seemed to us necessary and right to completely disqualify the men and institutions who had caused these ruins. We needed new schools, a new morality, and new guides. Work for all, education for all, national defense for all, unshakeable confidence in the destiny of our race: these were the slogans that spontaneously rose from the heart of a bloodied Paris and which in its eyes was embodied by the republic.

The siege left us militarily organized; this is why our revolution was both military and civil. The ruling classes had just given the measure of their criminal incapacity. This is why our revolution was proletarian and marks the pivotal fact of modern times, which is the direct access of the workers to the mysteries of power.

As for the Commune, for us as for those of 1792, it was the chance and provisional organism that is born at moments of crisis to take social evolution in hand and to lead it to its goal.

You already know how the struggle was engaged and what its course was. Thanks to the complicity of Germany, which purposely turned its 300,000 prisoners over to the Assembly at Versailles, Paris fell before numbers. But at least, by its heroic effort it gave republican France the time to take itself in hand. Formal commitments were made by Thiers with the delegates of the major, frightened cities. When the blood was washed from our streets it was discovered that Paris's program was the only practical one.

It is thus that from our holocaust, from our pain, from the tears of our mothers, that the republican pact was solidified. In the meanwhile, the municipal law was voted. On this point as well Paris won the day.

As for the economic transformation, it was put off for a quarter century. But who today would dare to say that it has not remained inevitable? Poverty grows along with mechanical progress. In this beautiful France, thousands of arms have nothing to do. The malaise of every class is betrayed by symptoms that are more obvious with each passing day. The impotence of old formulas, the incoherence of institutions and acts is clear for all to see. The hour is approaching when on this point too, the program of March 18 will impose itself by the force of circumstances. For we who wanted to advance it this hour will be that of historic justice.

Edouard Vaillant
Member of the Commune, currently Deputy

Without being as clear about it as I am now, I was nevertheless convinced from the beginning of the revolution of March 18, that there should be only one dominant preoccupation and goal: the fight against Versailles. To be or not to be—for the Commune that was the whole question. The facts, the circumstances had posed things in this way. If not to win, it had at least to last. However important it was to make manifest its revolutionary socialist character by all possible acts, nothing could better affirm this character than its very existence, its resistance. It was that and the rage, the fury of capitalism's reaction; the coalesced efforts against Paris of Versailles and Bismarck.

Those who during the siege had participated in the agitation, in the revolutionary socialist action concentrated at the Corderie, seat of the Committee of the Twenty Arrondissements and who, at the cry of "Vive la Commune!" had attacked the Hôtel de Ville on October 8, penetrated it October 31, and on January 22 had attempted, for the defense of the republic and for the revolution, to seize power, these people were not in a state of uncertainty. Throughout the siege they had seen the revolutionary movement grow, though it didn't attract the populace, duped by the lies and charlatanry of its rulers. They were able to foresee the popular anger and revolt on the day of disillusionment and open betrayal. And this is indeed what happened when, after having responded to our red poster that it wouldn't capitulate, the government capitulated and from hatred of the revolution, surrendered Paris and the country to the monarchic invader, which had become its counter-revolutionary ally.

Events had dispersed the committee of the Corderie and the arrondissement committees. Their most active members had made the mistake of going into the provinces, to such a point that they weren't at the head of the tumultuously growing movement that followed the governmental betrayal, where all the angered and rebellious currents of opinion would finally mix together.

The Central Committee of the National Guard was the expression of that uncertain and intermediary period, from which came, with the March 26th election, the elected Commune.

Several revolutionaries from the Corderie and revolutionaries and socialists from various groups entered the Commune. And so this election gave it a momentum, a direction, that was more socialist. The elected Commune was far from being what the committee of the Corderie would have been: a revolutionary Commune, master of power. It had neither that unity of ideas and action or energy. It was a deliberative assembly without sufficient cohesion, whose decisiveness wasn't on a par with its good will and intentions. What we can say in praise of it is that it was truly the representative, the socialist representative of Paris in revolt, and it did its best to represent it and defend it.

We can also add that most of the citizens who were delegates there did honor to their mandates. And we must pay honors less to them than to the revolutionary and enthusiastic environment that lifted everything up and made it grow. It was an environment that in those unforgettable and admirable weeks, made of the people of Paris in arms—at first to guard its weapons against reaction and the provocations of Versailles, and then increasingly for working class emancipation and the revolution—a people of combatants and citizens.

And in fact, as the threat of defeat became more pressing, the revolutionary spirit increasingly animated those who remained standing, those who lived, who fought. They truly represented Paris and its people. It is their fight and their death that constituted their grandeur in the eyes of the world, made all the greater by the ferocity of those who carried out the massacres: the grandeur of the Paris Commune.

When for many days Paris was isolated, in flames, slaughtered by the Versaillais assassins, was dying, in the eyes of all it became the incarnation of the proletariat fighting for its deliverance and the revolution militant. The prolonged fury of Versaillais reaction, applauded and assisted by the reaction and capitalism of all countries, spread this impression everywhere, confirmed this effect, made this calling to life of the organized revolt of all the poor, of all the oppressed more striking.

And so the struggle and the fall of the Commune, its history and legend, were the universal evocation of socialist and revolutionary consciousness. And in those countries where there had until then only been democratic demands, socialism was affirmed. If socialism wasn't born of the Commune, it is from the Commune that dates that portion of international revolution that no longer wants to give battle in a city in order to be surrounded and crushed, but which instead wants, at the head of the proletarians of each and every country, to attack national and international reaction and put an end to the capitalist regime.

M. Pindy
Member of the Commune

What do I think of the insurrection, of its organization? I think we acted like children who try to imitate grown-ups whose names and reputations subjugate them, and not like men with force (at least a certain force) should have done in the face of the eternal enemy. I am far from being a passionate admirer of what we did during the Commune, and I think that aside from a minority of our colleagues whose time at the Hôtel de Ville gave them the idea that they were statesmen, the others, and the people along with them, have become convinced that the best of governments is worth nothing and that authority, in whatever hands it is placed, is always harmful to the advancement of humanity.

Le Chaux-de-Fonds

M. Dereure
Cobbler

Elected in November 1870 to the municipality of the 18th arrondissement with Clemenceau, Lafont, and Jaclard, I remained at my fighting post, faithful to the insurrection. Elected a member of the Commune on March 26, I fought for its cause until the final day of combat.

Q: The parliamentary organization?

A: The Commune concerned itself far too much with details it would have been preferable to look after only after the military victory. It was powerfully organized. The Central Committee of the National Guard, which had been elected to prevent the Prussians from entering Paris and which met March 18 at the Hôtel de Ville , didn't understand its role and didn't want to take the responsibility for throwing its battalions at Versailles from the beginning. It left Thiers the time to organize the besieging army and it only worried about the elections to the Commune. Nevertheless, it had taken measures to seize the forts, but it sent the absinthe addict Lullier to Mont-Valérien; I had to shake Lullier, dead drunk, on a couch in the Hôtel de Ville . And based on the illusory promise of the fort's commander, the traitor didn't leave at the fort the battalions he had brought there. And after the sortie of April 3, a sortie that had been organized by some members of the Commune without the consent of the latter, the Parisians were stupefied and immediately demoralized at finding themselves under fire from Mont-Valérien. Confidence was lost. I estimate that after this defeat there weren't 40,000 men who in rotation defended Paris. I was often at the forward position and the constant request of the superior officers was, "We are lacking men; we need reinforcements." Towards the end of the Commune I was delegated to Dombrowski to keep an eye on his actions. Versailles had offered him a million to withdraw his forces from one of the gates; he had himself denounced this fact to the Committee of Public Safety. Did he betray? This is a point difficult to elucidate. I am convinced that he was not a traitor. What I saw was that it was absolutely impossible to send companies to the Point du Jour. The cannons of Mont-Valérien, of Montretout, and the heights of Issy rained down on it. Something interesting is that the chateau of La Muette, where the general staff was located, only received two cannon shots, one on the staircase and one in the stable. Placed as it was—within range of the cannons of Mont-Valérien—it should have been pulverized. There must have been two or three informants on the general staff whose lives had to be preserved.

Q: Financially?

A: If the Commune would have placed an embargo on the Bank [of France] everything would have worked much better, and it's not just a question of that Bank, but of all the banks. And they should have also seized the daily receipts of all the railroad companies. A detail: I remember seeing the directors of these companies at the ministry of Finance, where Varlin had invited them. They were across from two workers, Varlin, a bookbinder and me, a cobbler. And these people who are said to be so arrogant, showed such obsequiousness that I'm still disgusted by it.

Q: Administratively?

A: All services were easily reorganized and functioned with no difficulty.

Q: What do you think of the role of the Central Committee after the elections to the Commune?

A: There was a harmful duality, but it was impossible for the Commune to smash the Central Committee, which had the National Guard in its hands.

Q: Did you have the illusion that you could emerge victors?

A: We had no illusions. And in general the members of the Commune sacrificed their lives. But with regard to the masses, we didn't think the repression would be so ignobly cruel.

Q: Once the Versaillais were in Paris, do you think that all the members of the Commune did their duty?

A: No, it seems that the primary concern of some among them was to hide. In the final hours I recall seeing Ranvier, Varlin, Ferré, Gambon, Theisz, Jourde, Serrailler, and Trinquet. Others were fighting at other points; others had been taken prisoner or had been blocked in their neighborhoods. Durand, Rigault, and Varlin were executed. Delescluze died at the barricades. Others were wounded: Vermorel, Arnaud, Protot, and Brunel. If, many were able to escape once the battle was finished, it's because the Empire's police had been totally disorganized.

Q: And the barricades?

A: The barricades were good, but we didn't make enough use of houses. The Versaillais, on the contrary, knew how to use them. In the final days, the best defenders of the Commune were unquestionably the children and the elderly.

Jean Allemane
Editor-in-chief of the *Parti Ouvrier*

March 18, 1871 was a day that was wished for and prepared by M. Thiers and his accomplices, determined to have done with the popular National Guard (the armed workers), in the same way that their kin of the provisional government of 1848 put an end to the workers of the national workshops.

The mistake these rotters committed was, in the first case, that of unmasking themselves by assisting the Bank of France in ruining hundreds of small merchants and factory owners by deciding the cessation of the deferral of commercial payments. This could very well have had serious consequences if, instead of well-intentioned citizens and unknowing socialists, the Central Committee had been composed of determined men capable of guiding affairs by beginning their attack at the true center of resistance: the Bank of France. The members of the middle class, who were already overexcited by the patriotic disappointment, would have applauded the most daring measures.

Had determined men been in power during the insurrection, Messieurs Thiers and de Ploeuc, authorized representatives of the upper bourgeoisie and high finance, would have had nothing left to do but say their mea culpa for having unleashed the hurricane. But the members of the Central Committee—as was later the case with those of the Commune—were motivated strictly by sentiments. Their lack of resolution, compounded by economic ignorance, made them lose the benefits of an exceptionally favorable situation, since in the eyes of all concerned the government's attack had taken on the character of a monarchical restoration. This led sincere republicans to avoid placing any obstacles before measures that were clearly socialist and revolutionary.

The main thing was to move quickly, and this was precisely what wasn't done.

Proclamations, more proclamations, and still more proclamations. During this time the reactionary beast recovered from the turmoil caused by the unforeseen resistance and the incidents of the war. This resistance caused the finest flower of the canaille to scurry to Versailles and, assisted by all the cowardice and all the parasitism that was being held at bay, the reactionary beast prepared its revenge. A revenge which history will recognize was at the same high level as the braggarts that the flat-footed Maxime Du Camp called "the party of honest men."

March 18, 1871 was willed by its leaders and could have marked the epoch of a new world for the despoiled. But in order to do this, instead of chattering, it should have struck the bourgeoisie at its most sensitive point: the safe!

That done, all that would have had to be left was to use the gold to disorganize the Versaillais gangs, something much easier to do in Paris than should have been. Had they been deprived of their gold then steel, resolutely employed, would have put an end to capitalist resistance.

Too "48-er" to consider this, the men of the Central Committee unconsciously repaired the errors committed by M. Thiers and his accomplices, and allowed them to prepare the murders of the Bloody Week.

Jean Grave
Editor of *Les Temps Nouveaux*

Grave took no part in the Commune, but his opinion seemed of interest to us, the opinion of a revolutionary of today on the revolutionaries of the past.

What I think of the parliamentary, financial, military, and administrative organization of the Commune can be summed up in just a few words.

It was too parliamentary, financial, military, and administrative and not revolutionary enough.

To start with, while every day the battalions of Federals gathered at their meeting places waiting for the order to march on Versailles, a movement whose urgency was clear to all, the Central Committee, on the pretext that it didn't have regular power, thought only of organizing elections, while the army of order was reforming in Versailles.

The Commune, once elected, busied itself with passing laws and decrees, most of which were not implemented, because those they were aimed at realized that the Commune legislated much, but acted little.

Revolutionaries! That's nevertheless what they thought they were, but only in words and parades. So little were they really revolutionaries that even invested with the suffrage of the Parisians they continued to consider themselves intruders in the halls of power.

They lacked money, when hundreds of millions slept in the Bank of France. All they would have needed to do would have been to send out against the bank two or three battalions of National Guardsmen to have the Marquis de Ploeuc—who so easily fooled them—go flee into the shadows.

They voted the law on hostages and never dared implement it, while Versailles continued to massacre the Federals who fell into their hands.

I'm not saying that it should have executed the handful of gendarmes and obscure priests it had in its hands. Versailles could have not have cared less: the serious hostages were out of the Commune's reach. But it had the survey records, the mortgage office, the notary records, everything that regulates bourgeois property. If instead of making threats the Commune had actually set all the paperwork on fire, had taken control of the bank, the same bourgeois who insulted the imprisoned Federals would have forced Thiers to apologize to them on their behalf.

In a revolution, legality is not only a joke, but a hindrance; it can only serve the partisans of the order of affairs we want to destroy. It's not speeches, paperwork, or laws that are needed during a revolutionary period, but acts.

Instead of voting for the forfeiture of bosses in flight, they should immediately have placed their workshops in the possession of the workers, who would have put them in operation. And it was the same for everything. Instead of laws and decrees that would have remained dead letters, they needed facts. Then they would have been taken seriously.

They wanted to play at being soldiers, to parade in the uniforms of Jacobin officers, as if revolutionaries had to make a disciplined war.

Attacked by the government of Versailles, they should have contented themselves with self-defence. But they should only have given up ground foot by foot; they should have sapped terrain and houses so that every forward step of the soldiers of order would have been the equivalent of a defeat for them.

No, even backed against the wall in Paris they still wanted to develop strategy. They put up enormous barricades which, intended to confront a designated point, were turned by the enemy. Impregnable head on, they left their defenders wide open from behind. It would have been so easy to crenellate houses, to make each of them a fortress and only abandon them after having set them on fire or blown them up. The Commune respected property! Versailles, its defender, was less scrupulous and didn't hesitate to destroy houses when they had to turn a barricade.

Now, it must be said that the men of the Commune aren't responsible for what wasn't done. They were of their period, and in their time if there was a vague socialist sentiment, no one, neither leaders nor soldiers, had clearly defined ideas. So it was inevitable that everyone end up mired in uncertainty.

Triumphant, the Commune would have become a government like the others. A new revolution would have been needed to bring it down. Vanquished, it synthesized all proletarian aspirations, and gave momentum to the movement of ideas of which we of today are the product.

Louise Michel

For twenty-six years they've spoken of the victims of the Commune, about sixty whose names are known. The Commune's dead can't be counted. Paris was an immense abattoir where, after eight days of slaughter, the hordes of flies over the mass graves put an end to the killings for they feared the plague.

The number of dead of the Commune during the Bloody Week cannot be counted. They were buried everywhere, in the public squares, under the paving stones, in wells, in trenches dug at the time of the Prussians, in cemeteries, in casemates where they were burned. They were brought in wagons to the Champ de Mars, where they were also burned. The ashes weren't gathered and placed in urns; the winds that carried them away will tell neither their name nor their number.

And so the Commune, which naïvely waited for Versailles's attack and didn't plunge a spike in the stone heart of the vampire, the Bank of France, expiated its generosity.

But unvanquished under the avenging flames of the fire, it will be reborn even stronger, for it understood how useless political changes are that put one set of men in place of another set of men. It knew that the old parliamentary world would only ever produce what it produced on September 4, and this world has proved it since. Every revolution will now be social and not political; this was the final breath, the supreme aspiration of the Commune in the ferocious grandeur of its marriage with death.

The armies of the Commune counted few men knowledgeable in what is called the art of war, but all were equally brave. Cluseret, La Cécilia, Dombrowski, and Rossel were almost the only generals who came from the army, but enthusiasm and contempt for death have great value when the number of combatants is relatively small. This number was sometimes so small, as at Ivry, Clamart, and Neuilly, that it was an extraordinary stroke of luck that the enemy didn't know it. With combatants of this kind the Commune should have carried the situation from the first minutes. Already lost, the Federal hive for eight days halted the most formidable army that the Third Republic deployed.

It wasn't the moment for parliamentarism, and the Commune had no reason to praise the sessions it was engaged in, though it counted in its number eloquent men, like old Pyat, Vallès, and so many others. Majority and minority found themselves united at the final hour in the grandeur of same sacrifice.

You ask me, dear comrades, what my role was from March 18 to the end of May 1871. I went out with the marching companies of the Commune from the first sortie, I was a member of the Montmartre battalion, and I fought in the ranks as a soldier. In all conscience I thought this was the most useful thing to do. I continued fighting in Paris like the others, until Versailles arrested my mother in order to execute her in my place. I went to set her free (despite herself) by demanding that place for myself.

I have many times told how during the voyage to Caledonia I became an anarchist. But when people started to talk about the Commune again and question us, it seemed to me that the events of that period were as if a thousand years from us, we who are like shades, having passed through so many of the dead. Has the moment arrived when the specter of evil will be lifted?

London

Jean-Baptiste Clément
Member of the Commune

J-B Clément spoke to us about the frame of mind of his colleagues of the Commune.

Men like Theisz, Varlin, and Avrial went no further than mutualism. Vermorel was an enemy of communism. But was there even a question of communism? The Blanquists, especially Vaillant, had the best feeling for the situation and often sounded the right note.

Q: At the Commune you busied yourselves with decrees on payments due, on rents, on the municipal pawnshop.

A: The debts due! How much talk has there been about this! I said: "Does this have anything to do with the Commune? Then let merchants make arrangements among themselves." As for the setting aside of the rents, it was not without difficulty that the Commune voted it. And yet Paris was a barracks, and in a barracks they don't go so far as to make you pay rent.

At one session, having said: "Citizens, I thought we were here to proceed to social liquidation," Jourde heckled me. Since I got angry, Ostyn calmed me down, while Varlin approved Jourde. And the *Journal Officiel* of the Commune is full of the nominations of bailiffs and, what is less gloomy, devotes three pages to the regulating of the ham fair.

As for the Bank of France, Jourde and Beslay's way of acting was unspeakable. Had it condemned Beslay, the Commune would have been afraid to see him leave, and he was considered indispensable at the Bank. And he was also a proof of honesty at the entrance to the Commune. Varlin, who rightly left a great reputation of uprightness and intelligence made too many allowances for Beslay. Jourde was not without value, but he unfortunately had some financial capacities. Have they bored us enough, these honest men and these financiers?

Q: Did you believe in Paris's victory?

A: At best, Paris could have won out over Versailles. But to believe that would have implied that the triumph of the social revolution would be naïve, for the Prussians weren't far away, and the provinces were around us. No, there was nothing to hope for. The frame of mind was not what it is today. If Paris were to proclaim the Commune today it would find partisans in every village of France.

Q: During the final week?

A: I was in the 11th arrondissement at the barricade on the Rue Fontaine-au-Roi with Gambon, the two Ferrés, Géresme, Laccord of the Central Committee, and Penet, a wood sculptor who is still alive today. There and elsewhere I could see that in the streets Paris had no better defenders than the very young and the elderly. Even more, since its inception, the insurrection had given rise to much heroism: it had Duval, Herpin-Lacroix, and Dombrowski, the Dombrowski to whom I one day said: "Look, you are needlessly exposing yourself; you're going to get yourself killed," and who, rolling a cigarette answered: "Not at all; but I have to show these good people that the General of the Commune is not afraid." And with him that wasn't a pose, but rather the intrepidness of a hero of legend. And at the final barricades we saw Lisbonne offering himself as a target to the bullets, seated on a workhorse as big as an elephant and who, pointing to his men, replied to those who called to him: "I can't get down; this is the way they love me."

All this is perhaps secondary and the interest of so much Communard intrepidity seems to be of a decorative order. We lacked more precious qualities: initiative and the hatred of consecrated things.

Gaston Da Costa

Former Chief of Cabinet of the Committee of Public Safety, former Assistant Procurator of the Commune, currently reader in a major bookstore, author of the grammar book adopted by the city of Paris for its schools

Q: What was your role during the Commune?

A: The Blanquist party, of which I was a member, was primarily represented during the Commune by men of action such as Eudes, Granger, Girault, Fortin, Rigault, Trinquet, Regnard, Ferré, Breuillé, Brideau, Jeunesse, Genton, etc. Many were members of the Committee of Public Safety.

The latter reorganized the prefecture of police in the same way that it had previously functioned and as it still functions today, except that it was mainly occupied with political policing. I was particularly charged with the seeking out of former secret agents of the Imperial police. A certain number, who plotted alongside us under the Empire, were arrested, and the rest, declared hostages, were executed during the final days of the Bloody Week. I ran their pre-trial investigations and testified against them when they appeared before the revolutionary assizes whose juries were made up of delegates selected from the battalions of the Federals. This court had to judge, or rather declare to be or not to be hostages, policemen, priests, Municipal Guards, and individuals like Jecker, the man behind the war in Mexico. Once declared hostages, in keeping with the decree they had to be executed. In fact, the decree wasn't applied in the way it was written (three hostages were to be executed for each National Guardsman executed on the front lines).

Nevertheless, during the Bloody Week several hostages were executed at La Roquette and on the rue Haxo. They were held either at Mazas or at La Roquette. On May 25 both the Place de la Bastille and Austerlitz Bridge were attacked by the Versaillais. Mazas was threatened. I received the order of the Commune, which at the time was taking refuge at the town hall of the 11th arrondissement. The order, signed by Ferré, said to go to Mazas to carry out the transfer of the hostages from Mazas to La Roquette. This transfer was carried out in wagons which I requisitioned from the Compagnie de Lyon (it was the receipts that later caused my condemnation). While passing through the faubourg Saint-Antoine the wagons were attacked and, despite the escort, the crowd, made up mostly of women, wanted to lynch the hostages.

We had all the trouble in the world in getting to La Roquette. My role ended there. The next day Archbishop Darboy, Deguerry, several priests, and Jecker were executed. One shouldn't hasten to accuse the crowd of cowardice. One might say that this was a case of legitimate exasperation. You have to have lived the events to realize their state of mind. At the same spot the crowd, despite Delescluze and Eudes, had just executed the Count de Beaumont, who it accused of having misled it concerning the fate of a large number of dead in Neuilly.

I told you that I managed to save my convoy.

Q: Even so, without hesitation you executed Ferré's order, even though you had foreseen the consequences.

A: Exactly. What do you expect? We were living through a revolutionary torment. It was part of the struggle, the result of legitimate exasperation. These women were no more harpies than I was a bandit.

Q: And the other hostages?

A: Were transferred under the care of the chief judge of the court martial to the rue Haxo when Père Lachaise was threatened. On the rue Haxo it was said that forty were executed. They were mostly secret agents, Municipal Guards, the Municipal Guards in civilian clothes. Most had been taken in the barracks and died bravely. There were almost no more priests on the rue Haxo; the ones they were after were the police and the police informers. The people, the masses, didn't understand the meaning of the word hostage and naïvely translated it as priest, agent.

Q: What else did you do?

A: I signed all the arrest warrants. I am speaking, of course, only of arrests carried out regularly. But another fact contributed to my condemnation. It relates to Ruault, condemned under the empire in the Opera Comique Afffair, a plot against the Emperor in which, if I'm not mistaken, M. Ranc was accused. We all considered Ruault an old republican. When we had the proof that he was an agent you can imagine our indignation. When he was brought into my office I wrote some words on the back of his warrant that I showed him: "Save this canaille for the firing squad." The director of Mazas, a Blanquist as well, upon receiving this warrant placed it in his wallet. When I had the hostages evacuated from Mazas I had all the arrest warrants burned in the prison courtyard. Fifteen minutes after our departure the Versaillais entered, executed the director, found Ruault's warrant and my note.

Q: How old were you?

A: Twenty.

Q: And the organization?

A: I repeat: as far as I know only the personnel had changed at the prefecture of police.

In general, what the Blanquists wanted was a military dictatorship with the aim of defeating the Versaillais, to have a national convention named, and to continue the war. And this is why we expended all our efforts in trying to obtain Blanqui's exchange or escape.

All the offers of hostage exchange with Blanqui were sent from the prefecture of police, by the intermediary of Flotte, an old friend of Blanqui's. We offered all the hostages for Blanqui alone. We wanted to make Blanqui the leader of the insurrection. We didn't want to concern ourselves with parliamentary organization, administration, or socialism. Our sole objective was to go to Versailles, whose government was nothing but an usurper in our eyes. From this flowed the sortie of April 3: Eude's movements on Meudon in the center, of Flourens on the right wing on

Bougival, and of Duval on the left on Chatillon. The goal of this movement was to take Versailles, to dissolve the Assembly and continue the war. Revolutionary republicans, we didn't conduct ourselves like a government in struggle with another government, but like insurgents against usurpers who, above all, we had to overthrow.

Q: Did these projects materialize differently from the sorties you spoke to us about?

A: Between Rossel and the principal Blanquist leaders, it was question of carrying out a coup d'état with the aim of a military dictatorship, the sole manner in our opinion, of fighting and ceasing to deliberate. I recall a meeting held at the prefecture of police. We soon renounced our projects, seeing that it was too late. The proposal came from Rossel and was made just a few days before his resignation.

Q: And your opinion on the Commune, on its influence?

A: Well, when, after we returned after eight years of the penal colony, we saw the republic that had been made for us, we had to say that it wasn't worth the trouble.

Maxime Vuillaume
At the time, editor of the *Père Duchêne*.
Currently, editor of the *Radical*

Q: As someone sentenced to death by the military provost of the Luxembourg, can you tell us how justice was rendered during the last week of May?

A: My day was May 25. That day I heard many interrogations, which didn't take up too much of my time. Here was the formula: the provost asked: "You were arrested. Where?" "In my house tonight. I don't know why." The provost raised his eyes. And invariably, without any other explanation: "Put him in the line." Or more simply, with a glance at the door where four soldiers were standing: "In line!" Even so, for me it was a bit longer. I had been arrested on the street and I had the armband of the Cross of Geneva. "Why do you have that armband?" "I'm a doctor," I answered, "That's why I have the armband of the International Society for the Wounded, presided over by the Count of Flavigny. I was already a doctor during the siege." "And whose doctor are you now? Which wounded do you care for?" "All of them," I answered, embarrassed. "I cared for everyone during the battle, the soldiers of the army and those of the Commune" "You're not an army doctor?" "No, but..." "You remained in Paris during the Commune?" "Yes." The provost leaned over to the assistant and then, addressing the agents, said, "Take that man to the line."

Q: And this "line," what was it?

A: It was this. I left escorted by two agents with tricolor armbands. I found myself in the small courtyard of the senate. We turned to the left and an unforgettable spectacle suddenly appeared before me. Squeezed against a wall and surrounded by soldiers was a mass of men. Upon my arrival the ranks opened and then closed. This was what the provost called the line. Every few minutes a platoon of soldiers arrived and took away the first six. We then heard explosions. Hundreds and hundreds and hundreds of poor devils were executed in this way. There are piles of corpses under the two big gardens, and probably the body of Raoul Rigault.

Q: And yet you're here.

A: Thanks to the intercession of a sergeant of those troops who was a medical student: group solidarity!

Q: But you weren't a doctor!

A; Not in the least. I was editor of the *Père Duchêne* with Alphonse Humbert and Vermersch, and I had fought at the barricade on the Rue Monge. But if I really would have been a doctor, or even a supporter of Versailles, things would have gone the same way, except I would perhaps have been executed.

Élisée Reclus

My role during the Commune was officially nonexistent. I found myself among the anonymous mass of combatants and the defeated. A simple National Guardsman during the first days of the fight and then, after April 5 and for a year, a prisoner in the prisons of Satory, Trébéron, Brest, St-Germain, Versailles, and Paris, I can only formulate an opinion on the Commune from hearsay and the subsequent study of documents and men.

In the first years that followed the Commune it seemed to me that all those who had taken part in the movement were united due to the repression and the outrage suffered in common. I would not at that time have allowed myself to judge men who, in my opinion, were not worthy of the cause they defended. But the time has come to speak the truth, since impartial histories are beginning to be written and it is a matter of gathering information with future events in mind. I can thus affirm that during the first days of the Commune the military organization was as grotesque and worthless as it was during the first siege under the leadership of the pitiful Trochu. The proclamations were as bombastic, the disorder as great, the actions as ridiculous.

We can confirm this from this simple fact: General Duval, who was on the plateau of Chatillon with 2,000 men lacking in food and munitions, and who was surrounded by the growing mass of Versaillais, had requested reinforcements. We beat the call to arms in our arrondissement near the Pantheon, and at about 5:00 p.m. approximately 600 men were gathered on the square. Full of ardor, we wanted to march immediately to the fight, along with other corps sent by the southern quarters of Paris. But it appears that this movement would not have been in conformity with military precedent, and we were led to the Place Vendôme where, deprived of any food or camping equipment, for more than half the night we had no other comfort than hearing the brilliant officers of the new general staff say from within the nearby ministry: "Drink, drink to the independence of the world!"

At 2:00 a.m. an order from the general made our troop, already largely diminished through desertion, leave the precarious shelter of the Place Vendôme, and we were taken to the Place de la Concorde, where we tried to sleep on the stones until 6:00 a.m. It was then that we were led to Chatillon, our bones broken by this first bivouac and without any food. During the march our little band continued to melt away, and though we were 600 on our departure, 50 arrived on the plateau a half-hour before the Versaillais troops, pretending to go over to the cause of the revolution, were helped to climb the ramparts to repeated cries of "We are brothers! Let's embrace! Vive la République!" We were taken prisoner, and all those recognized by their uniform or their bearing as having once been soldiers were executed near the fence of the neighboring castle.

According to what my companions told me, I have every reason to believe that in other acts of war our gallant chiefs, at least those who commanded the first sorties, demonstrated the same lack of intelligence and the same negligence. Perhaps the government of the Commune had more capacities in other areas; in any case, history will say that these improvised ministers remained honest in exercising their power. But we asked something else of them: to have the good sense and determination that the situation required and to act in consequence. It was with real shock that we watched them continue all the same errors of official governments: maintaining the whole state governing system while only changing the men, keeping in place the entire bureaucracy, allowing tax agents to function in their booths and protect the money that the Bank of France sent to Versailles? The vertigo of power and the spirit of stupid routine had seized hold of them, and these men, who should have acted heroically and known how to die, had the inconceivably shameful naïveté to address diplomatic notes to the great powers in a style of which Metternich and Talleyrand would have approved. They understood nothing of the revolutionary movement that had carried them through the doors of the Hôtel de Ville .

But what the chiefs didn't know to do, the nameless crowd did. There were many of them, 30,000-40,000 perhaps, who died around Paris for the cause they loved. There were many as well who, within the city, fell before the machineguns shouting; "Vive la Commune!" We know from the first days of the Assembly in Versailles that this slaughtered people by its attitude saved the republican form of French government. Nevertheless, the present republic, a servant in the service of the Tsar and the Kaiser, is so far from any practice of liberty that it would be childish to be grateful to the Commune for its having saved this vain word for us. But it did something else. It held before us for the future, not through its rulers but through its defenders, an ideal far superior to that of all the revolutions that had preceded it. It commits in advance those who want to continue it—in France and throughout the world—to fight for a new society in which there will be neither masters by birth, titles, or money, nor servants by origin, caste, or salary. Everywhere the word "Commune" was understood in the widest sense, as having to do with a new humanity, formed of free and equal companions, ignorant of the existence of ancient borders, and assisting each other in peace from one end of the world to the other.

An Insurgent from Lyon

My role, from September 4 to March 22, was that of an ardent propagandist of the revolution, preaching in the workshop, involving myself with every movement, all the little riots that took place between these two dates. This attitude got me elected member of the Lyon Commune. Instinctively, through intuition rather than through reasoning, I felt that I was guilty of illogic by preaching freedom and accepting to be a new master. But how could I refuse without being taken for a coward? There was danger and I accepted it. I have been angry at myself ever since, though at that time I was one of those who believed that something could be done by a revolutionary government. I hadn't yet understood that if the revolution isn't created first as an idea, it's not possible as an action, and consequently, if it is made and passes into ideas it is pointless to elect a government to make it succeed. This was so logical that I hadn't even thought of it.

My role on the Commune was the same as any ruler's: it was absolutely useless when it wasn't harmful. I was Delegate for Public Works, which almost earned me delegation to forced labor. I thought it would be easy to sweep away Versaillais reaction, represented by Andrieux, Barodet, Gailleton, Perret, and Le Royer, among others, all of whom were later rewarded for their attitude during that period. I thought it would be enough to call on the people who had just mandated us to carry out this cleanup and they would come to the rescue. But they thought that their effort in electing the revolutionary Commune was enough, and they relied on us, who could do nothing without them. Three days passed with each of us counting on the other, at the end of which we all fell asleep, only to wake up with the red flag lowered and the tricolor flying.

Why this impotence on one hand and abandonment on the other? There were two causes for this. Paris, when it started to act on March 18, at first only called for its autonomy. But Lyon already had this communal autonomy, and because of this had difficulties in supporting Paris. Reaction didn't fail to exploit this situation, saying that Lyon had no reason to rebel in order to obtain what it already had. The agitation was carried out in a void, since the argument convinced a good number of people and Paris sent us its delegates *before* the timid reforms that it later demanded were implemented. Despite the people's ignorance and their faith in their rulers, the results would have been completely different if they had waited for the reforms proposed by the Paris Commune. Perhaps Lyon would have abandoned the communalist idea and taken up the economic idea, and then, having a clear field of action, things would have been different. But there you have it; at the time we waited for the Paris initiative, and it came too late.

The other cause of impotence resided in the absence of material and moral force on our part. Despite the proclamation of the Commune, reaction was still the master of Lyon because it held all the forts, which as everyone knows were built with nothing but an internal revolution in mind. It had the army and it had the money, which is what allowed it to function, for in fleeing and saving itself it had saved the cash box. On our side, we had the rifles of the National Guard and some cartridges, plus a pitiful little fort with its spiked cannons. Facing the army in these conditions could only have produced a useless hecatomb.

A member of the Commune told us that we had the canals and the torch at our disposal and that, not being able to seize the owners—who had sought refuge with the army—we could take what was their strength and our weakness: property. We could do this by calling on the people to act like communist revolutionaries, to leave their shacks to live in the empty luxurious palaces and houses, to eat their fill by expropriating the accumulated foodstuffs, to dress themselves by using the products woven by them and held by the Jews—in Christian or other form—and in this way they would attain two goals. The first was that of meting out justice, and the second that of leading Versailles to dismember the army that was before Paris and thus unblock that city. But either the word "communism" might have spread fear, or it was judged that popular morality was not yet ripe for these demands. The motion was rejected, and as a result we didn't roast property; it was property that let us stew in our own juices.

I was foolish enough to accept a power that tied my hands while giving me the right to tie that of others. I here make my mea culpa; I would never make that mistake today.

My opinion is that the insurrection of 1871 could not succeed, precisely because it left the insurrectionary state behind in order to enter the governmental state. I believe that any insurrection that marches to the conquest of a new government is sterile; that any insurrection that names chiefs is stillborn. The insurrectionary state is one in which the people alone, without leaders or chiefs, can specify its desires, its wishes, its aspirations and its needs. As soon as there is a chief, there is a master; the insurrectionary state comes to an end and gives way to slavery. And it is idiocy to say that you can give yourselves chiefs who will command you to go to Versailles because you command them to lead you. Paris, Lyon, and the other Communes of 1871 died because of their chiefs, of parliamentarians, even the best intentioned. Whether we want it or not, things are and always will be thus.

The influence of these insurrections is great precisely because of their defeat. Until then the provinces were used to following Paris, and they believed themselves powerless if Paris didn't take the initiative. They didn't believe themselves to be a force without Paris; there was a kind of centralization of brains from which everything radiated. Paris seemed to be the center of this radiance. In a way we acted as we would under a form of militarism, where everything is concentrated on one point, everything seems good if this center is the victor, but everything seems and is defective if it is vanquished. It is then that the guerrilla army begins to form, which, with its small numbers, succeeds where a larger army couldn't. A defeated Paris, having in hand an imposing force and seeking to create communal guerrillas, proved to the provinces that even alone they are a force. They no longer wait for Paris to give them ideas; they break themselves up into smaller groups in order to advance more quickly. As proof of this I only have to give the trials and sentencing that took place in the provinces well before those of Paris, the trial in Lyon having preceded that of the Thirty in Paris.

Political and administrative decentralization has been spoken of; the decentralization of brains followed. If we were to investigate, if we were to ask provincial revolutionaries what they would do today if similar events were to occur, there would be a unanimous response: we wouldn't accept battle with soldiers who, after all, are our kind. We would fight against wealth, and if we couldn't pinch the owner we would wipe out what constitutes his joy and his strength. We would flee, leaving nothing standing behind us. People add, with some reason, that they believe that they wouldn't be forced to go to these extremes, and that as soon as the forward march would begin the frightened bourgeoisie would come to its senses. Are they right in all this?

Whatever the case, these ideas are born under the influence of the defeats of the working class. I believe that several insurrections at once at several points are possible, all marching towards the same goal, towards the satisfaction of material needs *before* that of moral needs, something I wouldn't have thought possible before '71. Unlike that period, today the people know full well that it is a matter of indifference to them if they are taught to read that there is much wheat in America if they are prevented from eating it. They know that if their bellies are empty that it makes no difference to them to know that the moon transmits thirteen times less light than we transmit to it. They want to live, and to live well, since they produce everything. They thought they could obtain this well-being through political revolutions; our defeats have shown them that they can't. If the defeats have done nothing but demonstrate this they would be worth it.

To finish, I confess to having many regrets that I couldn't do more. But my most crushing regret is that of having deserved this terrible slap in the face: I was in exile, arguing with Jacques Gross, who has since become one of my best friends, when he threw this in my face: Shut up, elected representative!

P-O Lissagaray

M. Lissagaray wrote The History of the Commune of 1871 in 600 thoroughly documented pages. There was thus no call for a long interview. We first asked him for some anecdotes.

Q: Did women have a role?

A: We see many of them behind the barricades. As for the *petroleuses*, these were chimerical beings, like salamanders and elves. The military tribunals didn't succeed in exhibiting a single one. These tribunals sentenced many women, few of whom had been widely known during the events. Louise Michel was an exception. In front of the judges she was as aggressive as she was in battle and took on the role of accuser. Another, whose name was Dimitriev, was a fantastic creature on a tragic background. She came from Russia, where she had left her husband. During the Commune she was seen in a fabulous red dress, her belt crenellated with pistols. She was twenty years old and beautiful. She had adorers but either "the bare-armed" didn't please her behind closed doors or, for her, love was an exclusively feminine sport, and no one could melt this young ice cube. And it was chastely that she took the wounded Frankel in her arms on the barricades, for she was at the barricades, where her bravery was charming. We must mention her attire: a fancy outfit of black velvet.

Q: She was seized?

A: No, and a few weeks later she was installed in Switzerland. Quite wealthy, she had a hotel on the banks of the lake and nursed refugees. In her salons there was a brilliant society of "forced laborers" and other exoticisms, along with a few men under the death penalty. She then returned to Russia to rejoin her husband, who died soon thereafter. There was a trial where she appeared as a witness. The lord had apparently been poisoned. The overseer was sent to Siberia, where she hastened to join him. No one ever heard from her again.

Q: How would you summarize the causes for the fall of the Commune?

A: The capital errors of the beginning were not having occupied Mont-Valérien and having waited until April 3 to march on Versailles. The Central Committee's interference in affairs after the elections, the manifesto/split of the twenty-two of the minority (May 15), and the Commune's mania to legislate when it should have been fighting and preparing the final struggle were all seeds of the defeat. And once Versailles was inside Paris the defeat was hastened by Delescluze's proclamation of May 22 putting an end to any discipline through the dispersion of the members of the Commune in their neighborhoods (the defense was from that point on decapitated), by the virtual inaction of the artillery park of Montmartre, and by the burning down of the Hôtel de Ville . Before May 21, the day of the invasion, nothing, or almost nothing, had been done for the defense of the streets. They had offered 3 francs 75 to laborers, but hadn't found any takers. They had laborers for free; they had an entire people during the tragic hours, but it was too late. Two hundred planned, strategic, and unified barricades were needed, which 10,000 men could have defended. We had hundreds and hundreds of barricades, but they were uncoordinated and impossible to man. Alas, the Commune hadn't spent money for its defense. Its munificence had only gone as gone as far as the daily 30 sous of the National Guardsmen. They should have put pressure on M. Thiers by seizing the Bank of France as a guarantee. There was no argument that would have been more decisive. Even more, in the Bank, among other docile riches, there were blue bills with a value of 900 million which only waited for an engraver to be put in circulation. It is truly sad that in the course of an insurrection that counted so many workers in the arts that one wasn't found.

Alphonse Humbert
At the time, editor of *Père Duchêne*; since then
President of the Paris Municipal Council and currently Deputy.

I consider the Commune a heroic act; this and nothing else, for I don't think it marked a date in the history of socialism.

Q: Can you give us some anecdotic details on the final days?

A: The Thursday of the final week, May 25, I was with Lissagaray, Jourde, Larochelle, the Commune member Johannard, etc., on the barricade at the entry to the Boulevard Voltaire. Delescluze had just died; over the barricade we could see his corpse. I remember that we had among us a big, colorful lad, a kind of rustic gentleman who in the midst of the flying projectiles shouted, "And to think I came to Paris to have some fun." He was shot in the calf. It was 5:00 or 6:00 p.m.; the barricade, being untenable, was evacuated. The firing from the barracks occupied by the soldiers swept the boulevard. We answered them from a balcony. There was a variety of faces there, among which I recall Johannard in a state of mad exasperation.

Q: And the following day?

A: The evening of the following day, while returning from I don't remember where and going up to Belleville, Jourde, Lissagaray, the medical student Dubois, and I met a group of National Guardsmen. One of them, Carria the younger, told us, "We're going to relieve the gendarmes." I think he was alluding to the Parisian gendarmes from the Roquette quarter. A little later, in the Lake Saint Fargeau quarter, we were dining at the Lapin Vengeur when we heard rifle shots. Suddenly it hit me: "My God, those are the gendarmes that are being executed." The hotel owner came in with a plate of rabbit in his hands, into which tears were falling. I wasn't wrong; it was the hostages. We were only a few steps away from the Rue Haxo.

Q: Once the Hôtel de Ville was evacuated, did the members of the Commune personally take part in the defense of the barricades?

A: Almost all of them, which is something unique in the history of governments. They set an example of intrepidity. What a generation!

Q: How were these fighters of the final moments able to avoid falling into the hands of the Versaillais?

A: It was relatively easy to leave during the battle, but afterwards the exits from every neighborhood were guarded by soldiers, and when you arrived at them you had to submit to an interrogation. After adventures and alerts, Lissagaray and I were able to leave via the 11th arrondissement, thanks to a curvaceous and jovial hotel keeper. That night we asked Suzanne Lagier to put us up and she refused. We had to look elsewhere. For several days we went from place to place, and then Lissagaray was able to leave Paris. As for me, I was captured two weeks later after having been denounced by a concierge. I have since learned that she was condemned by a military tribunal for having turned in Versaillais soldiers during the Commune.

Q: Do you think that one of the results of the Commune was the maintaining of the republic?

A: Yes, since after the execution of the Commune, the period during which it would have been propitious to execute the republic had passed.

Q: Were those of you at the *Père Duchêne* favorable to the majority or the minority on the Commune?

A: Vermersch to the majority, Vuillaume and I more or less to the minority. The latter was made up of the most intelligent men, but I now recognize that the revolutionaries of the majority, with their less theoretical bent and their decisiveness, saw things more clearly.

Q: What is your opinion of the military leaders?

A: Cluseret was a poseur. His thing was to show that he was brave (and he was) and to impress the National Guardsmen. When Federals brought him bad news or asked for reinforcements he calmly answered them, "Go back, boys, I've got things under control. Everything is fine." The men went back saying, "What a man; what calm." He would then pick up his pipe and, comfortably seated in his easy chair, would stretch his legs under the table. As for Rossel, he was a religious fanatic and a patriot. Without being a professional soldier in the worst sense of the term, he didn't much believe in the National Guard, and in fact during the two months of struggle almost the entire military effort was borne by 8,000-10,000 men of the free corps.

The Commune couldn't introduce discipline among its troops; it couldn't quarrel with anyone. Rigorous acts of repression were impossible for it. For me, Bergeret was a faker. Eudes was completely unaware of his role. His bravery, like that of Duval, was amazing. Dombrowski was used to war on the barricades. He was an admirable leader and was brave as a Pole. Was he listening to Versailles' proposals? Did he want to fool the enemy? Wanting to clear himself of any suspicion, he got himself killed at the barricade on the Rue Myrrha. Wroblewski was very intelligent, La Cécilia very brave, but he lost his head when faced with the responsibilities of command.

Q: And from a financial point of view?

A: Jourde wasn't a high financier, but a precise and honest accountant. He limited his role to distributing to the arrondissements the money that was indispensable. Beslay wasn't able to take full advantage of the bank.

Q: And life in New Caledonia?

A: Sinister beyond words. Nevertheless, there was a glimmer of hope when Grévy was elected to the presidency. We were invited to submit requests for pardon, and we were promised they would be accepted. Those sentenced to simple deportation were, but this was less the case for those sentenced to deportation to a fortified place. Where I was, in the penal colony, there were almost none; these were the most compromised men. In the colony there were workers, the humble who didn't have to pretend because they were hoping for a seat at municipal councilor or deputy, and they wrote furiously indignant letters in response to the offer.

I have maintained a profound admiration for the anonymous mass that defended the Commune. The leaders were no less courageous. I can still see Jaclard on horseback and in the uniform of a colonel in the Commune's final moments when disguise was needed in order to flee. Yes, they were all intrepid, and were so gaily and without posing.

G. Lefrançais
Member of the Commune

The degrading situation that the French Republic now finds itself in, a situation wanted by all those who have held the government in their hands since September 4, 1870, faithful continuators of the system inaugurated by the republicans of February 24, 1848, clearly proves that the proletariat has nothing to hope for from those who don't recognize that revolution and authority, be it republican or royalist, are antagonistic.

This was this profound conviction held by most of those who composed the minority of the Commune of 1871 that led them to separate from their Jacobin colleagues, while recognizing their sincerity and their devotion to the revolution of March 18.

The twenty-five years that have passed have convinced me even more that the minority was right and that the proletariat will only succeed in truly emancipating itself on the condition that it rid itself of the republic, the last, and not the least maleficent form of authoritarian governments.

But if it persists in its mad hope of arriving at its emancipation through the famous "conquest of governmental power" it is certainly preparing for itself a new and bloody disappointment from which it will likely not recover for quite some time.

M. Brunel
Currently professor at the Dartmouth Naval School

1. Named chief of the 107th battalion on March 19, 1870, successive acts of war led me to be General-in-Chief of the Central Committee head of the 10th Legion and then member of the Commune. The principal events I participated in were the taking of the barracks of the Chateau-d'Eau and the occupation of the Hôtel de Ville on the afternoon and evening of March 18 and the seizing of the ministries on March 19.

(During the German war I took part in the defense of the fort of Issy and the capture and occupation of the heights of Buzenval, despite the attacks by the Prussian troops. For this feat of war I was proposed for the cross, but I refused.)

When we had to retreat, surrounded on all sides by houses in flames and troops that threatened our retreat, we occupied the 10th arrondissement and then the barracks of the Place de la République where a wound led to my removal from the battlefield.

If I add that I was sentenced to the death penalty then I will have finished with all that concerns me.

2. The insurrection of 1871 is still misunderstood. It was first provoked by a patriotic sentiment and by the determination to prevent the monarchical form of government from taking possession of the country. Almost all the men placed at the head of the movement proved themselves before the enemy and actively professed republican ideas.

The starting point was thus patriotism and the republic.

Could we have succeeded, and why were we defeated?

In a revolution it doesn't suffice to have generous tendencies and to count too much on the enthusiasm of the masses. If we fight against hardened troops we must know how to imitate what constitutes their strength, and even surpass them in valor and discipline. A scattered command cannot hope for victory, and this is what the Commune didn't understand.

Made up of men whose sincerity was indisputable, but whose heads were filled with ideas and who understood nothing about how to conduct a war, the Commune unfortunately suffered the influence that can be seen in all political bodies. Instead of constituting a mighty political power it failed to ensure unity of action and gradually allowed all its forces—the 250,000 men who made up the defense of Paris—to be dispersed.

3. The Commune preserved a republican center in monarchical Europe.

It gave the people of Europe a banner.

It raised an insurmountable barrier between the two social forms.

Its hecatombs showed the entire world what the enemies of progress and all great reforms were capable of doing.

It also showed that blood and steel alone can smash age-old obstacles and give birth to a new society.

This anticipated revolution, which is only a precursor, clearly shows apparently degenerate France that it can no longer hope for anything from the men who govern it.

We have gone from defeat to defeat since 1870. Formerly powerful, we are now nothing but satellites.

And as if nature has abandoned us, we increasingly lack the force to reproduce.

But all of this is due to the causes inherent in the regime we allowed ourselves to be governed by. Once these causes are destroyed we will resume our place in Europe. Imminent events will complete this metamorphosis; we will no longer commit the same errors as in the past, for we now know where we want to go.

Léo Meillet
Member of the Commune,
currently professor in Edinburgh

Your questions require a lengthy analysis which I am not able to provide, first because I don't have the time, and then because, leading a retired life and having spent twenty-five years outside of France I've never thought of coordinating my memories or analyzing my impressions.

From March 18 until the end of May I was overloaded with work. As deputy mayor of the 13th arrondissement and charged with administering my district on my own I participated in many meetings with my colleagues at the town hall of the 2ndarrondissement on the Rue de la Banque. And then on the Commune, little by little I accumulated the functions of a member of the justice commission, of the external relations commission, president of the appeals court of the courts martial, quaestor of the Commune, member of the first Committee of Public Safety, governor of the fort of Bicêtre, Civil commissioner delegated to the southern army, all the while administering my arrondissement, a task in which my colleagues took no part.

You can easily understand that everything is jumbled up in my head. Nevertheless, in order to cooperate as much as possible in the speedy publication of your investigation, I will risk sending you the few reflections that particularly come to mind.

I consider the revolution of March 18 an entirely spontaneous manifestation of popular instinct. It was the unthinking élan of a people that felt itself betrayed and threatened, but whose forward march, instead of being based on an analysis of its sufferings and the consciousness of its needs, had no other guide than the abstractions of historical memory and vague ideal aspirations. This is enough in order to fight and die heroically, but not enough to triumph and live. All of our errors are summed up in these words: "Not to know," with their mandatory corollary, "Not to dare."

It's because the Central Committee *didn't know* that from the time it entered the Hôtel de Ville its only concern was to leave it and it *didn't dare* to attempt (and this was something quite possible at that moment) to revolutionarily take control of Paris and take hold of Versailles before Thiers could assemble his army. A revolution that begins by legislating for ten days is condemned to death, and the Commune could have no other end than that of being the registry room of the people's defeat.

The hesitations and tergiversations of the Commune can also be attributed to this same initial defect. Born of the interminable negotiations of the second half of March, at the beginning it lacked the revolutionary sentiment that progressively developed within it as its fall became imminent and which, had it been produced earlier, could have delayed its defeat by several weeks.

In the absence of documents, and only having vague memories at my disposal, I don't dare risk speaking of the Commune's parliamentary, military, financial, or administrative organization, but it is my opinion that if, from the revolutionary point of view, it left much to be desired, it can be compared positively—except from the military point of view—to all the governments that preceded and followed it. And the honesty and disinterestedness of the members of the Commune and most of its agents is only contested by parvenus of letters and pillars of the bank and the sacristy.

I can't speak about the influence of the Commune on events and ideas; I'm afraid I'd be led astray by my personal sympathies. And yet, it can't be hidden that it was very great. It is generally admitted that in France it saved, if not the republic, at least the republican form. The duration of the resistance and the immense massacre that marked its epic end have drawn the attention of even the slowest to be moved of proletarians, and the thousands of exiles that its fall scattered around the civilized globe have constituted so many rings destined to connect France to the great international socialist movement.

Nadar

To the right of the boulevards there came a sound that was distant, intense, deep. As it grew nearer, the sound grew louder by the minute, and the crescendo exploded beneath us. Something extraordinary was surely happening.

The people in the apartment all rushed to the windows. Sick and, unbeknownst to me, condemned by the doctors, I dragged myself to the window as well, driven by an unhealthy contagion of curiosity for which I would be punished.

After so much pain, sorrow, and horror, here is what I saw and heard in the middle of Paris, the center of human civilization.

Behind a platoon of chasseurs on horseback, their muskets standing upright on their thighs, between two rows of horsemen there filed endlessly, four by four in the middle of the street, an uncountable number of men. Prisoners grabbed individually or in sweeps, sometimes based on their appearance, or on the look of their shoes, or on nothing, on the whims of choice. There were neither women nor children in this convoy. But there were many young soldiers, their caps inside out, from the two regiments which, engaged deep within Paris, were forgotten there on March 18 by their chiefs as they fled to Versailles. These men couldn't leave once Paris was evacuated by the civil and military governments, since the strictest rules forbade the departure through the gates of Paris of any man under 40.

Among these soldiers, now without chiefs and absolutely abandoned to themselves in the middle of a general insurrection, some had been incorporated into National Guard battalions. As was well known, others in large numbers resolutely refused to march against the Versailles troops and, as we learned from the newspapers, a special barracks had been granted them, after a stormy discussion in the Commune.

What exactly were those who, momentarily degraded, filed along before our eyes, while waiting for the rest of the men?

Which among them were faithful and which were enemies? What was the difference? They marched quickly, pushed along. Most had their heads bowed and alongside them was a confused mass of other prisoners of all kinds and dress: National Guardsmen, workers, bourgeois, marching under the deafening clamor of insults, jeers, and threats. The two rows of horsemen occasionally swayed under the terrible pressure of the spectators, protecting the captives with difficulty; men not sentenced, not judged, not even interrogated yet. Well-dressed men and ladies banged into each other, pushed each other so they could insult the prisoners from up close, these prisoners who were neither condemned, judged, nor tried. And at the height of the bloodthirsty madness, unanimously, without a protest, without challenge, they cried out, they shouted these terrible cries that I can still hear: "Death! Death! Don't take them any further! Here! Right now!"

How many pent up cowardly terrors had there been for them to be unleashed with such ferocity?

The prisoners continued to advance, seeming not to want either to see or hear. But one of them turned and cried out, waving his fist: "Cowards!" At that moment, like a rocket, an old and fat decorated gentleman, dressed respectably, flew from the Café de la Paix, and breaking through the crowd, beat the prisoners with his cane.

But all of this—shouts, threats, insults, screams—was still nothing. A formidable, deafening clamor burst out, and in this mass there was a furious movement where prisoners and escort seemed to mutually annihilate each other.

Above them all, there advanced like a ghost, pale, bloody, haggard, his hair standing on end, rocking side to side and supported on each side, a man wounded in the back, it was said and who, unable to march any longer, had been hoisted onto the horse of one of the men of the escort.

Who was this unfortunate? Was he really one of the leaders, or was he taken for one because he alone was on horseback? Whatever the case, the look of this moribund (he was going no further, we were told, than the church of the Madeleine) was able to accomplish the unlikely feat of further increasing the homicidal delirium of these lycanthropes.

And above the shouts and roars of the possessed: "Death! Here! Now!" we heard a strident voice from among them, the voice of a woman, shrieking towards the clouds in a falsetto: "Tear out their nails!"

Yes, this is what I saw, this is what I heard, in the middle of Paris, the center of world civilization.

And as a sincere, disinterested witness, with other similar testimony at hand, historically, as is my duty, I testify.

General de Gallifet

Sir: It is impossible for me to answer the questions you do me the honor of posing.

Please accept my most humble respects,
General Gallifet

Élie Reclus:
The Paris Commune Day by Day

Élie Reclus's *La Commune de Paris au Jour le Jour* gives us the opportunity to see the Commune's seventy-two days as it was lived on a daily basis by a committed but critical observer. In these pages we see and hear how the events were lived and experienced on the streets of Paris. Though called a "journal" it is clear that most of these entries were written after the fact, but they are nevertheless an accurate reflection of the contemporary thoughts and feelings of a revolutionary figure of no small importance.

Élie Reclus (1827-1904) was the brother of the great anarchist geographer Elisée Reclus. Son of a Protestant pastor, he was himself ordained, though he left the church almost immediately after his ordination, becoming a convinced Fourierist. After Napoleon III's coup in December 1851 he fled to England, though he returned to France in 1855, earning his living as a writer and journalist, even writing for a Russian newspaper. In keeping with his Fourierist cooperative interests, much of his writing dealt with cooperative societies in France and around the world. In 1865 he and his brother joined Bakunin's Social Democratic Alliance, and like so many French radical and revolutionaries he also became a Freemason.

During the siege of Paris he was in charge of welfare work in Paris's 5th arrondissement and served as a stretcher bearer for the National Guard during the first six weeks of the Commune. He was named director of the National Library on April 29, but he was only able to enter his office with the assistance of a locksmith.

Fleeing France after the defeat of the commune, he lived in Italy and Switzerland. He was sentenced in absentia to deportation by a military tribunal in October 1875 and pardoned in March 1879.

During the interim he had spent time in the United States, where he was housed by a relative of the most important early American anarchist, Benjamin Tucker, writing for one of the latter's reviews.

Returning to Europe he taught at Brussels's Free University and wrote for Jean Grave's anarchist paper *Les Temps Nouveaux*. He died of infectious influenza February 11, 1904.

Paris, March 22, 1871

Three or four days separate us from the memorable day of March 18. A sudden gust of wind swelled the sails of the republic; the masts cracked, but they are still standing, and we have set out into uncharted waters, through unknown archipelagos, not knowing where our impetuous course will end: against rocks or at a safe harbor. The storm rages, we plunge into the abyss and then climb again to the crest of the waves, but our prow breaks through the foaming sea. We go ever forward. The storm makes men of us men; it is in the face of thunderbolts that we feel ourselves to be like a fountain sprouting life and determination.

Suddenly borne to power, the Central Committee, made up mostly of honest and determined men of a simple, ordinary intelligence, didn't know, still doesn't know what it represents. In fact, no one knows, the most intelligent less than the others. It is the situation itself that is undecided and confused. It is the most glorious anarchy imaginable—a dark night, illuminated here and there with lightning bolts.

And so the Central Committee, which on March 17 was just one of the barely noticed gears of the enormous social machine has, in the middle of the complications that have arisen, found itself to be the most important piece of the mechanism, the piece upon which depends the entire functioning of Paris, and even more than Paris. Through his coup d'état, M. Thiers has upset the situation to his benefit. He didn't succeed in what he set out to do, but he still upset everything.

In fact, this Central Committee is entirely lawful. We are in a revolution, and just as the revolutionary fact substitutes itself for prior legality, and just as the new law takes the place of the old law, the men of the Central Committee are new men. It is because they're new that they have been brought to the Hôtel de Ville to do new things. They must innovate, of course, but what should they innovate, how much should they innovate? This is the immense difficulty. In order to properly answer the question, one needs the most delicate of instincts, supreme tact, or the most scholarly of analyses. But how can we expect to find these traits in these brave men in the midst of unexpected events, in the midst of strange and fantastic occurrences? Should the Central Committee have immediately arrogated all power to itself? Should the Central Committee deliver Versailles the same blow that Versailles wanted to deliver to Paris? Because Versailles failed in its blow against Paris, must Paris attempt a coup d'état in its turn against Versailles, risking failure as well?

In the final analysis, the Central Committee, personification of the National Guard, is nothing but armed universal suffrage, but there is universal suffrage and there is universal suffrage. There is universal suffrage in civil matters, and this is the municipalities and the town halls of the twenty arrondissements of Paris; there is also universal suffrage in political matters, and this is the representatives of Paris, who are themselves but a fraction of the National Assembly. There are thus three expressions of universal suffrage which, formulated at different moments, have different meanings, meanings it is impossible to reduce to the same formula.

If at least the Central Committee could be summed up in a simple "yes" and the municipalities and the deputation at Versailles were summed up in a simple "no" the poor Committee of the National Guard would be free of any problems. It could open the doors to the temple of Janus, brandishing its lance to the four corners of the heavens while crying out: *mens vigila*! But can it, should it go to war but against its inveterate enemies and against its disconcerted and surprised friends? As for the municipalities, a good third is on the side of the Central Committee, another third can be won over, and the final third will remain hostile. As for the Paris deputation, the most ardent revolutionaries have long since sent their resignation letters to the reactionary Assembly, but honest men, devoted men have thought it their duty to remain there. And so Louis Blanc, representative of Paris, sits in Versailles. He is seated there under the command and the authority of Messrs Thiers and Dufaure, also representatives of Paris.

Tossed between these contradictions, the perplexed Committee lacks logic and consistency. It recognizes or denies the representatives and the municipalities of Paris according to whether the municipalities or representatives seem to deny or recognize it. It sometimes acts as simple director of the National Guard, sometimes as dictator, invested with all powers.

There is only one way to escape from this inextricable confusion, and the Central Committee has the merit and, even more, the honesty to immediately understand its necessity, to proclaim and not to back off from it. This method is the appeal to the people of Paris by the convocation of all citizens to the election of new municipalities. And the election of new municipal councils, or the re-election of the old ones, would have as the necessary consequence the resignation of the Central Committee, or it least its retreat to a secondary role. For the most recent expression of universal suffrage is always supposed to be the truest one. If, after the elections, the Central Committee continues to exist, it will only be as the armed forces of the new Commune.

We say Commune this time with a capital C, because only a dictatorship can result from this abnormal situation. If it is republican it should take as its motto: "Save the people at whatever cost!"

Paris, March 25, 1871

Whatever happens, we must vote. Come what may, we must line up behind the Central Committee. Paris's universal suffrage is split in three parts: deputation and municipality against the popular National Guard. We must be on the side of the third party. Legality is doubtless on the side of the mayors and the deputation, but the mayors and the deputation are firmly tied to the government of M. Thiers, who is hardly bothered by legality. He makes and unmakes laws at will, for he places himself above the law and is preparing coups d'état in the shadows. And in time of war what does this word "legality" mean? Everything that is done today will be illegal tomorrow, and if we had to return to strict legality we would have to reinstall Napoleon III in the Tuileries, unless we preferred reinstalling a prince from the house of Orleans there, or a Bourbon, or even the constitution of 1792. So be it; let's go back over the chain of time to the first year of the French Republic. Here it is legality that is against the law; it's the letter that kills. For republican law insists that in all great circumstances, and especially during unforeseen events, an appeal to the people be made. Well, now is the moment for an appeal to the people. The Committee interjects an appeal and M. Thiers, the assembly in Versailles, and the mayors oppose it. Too bad for the opposition!

The immense difficulty is this: voting is the affair of the municipalities and not of the National Guard; it's up to the mayors to call on the voters, it's in the town halls that the voting lists are held, and without which no control is possible. And elections without controls would be too easy to criticize and consequently, to invalidate.

Nevertheless, most town halls are in the hands of the Central Committee. Despite much clamor, several were occupied by National Guard battalions that immediately installed new mayors and provisional deputy mayors to temporarily function during the balloting. This isn't legal, but it's on the road to truth; it's part of the needs of the situation. There remain only two or three town halls still occupied by bourgeois battalions with rifles and machineguns, and they appear ready to use them. As a prelude to the vote must citizens kill each other, open the discussion between bayonets, arrange things so that gunfire converses with gunfire? No, a thousand times no! Let us not begin the hideous civil war. Since we can vote in seventeen town halls out of twenty, if need be we can ignore the three that persist. Seventeen voters convoked of twenty can pronounce a valid and sufficient verdict, as long as the verdict is pronounced by a strong majority of seventeen votes, without pressure of any kind and in a way that is clearly free.

We didn't ask for it; we wouldn't have dared hope for it—hope came and took us by surprise. We chose to go forward all the same, and this was a desperate resolution, for it implied terrible necessities, accepting the inevitable nature of the situation. Inevitable: a euphemism expressing the total of lack of foresight, expressing the errors and crimes of which the French nation, torn into enemy factions, is guilty. We were going to gamble the existence of the republic on a throw of the dice when by a happy chance—which we are hardly used to—one of the three actors of the terrible drama that was about to explode allowed itself to be illuminated by common sense, by humanity. Suddenly, the municipalities have rallied to the elections proclaimed by the Central Committee. We will vote in the twenty arrondissements without shooting at each other.

Going down the Rue Richelieu I heard cries of "Vive la République!" All the rifle butts were in the air, people shook each other's hands, embraced. Already people were hiding and taking away the hideous machine guns. Members of the Central Committee fraternized with the mayors and deputies of the arrondissement; they traded sabers, belts, sashes. The mayors of Paris made the deputies of Paris understand the need to refer to the people of Paris in order to put an end to the abnormal situation of Paris, an abnormal situation that is the fatal consequence of the coup d'état machinated by those legally in power. Tomorrow, in front of the ballot boxes, we will commit an act of concord and civic-mindedness. Like coming out of a painful illness, we are being reborn to joy, to moral health. We are happy to live and to act in this great drama which, in these vast whirlwinds, carries away our frail and petty influences.

At night almost 100,000 souls crowded the boulevard. All the faces were glowing, all eyes smiled, all voices were gentle and friendly. We all loved each other, we were all happy. It was by the act of federation that the first republic was founded; it is through a similar act that the republic of 1871 will be founded.

Paris, March 27, 1871

We had our elections; we had them.

The Central Committee, a product of chance—happy chance this time—gives way to the long awaited Paris Commune, to the regularly elected Commune, to the Commune with legal origins and thus legal authority.

It received 250,000 votes, many more than the mayors and deputies elected under the rule of the Fabre-Trochu plebiscite. Two hundred fifty thousand voters have just pronounced themselves against the monarchic coup d'état. Paris wants the republic; despite the royalists leagued against them, they want the program of the revolution to be carried out.

The new revolution now has body and life; it has a civil existence. Born prematurely on March 18 as the result of an accident—an evil blow by the evil Thiers—the revolution was left lying there in the street. Would the revolution live? Yesterday its legitimate father, the people of Paris, picked it up, took it in its arms, and showed it to the world. It recognized it in keeping with the rites and formulas of legal adoption: here is my child.

Will the child live?

Who knows? It is the child of our sufferings. How much pain and anguish it costs us. What a trial it was to bring it into the world. It was conceived of our stifled tears, of our choked back sobs, of our bitter bile, distilled in nights of feverish insomnia, in days of painful waiting. You were born in blood and mud, in the mire into which France was thrown, through which it was dragged by the wretches of Sedan, by the capitulators of Paris. You were made to wallow in the blood that still flows from our thousand wounds.

But you were finally born. Will you live? I think so.

If you live, if you justify our hopes, if you show yourself to be the child of our desire and love, we will regret nothing. We will applaud ourselves for all the suffering and pain you cost us. You will bring it into the world in joy and happiness. If you are what we think, you are the new era, you are the republic of the United States of the World; you are the universal Commune!

Live, dear child, hope of heroes and martyrs, awaited for generations.

Paris, April 1, 1871

Succeeding the Central Committee is the Paris Commune. Succeeding de facto power, improvised from necessity, is de jure power. It is de jure power because universal suffrage, pronouncing itself by a large majority, has ratified the state of affairs created by the Central Committee, itself produced by the counter-blow of M. Thiers' treasonous machinations. All ambiguity has ceased for Paris, where universal suffrage is no longer divided against itself, the National Guard on one side, the municipalities and deputations on the other.

If in Paris universal suffrage is once again homogenous it is so it can be in even more flagrant opposition to universal suffrage as it is represented by Versailles. Paris and Versailles are two opposing poles, two poles so close that they almost touch, but with opposite electrical charges, with an ever-increasing tension accumulating.

Is there a way of preventing these two enemy electrical charges from falling on each other? Hatred produces anger, anger engenders hatred, and their meeting is the lightning that smashes and tears. Can we avoid the storm and the hurricane?

There is a way, if we want to use it. The provinces must, in their turn, do what Paris just did; they must proceed to general elections. The provincial Assembly was voted by our farmers to the cry, the sole cry, of "Peace! Peace above all and at whatever price!" The Assembly voted for this peace within twenty-four hours; it paid five billions for it plus France's dishonor. Since the Assembly has fulfilled its mandate, since it did what it was told to do, all that's left for it is to go away.

It is now a question of something more terrible than that of war or peace; it's a matter of knowing if France will be regenerated by the Republic or if it will allow itself to be rotted by the Orléanist decay or the Bonapartist gangrene. Now that France has been separated from Alsace and Lorraine and must pay both for what it has and what it no longer has, it's a question of knowing if it will finally enter an era of justice, truth, and labor. We love France, but we prefer honesty and morality. When it stupidly, foolishly, and criminally set out to war behind Monsieur Bonaparte and attacked Germany we sternly told it what we thought. We would, with no rest or pause, have protested against its success. In an unjust war we would not have preferred it victorious; we wanted it vanquished. Now that it is more vanquished than is necessary we still love it—we love it more than ever. Now that it is no longer the republic of nations, now that the former Grand Duchess of Gerolstein, betrayed by her chamberlain, half-killed by her General Boom, poisoned by her Prince Paul, turns its suffering gaze to us, we learn how sweet, profound, and tender our love for it is. "But you must change your ways; you have to want to be reborn, to make a new life for yourself. If not, die!"

Paris wants the republic, the true one and not like that of Louis Philippe which, according to M. Thiers and his fellows of the July monarchy, was the best of republics. We have already had the Thiers, Guizot, Falloux, and Montalembert republic; it gave us the June days and the December night[1]. We today have the Thiers, de Broglie, Favre, Picard and Simon republic. We had it in Bordeaux, we still have it in Versailles, but we no longer have it in Paris, and we don't want it anymore. Let France rid us of it with a new vote. "May the charter finally become a reality," as was said at the time of Louis-Philippe; may the republic that since September 4 exists strictly de jure, exist de facto, if only in humble and modest conditions, but may it exist! We are tired of these treasons and lies that are imposed on us as precepts of wisdom and rules of good sense. We don't accept the fact that in a republic those who cry "Vive la république" are thrown in prison as disturbers of social order. We don't accept that in a republic it's necessary to have shown proof of Bonapartism to be a general officer or police prefect, that you have to show proof of Jesuitism to occupy high positions in the university, show proof of legitimism to enter into the diplomatic service, proof of Orleanism to enter the tax service, proof of servility to be kept on as prefect, teacher, or game warden.

The Versailles Assembly is the permanent conspiracy of the monarchists of all tendencies against the republic: this is a widely known secret. The Assembly itself has not deigned to hide this a single minute. Its first plot failed. Let it accept this and go on its way with the congratulations of M. Bismarck. And may France replace it with a new deputation that is simply, modestly, and honestly republican.

There is thus a simple and practical way to pull us from this difficulty and to perhaps avoid terrible catastrophes. But what is rarer than pearls and diamonds? It's good sense, common sense. And if the thing that would at one and the same time be simplest and the most practical is at the same time that which no one wants, then that very thing is what is most impractical!

Who exactly are the people who make up this Commune, these men to whom the hazards of the ballot have just confided our destinies?

The Commune, composed of about a hundred members, includes in this number about twenty who are fairly well known. Who are the others? The future will show us.

Paris, April 3, 1871

Yesterday on the calendar was a holiday, Palm Sunday, festival of nature reborn, of the joy of blossoming and renewal. Devout men and women were going to or returning from church. On the streets and on the squares, citizens discussed public affairs. Women with new ribbons on their dresses asked each other at the bus stops: "Should we go see the devastation in Meudon or Ville d'Avray? Why don't we go instead to see what's left of the city of Saint Cloud after the cannonade and bombardment? What's left of Château, torn apart, sacked, burned?"

Amidst these conversations could be heard the sound of cannons. At first we didn't pay much attention. During the siege our ears had grown accustomed to it. But the detonations continued. Perhaps it was a noisy celebration, probably some suburban locality also proclaiming the arrival of its Commune. But listen closely to these discharges. They're cannon volley. There have never been cannon volleys at celebrations!

Alas, it is true. Two cannon shots from Versailles gave the signal for the civil war. Forward marched the Catholic volunteers, the pontifical Zouaves, the Breton monarchists, Trochu's favorites. There followed the regular troops, the Chasseurs d'Afrique and others. Behind them came the municipal officers and the gendarmes, the Bonapartist sergeants who Paris hates and who hate Paris. It is said that they were commanded by the Bonapartist Baron de Vinoy, by the legitimists Baron de Charrette and Cathelineau. It is said that during the action they unfurled a white banner and that cries of "Long live the king" were heard.

I went to the site and gathered the most varied and fantastic information, and in the end I understood that things must have happened in this way: at approximately 9:00 the National Guardsmen, posted on and around the Neuilly Bridge, were still sleeping, preparing their food, eating, drinking their coffee or wine, when an as yet undetermined mass of Versaillais troops, whose approach no one had signaled, spread across Courbevoie and Neuilly. At the roundabout a National Guardsman suddenly sees a band of soldiers, preceded by a man who then disarmed or feigned disarming a boy belonging to the post. The National Guardsman immediately fires at the leading man and lays him out dead.

(The supporters of Versailles later said that he had killed a parliamentarian, the Surgeon Major Pasquier. It's possible, but this parliamentarian was carrying out his functions in an irregular fashion.)

He had barely fired his rifle when he himself fell under the bayonets and was finished off with the blows of rifle butts. The entire post is invaded and massacred, except for a few individuals who flee and who aren't touched by the bullets. Cannons and machine guns are then installed on the roundabout, which dominate the large and wide triumphal avenue. The Versaillais sweep up Courbevoie and Puteaux; they descend on Paris. A patrol of gendarmes advances up to the Neuilly Bridge and calls on the National Guardsmen on duty to retreat. The latter respond by inviting the gendarmes to make common cause with the people. The sergeant gives the order to charge, but the National Guardsmen riposte and the gendarmes retreat. Several companies of Nationals set out after them and reach the roundabout. There they are received by the fire of Charrette's Zouaves hidden behind a barricade, who fire on them to cries of "Long live the King!" Surprised and decimated, the Nationals beat a retreat, with Zouaves, gendarmes, police, and regular soldiers behind them. The battle withdraws to the Maillot gate, which for a moment appeared to be in danger. There then arrived some *tirailleurs*, about a hundred Garibaldians who re-established the combat. Little by little National Guardsman arrived en masse, and upon seeing them the Versaillais beat a hasty retreat from the other side of the bridge.

While most of the National Guardsmen, shot at from the heights of Courbevoie, beat a retreat, two hundred men of the Commune, surrounded by the gendarmes and the soldiers, were about to be taken when the regular troops raised their rifle butts in the air, shouting "Vive la République!" The gendarmes then turned around, while one or two hundred soldiers joined the Nationals. I saw them going towards city hall; the crowd greeted them with enthusiastic acclamations: "Long live the army! Long live the army!"

We heard it said with horror that all former soldiers found in the ranks of the National Guard by the Versaillais were executed. Thus two hundred would have been killed in one place alone. It appears they truly want to massacre all soldiers who fraternized with the people, but this is impossible. They would be forced to execute hundreds and even thousands of men.

Starting at noon everything, little by little, returned to silence. Satisfied with his brilliant initiative, happy with his coup d'état, proud of having shot down Frenchmen, as on January 22 and December 2, General Vinoy returned to the road to Versailles, taking with him a few hundred prisoners swept up in his razzia.

In the evening we feverishly wandered the streets, listening to the rumors, interrogating physiognomies, scrutinizing expressions. The animation grew by the hour. With bright eyes, an ardent voice, we read the proclamations of the Commune.

What is to be done now?

In the groups around city hall the most popular opinion is that, without wasting any time, we respond to Versailles' *coup de main* by a *coup de main* of the Parisians against Versailles.

We've already wasted too much time. If the Central Committee had had the spirit to have Messrs Thiers, Favre, and Picard pursued to their refuge in Versailles by a few battalions of National Guard after these men had failed in their underhanded blow of March 18, the monarchists would already have been scattered to the four winds and would cause the republic no more worries. Communes are being formed in Lyon, Limoges, Toulouse, Marseilles, Narbonne, Carcassonne, and all over France. Help them by making an energetic effort. Let us profit from the moment, which is always propitious. Two weeks ago the army declared that it was with us; today its disposition is still excellent. Every day republican soldiers come to us who throw away their rifles, not wanting to fire on the people, for they are of the people and they know this. They hate their generals who are cowardly and inept. They would be horrified to wash away the shame of Sedan and Metz with the blood of their brothers. But we shouldn't leave Thiers, Canrobert, Gallifet, Charette, Vinoy, and Valentine the leisure of reconstituting an army with gendarmes, pontifical Zouaves, and policemen as its nucleus. They have already thought themselves strong enough to attack us. We victoriously repelled them. Let us pursue them to Versailles.

I listened, not daring to give my opinion. I travelled with soldiers ordered up in haste by M. Thiers: they didn't look as intelligent and fraternal as all that. In *Le Monde Illustré*, I had just seen a fearsome description of all the pieces of artillery piled up in Versailles. Nevertheless, a vigorous expedition there would have a good chance of success. "Audacity," Danton shouted to the revolutionaries, "Audacity, and more audacity." Fortune loves the audacious. How happy I am not to be on the Commune and not to have to pronounce on what I don't know! But obviously, the Commune knows.

We hear the rolling of drums, and there they are coming from the depths of the Saint Antoine quarter, coming down from Belleville and Montmartre, battalion after battalion. They've unfurled their red flags, they sing the "Marseillaise," they shout "To Versailles, to Versailles! We're going to Versailles!" It was 11:00 p.m.. At midnight they were still marching by. I left, pensive.

I don't know who slept that night. Early in the morning you still met National Guardsmen who'd been held up. Two or three at a time, twelve or twenty at a time, even alone, they went off to war.

"We'll join up with the others somewhere."

"You have cartridges?"

"We'll find some there. Anyway, will we need them? The soldiers are for the republic; when they see us arrive en masse they'll fraternize with us."

Three columns of expeditionaries set out from Versailles we are told. One by the Left Bank, Clamart, and Meudon; the two others are to go via Reuil, Bougival, Garches, each one to bypass Mont-Valérien. People go to the ramparts to have news sooner.

Around noon the falling tide meets a few waves of the rising tide. National Guardsmen return scattered, covered in powder, lame, shamed, wrathful, everything all at once.

"What? What is it?"

"We've been betrayed. We were told that Mont-Valérien was ours. Not at all. The Versaillais are holding it. They waited for us to be gathered together in a mass on the road and while we filed by them, not thinking anything at all, they suddenly machine gunned us. Panic and rout! They made more noise than they did harm, but even so we left comrades there who'll never return. They cut us in two; the first third continued on its way forward, but it was impossible to rally the others. It was a mad disorder. I saw men who shot furiously in the air against the fortress. One of our men, madder still, killed the horse that was dragging a cart. To not even know if Mont-Valérien was for or against us—to not even know that!"

So the expedition begins with a failure. Our National Guardsmen are novices; thanks to M. Trochu, four-fifths of them never saw fire. I'm beginning to think that our men made a big mistake in their coup de tête, responding to a carefully thought-out attack by an improvised one. When right is on your side you have strength on your side by remaining on the defensive. But enough of these reflections and moralizing, which won't hold up a minute against the news of a victory. The events have begun, and it is impossible to hold them back.

The poster says: "Colonel Bourgoin to the Director General, 11:20 a.m.

"Bergeret's and Flourens's forces have met. They are marching on Versailles. Success certain."

Bergeret and Flourens are the two generals who were supposed to bypass Mont-Valérien. We are told nothing about the failure suffered by Bergeret. Will his vanguard joining Flourens suffice to assure success? Whatever the case, the Director General should have told us the whole truth.

We come, we go in a cruel, heavy state of expectation. How far Versailles is.

In the evening we took our meal, somber and silent. Suddenly, we hear the rolling of the drum sounding the alarm in our quarter. Our hearts beat faster: To arms, citizens! Raising my head, I see the great woman from Marseilles on the Arc de Triomphe. She flies in the air and, as she passes, gestures to us.

We are three brothers; we set off together. Two have their weapons and some form of military accoutrement. With my wounded hand I can't use a rifle. It doesn't matter, I'll still take part. I'll carry the sacks of tired men; I'll pick up the wounded.

Instead of rallying, the armed National Guardsmen raise objections to receiving this bourgeois among them. "What's he doing here?" I have the honor of being slightly known by the captain, who vouches for me and authorizes me to join the ranks.

"Where should I go?"

"We don't know. We are ordered to go to the Place de la Concorde and to await a later command."

I carry the sack of one neighbor, the rifle of another, and I clumsily join the march. We were generally silent; we heard the echo of our steps in the dark streets. Alert to the least detail, I nevertheless dreamed. I felt like I was marching along the sea, the waters of the beach raised the heavy stones with difficulty; then the falling water receded, and the crying stones rolled and fell heavily behind them.

No order awaited us on the Place de la Concorde. After a half an hour we were told to halt, break ranks, and pile up our arms. Before us, not far away, rose the obelisk of Luxor, so strangely disoriented; it doesn't know what the city and the generations of men who surround it signify. Its foundations are still damp with the blood of Louis XVI and Marie Antoinette, of Chénier and Charlotte Corday, of Danton and Saint-Just that spreads around it. While waiting for destiny's signal of what was going to be carried out, it was the time and the place to again think about one's life and question oneself. What have you done? Why are you a revolutionary and socialist republican?

Here and there a few dark shadows noisily move about on the black-top. Above the tenebrous earth, the shining, serene, and sorrowful moon floated solitary in the empty heavens. Starting at 11:30 a few staff officers pass at a gallop. The men shout at them: "What's the news? What's the news?"

"Everything is fine. They should be in Versailles now. The Assembly didn't wait for them. The monarchists have left; they fled, the Orleanists on one side, the legitimists on the other."

Every messenger brings different news. According to some of them we aren't yet at the gates of Versailles, but all say: "Everything is fine; victory is won."

Our battalion receives the order to fall back to the Place Vendôme. It's doubtless only a matter of passing a bad night sleeping little if at all on the streets. I prefer my bed. Plus my position as amateur baggage carrier or unofficial nurse has earned me some disagreeable occurrences. I've already been stopped two or three times: "By what right are you here?" After five minutes the captain rescued me, but now I myself believe that I am posing. Let us peacefully go off to sleep, announcing the good news to the people we pass. "Good night, my friends."

On the Pont des Arts I wanted to give my heart, swollen with joy, made tender by hope, an extra half hour of joy and so I sat on a bench. The silent air was filled with a vast clarity; the deep waters seemed made of shadow and light intimately linked, like our poor human soul. The waters flowed powerfully and hurriedly. They ran up against the scattered obstacles with a silver sparkle and a weak murmur, softened by the distance. Thus go the generations, gliding rapidly and inevitably towards the ocean of eternal death and eternal rebirth. The waves encounter a rock or themselves, and from the shock there spurts a ray of light and a cry of pain, gentle for whoever hears it from afar. The revolution carries and drags us, but to what breaker?

Paris, April 4, 1871

The news isn't true. Alas, good news, false news.

Yesterday Bergeret's men failed in their bypassing of Mont-Valérien, and Flourens's men failed on the other side. Flourens was even killed, and if the two vanguards joined up they did it among the dead. The bands of the National Guard occupied Chatou and Bougival at almost the same time, on whose belfries the red flag flew for two hours. They rested there a bit, and doubtless lingered at lunch in the cabarets. They nevertheless set out on the march again, those most in a hurry in front, the others staggered out in keeping with their strength or their good will. It was then that the artillery and the cavalry riding at full speed from Saint Germain fell on them, chasing and repelling the National Guardsmen. Dumbfounded and in a state of total confusion, they successively evacuated Bougival, La Jonchère, La Malmaison, Chatou, Rueil, and Nanterre. At the same time soldiers come down from Versailles built up the works constructed by the Prussians on the heights of La Celle Saint Cloud and entrenched themselves there to block the road. Not for an instant did any of the soldiers think of raising their rifle butts in the air; they were preceded by gendarmes and had policemen at their backs. We have held—still hold—deplorable illusions about them. Several told of having seen Flourens's corpse; the gendarmes executed former soldiers; many prisoners were swept up and taken to Versailles, but in the rout it's impossible to know their number. All we know is that the escapade, for the attempt that the evening before last and even yesterday that we could think to be an outburst of heroic fraternity today fools no one: it was nothing but another foolishness of that poor Flourens.

But if the other column, that commanded by Duval, succeeded? Yesterday, Monday, it advanced towards Fleury and Clamart and captured the area around the chateau of Meudon and the Chatillon redoubt, which it seized from the Versaillais troops, who didn't expect this sudden movement. But when the National Guard saw itself attacked from the batteries of the chateau of Meudon and by those of the heights of Clamart they beat a retreat, for they had gone out to capture Versailles without artillery, without food, and without munitions.

It was to retake the Châtillon redoubt that the battalion I belonged to yesterday for four hours was sent out from the Place Vendôme. I can testify, alas, to the fact that it was lacking in everything; those who brought munitions were those who by chance had any in their homes. They had naturally thought that munitions—they could do without food—would be shared at the same time as the general's orders. But which general?

A general? Oh, yes. The overgrown children of the Commune showed real concern for strategy. They said to their battalions, "Quickly take your rifles, with or without powder; don't even take the time to load them, and run quickly to Versailles by three or four roads. Run; the soldiers are waiting to throw themselves in your arms."

I come, I go; it's impossible to get any news.

The forts of Vanves and of Issy, which are ours, fire all day. But is it certain they can aim at anything at all, and even more importantly, not hit our friends?

"At the Porte d'Issy many women wait," says the newspaper *Le Mot d'Ordre*, I think. They were pale but firm. The gate opens, the drawbridge lowers, the drum beats, the battalion passes. These men, smeared with dust, their clothes in tatters, advance. "Vive la République!" They say, "Everything is fine." Is everything fine? I don't know. Many have white hair.

The women throw themselves on the ranks as soon as they see those they love. They cover them with kisses and tears. One pulls out her husband, black with powder and the officer calls for him. "Oh, take it easy," she says, "I'll give him right back to you."

Further along the wounded came. We see a National Guardsman being amputated. His arm is thrown in the ditch.

Anger answers provocation; hatred answers hatred. Here is the decree with which our walls have been covered:

The Paris Commune,

> Considering that the men of the government of Versailles have ordered and begun civil war, attacked Paris, killed and wounded National Guardsmen, soldiers, women and children;
>
> considering that this crime was committed with premeditation and by surprise, against all law and without provocation,
>
> Decrees:
>
> Article One—Messrs .Thiers, Favre, Picard, Dufaure, Simon, and Pothuaua stand accused.
>
> Article Two—Their property shall be seized and sequestered until such time as they have appeared before the justice of the people.
>
> The delegates for justice and general safety are charged with the execution of this decree.
>
> The Paris Commune

One can feel that we are entering the path of terrible actions and reactions. Before allowing ourselves to be taken over by anger, before we too are swept away by the whirlwind of events, before having being led astray by the universal vertigo so that we no longer know to distinguish good sense and the right, let us stop at this first step and ask ourselves: is this decree just?

I think so. Unless the blood that flows in my brain has already troubled my vision and judgment, I say that Messrs Thiers, Favre, Picard, Dufaure, Simon, and Pothuau are criminals for having unleashed the horrors of civil war on France. They are criminal for not having listened to the answer that universal suffrage gave to their attempted coup d'état; criminal for not having exhausted all means of conciliation before resorting to blind cannons and ferocious bayonets; they are criminal for not having wanted to hear a single word of peace. Their crime is even worse: representatives elected by the city of Paris, it is they who threaten Paris with their bloody knife. There is parricide in their act.

Now, is it up to the Commune, their enemy, to decree their accusation? In the case of the Commune's victory, will it be up to the Commune to judge them? No, it is up to universal suffrage, consulted anew, to pronounce judgment. It will be up to the universal suffrage of all of France to settle the dispute between the old Assembly and the young Commune as quickly as possible. But alas, who can convoke it, this universal suffrage; who can save us from the gathering storm? No constitution has foreseen this case.

I hear the enemies of the Commune say that it is committing an injustice in provisionally sequestering the property of these men. We'll think about this later. For the moment it's a question of a few houses and some furniture.

Paris, April 6, 1871

The Paris Commune, in which the Blanquists are numerous, too numerous, affirms that Blanqui, sick and perhaps dying, was arrested in the night deep in a department of the south, where he had taken refuge during the siege. The government of Versailles, which seized him in the aftermath of its coup of March 18, refused him a trial, even by a military tribunal, imprisoned him no one knows where, and placed him in a location that is so well kept a secret that Blanqui's elderly sister has not been able to discover his prison or even learn if he is still alive. Thiers responded that he will give no information on this man until order is reestablished.

For a government punctilious when it comes to legality, for a government that doesn't even deign to enter into negotiations with the elected representatives of 200,000 voters, and doesn't hesitate to resort to cannons and bayonets because it claims that Paris committed the wrong of conforming to certain legal forms rather than others, this is treating equity, and not only justice, but the law, quite cavalierly. The law had never permitted the suppression, that is, the disappearance of the accused who, the Code Civile says, "must always be presented at the first requisition of the family," so that it can be verified that the prisoner was not murdered in the prison by his enemies.

Blanqui was condemned to death by his enemies, Jules Favre, Simon, and Trochu, for his participation in the events of October 31. He was judged and sentenced in absentia. The trial should be conducted again. Since that time he has been elected a member of the Commune by the people of Paris. He has never taken his seat, and we don't even know if he has accepted. It is true that he fought all his life to have a Commune in Paris; his utopia, his dreams were suddenly realized, more as a result of M. Thiers's mischief than as a result of Blanqui's long conspiracies. The Blanquists of the Commune would like to name him honorary president of the Commune, but Delescluze and several others have declared that if that were to happen they would hand in their resignations. Blanqui, the official father of the Commune, plays no role in the actions of his child, and it is supremely unjust that M. Thiers holds him responsible and has his fate depend on the "re-establishment of order."

Illegality engenders illegality; one injustice produces another injustice. Citing Blanqui's sequestration, the Blanquists of the Commune have demanded that we take hostages and that Versaillais prisoners guarantee the fate of Parisian prisoners or their friends. We have returned to the morals of the Middle Ages, to patriarchal justice—hostages and reprisals, an eye for an eye, a tooth for a tooth, imprisonment for imprisonment, murder for murder.

During the night of April 4-5 Father Deguerry, curate of the Madeleine, one of the most influential men of the Catholic party, Monsignor Darboy, and two of his vicar generals along with Senator Bonjean were arrested and sent to the Conciergerie.

The road M. Thiers is entering, and upon which the Commune is hurrying to follow him, is dangerous. It was with a shiver of fright this morning that we read the decree posted on the walls: "Every execution of a prisoner of war or of a supporter of the regular government of the Paris Commune will be immediately followed by the execution of triple that number of hostages." This word "triple" particularly displeases us. If the Versaillais scalp Parisians, we ask that the Parisians in turn only scalp one Versaillais for one Parisian. If these attacks on humanity are committed inside or outside the walls of Paris, it is shameful for the legal Assembly; it is shameful for the revolutionary Commune, if the latter is forced to it or not.

Saturday, April 8

The combats are unfavorable to us, and we are suffering misadventure after misadventure. The day before yesterday the troops of the Commune tried to retake possession of Courbevoie. A few battalions of good will went there, brave, astonishingly brave, but too few in numbers and with officers even more novice than the men. We know the story. After having won terrain through the liveliness of their assault they were repelled. They defended the soil inch by inch but lost it, and finally, after superb acts of bravery they lost all of Courbevoie and even the bridge, only one end of which they held.

And yesterday they completely lost it, this bridge of capital importance. They had started to build a barricade there, but it was too late; it was carried by the cannons before being seriously defended, and immediately thereafter the Versaillais spread across Neuilly and the Bois de Boulogne. They hold both banks and they swarm as far as our walls on a line of two kilometers.

Easter, April 9

My brother disappeared during the combat at Chatillon. We have some reason to believe he is a prisoner, but no one we know saw him either in Versailles or Satory. We have visited the neighboring forts, from Bicêtre to Issy. The headquarters at the Place Vendôme sent us the list of the wounded, we have searched in many hospitals, many ambulances. There remains a final inquiry. He is perhaps among the unknown dead, buried at the cemetery of Montmartre. A friend is accompanying me there.

The sun shines brightly; the trees and vegetation are in festive spirit. We are not alone in making the painful pilgrimage; in silence, we climb the tortuous path. We finally enter the sanctuary of death; he wasn't there.

Five corpses were laid out there, two young men and two with hair going gray. There were no hideous wounds; the purplish faces were calm, sad, honest. They were obviously workers, and not pillagers and assassins, which is what M. Thiers shouts to France. The spectacle was of an august melancholy. These five working men laid out dead seemed to say: "Our cause is immortal."

If only the representatives of Paris could summon the Assembly around these corpses: "Come closer, Lorgeril! Look, Belcastel! And you, Duke d'Audifret Pasquier, touch this bloody forehead!" If those who decreed the war could for once contemplate the painful reality one on one, confronting their consciences, would they shout at Vinoy "Kill more!"

How sad a thing is civil war. Yesterday a poor woman in mourning told a group on the Place de la Concorde that in the morning they had brought her one of her children, wounded by the explosion of a cannon ball in Neuilly. "I would console myself for this misfortune," the unfortunate woman said, "if my two sons fought in the same ranks and for the same cause. But one is in the 168th battalion of the National Guard and the other is a non-commissioned officer in the army of Versailles. When I hear a cannon shot from one side or the other I die a little inside."

Wednesday, April 12

The fact is that Paris is jolted, surprised by the formidable racket, and with every passing minute worry increases along with the noise. It came both from the south and the west. The walls were attacked at several points, in the direction of Montrouge, Vanves, Issy, and Asnières; Asnières was taken in a daring blow by General Dombrowski so as to have a toehold on the other bank of the Seine and to take the attackers from Neuilly by the front.

The shops closed hastily, the cafes emptied, numerous groups formed in the streets and on the squares. The heights of Montmartre and Belleville were covered with the curious. Looking at the lights that crisscrossed the sky one would have said that Paris was being attacked in the night by thunder and lightning.

It was the great attack announced by M. Thiers to his faithful; the great victory of Mac Mahon promised to the monarchists of the Assembly. The assault from without was to be accompanied by an uprising from within, but the conspiracy failed, nothing particular was remarked by the groups. The sole proof that treason is lurking in the shadows is that all the spots where the National Guard gathers are regularly visited by cannon fire.

I was in the center of Paris when I heard the first detonation. My heart beat. These cannon shots, these machineguns, these scything of ranks and platoons which follow each other without interruption put it in a state of turmoil. I hurriedly went to the spot that seemed the most threatened, that of Montrouge. Along the way three horsemen appeared for an instant, leaving a red trail in the darkness. It was the noisy vision of the members of the Commune with their sashes: they have made it a law always to have someone present wherever there is danger.

I see the citizens working in the shadows on barricades. "Rest easy, citizens; the Versaillais have already been repelled."

Tuesday, April 18

After laborious discussions which took up several sessions, the Commune has just promulgated its decrees on payments whose due dates have been delayed since the day France went lightheartedly off to war behind M. Ollivier and the Emperor.

In substance it was decided that until next July 15, i.e., until the end of the civil war, every legal demand for reimbursement is postponed and that from July 15 debts of all kinds will be paid in twelfths, payable quarterly, consequently spread over a period of three years.

You will recall that the Commune refused from the start to make a decision on this question of payments due, which is full of difficulties. It had wisely resolved to first consult the syndicates of merchants, industrialists, and working-class corporations. The results were not as liberal for the debtors as we could have hoped, given the example of the United States. After the war against slavery, the Americans, a practical, commercial, and industrial people in their souls, bravely granted a general delay of five years for the liquidation of debts and loans between individuals. The Commune has greatly facilitated reimbursement. Bad years are spread out across three in a continuous way. The arrangement, though less radical than that determined in Washington and New York, is no less practical. Commerce declares itself generally satisfied. We hear on all sides that too much was done, or not enough, but the principle is accepted without contest.

Here again we clearly see the difference in spirit between the Assembly seated in Versailles and that in Paris. Against the first law, called the law of a thousand bankruptcies, which was voted by Versailles in an access of stupidity and under the high inspiration of Messrs Thiers and Dufaure, stirring protests were raised by both large and small Paris businesses. Petition after petition addressed to Versailles contained their pressing demands. The minister of the interior, M. Picard, from the height of the tribune, didn't hesitate to attribute to this measure the Parisians' indifferent or hostile attitude towards the government of Versailles as expressed in risking the adventure of March 18. The rural Assembly recognized the necessity of modifying the law; M. Dufaure himself rallied to the emergency proposal. In recognizing its error the Assembly could have corrected it and diminished popular anger. It set to work, and aside from one or two formal alleviations, it maintained its law bearing the quasi-immediate payment of all debts coming due. And these men call themselves practical!

Wednesday, May 3

Clearly Paris's weakest point is the one that should be the strongest, the central point of the Hôtel de Ville . What is least reassuring about the Commune is the Commune itself. The newspapers give us an account of the deliberations, in which we learn that we are at the mercy of a new dictatorship which dares to take the terrifying name of Committee of Public Safety. The measure is totally impolitic. The proof of this is that it causes neither fright nor enthusiasm. This appellation, the most frightful for French ears, will be in no way justified by the five gentlemen who were decorated with it. The committee of 1793 plunged its hands in blood, but saved France. The new committee will probably dips its hands in ink and issue many decrees, but if the committee won't destroy us, it won't save us either. Neither friends nor enemies take it seriously. With a disdainful pout and a shrug of the shoulders we have learned the names of the individuals now responsible for the salvation of the fatherland. A big word for little men. The title of Committee of Public Safety doesn't give them an atom more power, but could cause vain fright and unjustified repulsion if it didn't, above all, appear ridiculous. One could say they are mandarins who put on a frightening costume with slogans written on the belly and back saying, "Tremble! I am the invincible tiger!"

In vain, a few orators have affirmed that we are surrounded by rascals and that we have to chop off the hands of a few traitors. The public wasn't moved. We would pardon the thing, but everything that resembles pastiche and declamation makes us singularly uncomfortable.

Right or wrong, people were unhappy with Cluseret; he was suspected of leaning towards dictatorship and of being, despite his ambition, an incompetent, and the Commune gave all power to an Executive Committee that it has just overthrown to the profit of the Committee of Public Safety. The name is changed, the individuals are no longer the same, but for all that the situation hasn't improved; there has only been one more false step that has been taken.

Citizen Langevin said: "What do we see? We see the Assembly naming commissions and not referring to them, not discussing the way in which they execute the details of their work."

Citizen Paschal Grousset said: "Conflicts of all kinds have arisen. The Executive Commission gave orders that weren't executed. Every individual commission, believing itself sovereign, for its part also issued orders. All this was done in such a way that the Executive Commission could not have any real responsibility and, making super-human efforts to see to everything, in the end succeeded at nothing."

Citizen Vaillant said: "Let's not make a revolutionary pastiche. The important thing would be to transform the Commune itself, to make of it what the first Paris Commune was, a group of commissions working in concert. It should start by reforming itself and ceasing to be a talkative parliament, smashing tomorrow what it created today in accordance with its whims, while throwing itself in the path of the decisions of the Executive Commission."

Tuesday, May 9

As the battle heats up between Paris and Versailles, the number of women who take part in the struggle increases. Many have taken up the rifles of their slain husbands, of their brothers or lovers. Most nurses fire from time to time. Some women have disguised themselves as men and fight in the vanguard. But no one thinks of implementing the idea put forward by Felix Belly during the first siege of Paris, the creation of female battalions under the name of Amazons of the Seine, with sparkling costumes and toy guns. The idea couldn't be sustained, it wasn't even decent that women be enrolled in these companies, impelled by the purest and most ardent patriotism. Patriotism pushed to this degree made people forget the ordinary weaknesses and conventions of the sex, and particularly forget the faded finery of costumes. The women who fought behind the barricades of Neuilly go with their husbands and neighbors in their everyday clothes, with or without putting up their hair, as if they were going to the bakery. Women only have the right to go to battle if they have the passion for the right and that passion alone. Mme André Léo, a valiant woman who left the peace of her province to share the danger of her friends, but who has thus far only fought with her pen, nobly spoke to women the other day:

It is no longer a question of national defense. The field of battle has grown; it's a question of humanitarian defense, of the defense of the right to freedom. Today the fate of right in this world is tied to the fate of Paris. The assistance of women today becomes necessary. It is up to them to give the signal for one of those sublime impulses that carry before it any hesitation or resistance. We see them, anxious, enthusiastic, ardent, their souls attached to the hazards of combat, their eye more filled with fire than with tears, give themselves wholeheartedly—the women of the people especially—to the great cause of Paris. May they enter the fight through action as much as through their hearts. Many wish for it, and many can do it. Louise Michel, Mme Eudes, Mme Rochebrune, and many others have already provided an example. They are the pride and admiration of their brothers in arms, whose ardor they double. When girls, women, mothers will fight alongside their sons, their husbands, their fathers, Paris will no longer have only the passion for freedom, it will have the delirium.

Many are those who every morning are more tenderly embraced by a woman, for in the evening they could be killed, these objects of so much care and affection. Character is tempered, morality is transformed without their even knowing it. And many are the heroines immersed in the people who don't know that they are worthy of admiration, and who will never know it.

Sunday, May 14

The people is a woman, as has long been said. More than any other, the people of Paris is a woman. In a word, it is a Parisienne. I love her, I admire her, I approached her, I lived with her; I often enough reproached her for her faults, knowing them only too well. I never flattered her, I never lied to her to earn her good graces; I love her too much for that. Of course I held her in high esteem, but today, after a year of terrible tests, I am happy to state that she has far surpassed my expectations. In the history of the last twenty-five centuries the story of the two sieges of Paris is worthy of being counted among the cruelest, most painful, most important events. The population has remained the equal of events, and it even dominates them. Prussians and Bavarians keep it locked in. The Germanic soldiers, chewing on their pipes, full of our meat, their thirst quenched with our best wines, contemplate our disasters; their eyes round and rolling, they accompany the shots of the Versaillais soldiers with a loud and vulgar laugh, making holes in houses and breasts with their cannon balls. And even so, despite the terrible defeats we suffered at the hands of the enemy, despite the cruel humiliations he inflicts on us, Paris still has the red flag of the brotherhood of peoples flying over city hall, and it still goes into combat to the cry of "Long live the universal republic!" Paris is aware that it must conquer and perhaps die to accomplish the great modern social renovation, the freeing of labor exploited and ransomed by capital.

If Paris must die it will die, and without many regrets, for since it ended all relations with "a certain God" it no longer fears death. Ever since it has become convinced that when we are dead we are dead for a long time it is more generous with its brief life, the sole one it will have. In ceasing to be spiritualist it has become heroic, like Molière's Don Juan: impulsive, gay, and generous with its life. It abandons heaven to the valet Sganarelle, cowardly, cuckolded, and pietistic. Its enemies say it is debauched, drunk, lazy, and dissipated and they attribute to it all the infamies of Rome, of Sodom and Gomorrah. But the people of the workshops are not the people of the Jockey Club, of the stock exchange and the Maison Dorée. The truth is that there is no big city whose population taken as a mass is more intelligent or morally healthy, more sympathetic, more just. The city with its 1,500,000 inhabitants, not counting those who fled, the city with its immense public and private treasures, absolutely belongs to 200,000 hooligans, as they say, to the crooks of Montmartre and the lowlifes of Belleville, to use the elegant language of the friends of order. Never was a city better behaved, more peaceful internally. People peacefully eat their soup with their families while the Thiers bombs fall here and there in the quarter. People go about their affairs, walking pressed against the houses for fear of cannon shells. When his shift arrives, or when he is awakened suddenly by the rolling of drums, populating with alarms the silence of the night, the simple National Guardsman, the brave Federal again embraces his wife, kisses his youngest child one last time, and goes to handle his bayonet in Neuilly, Asnière, or Montrouge. It would be less dangerous to go hunting for tigers in the jungles of India. In going to battle, perhaps to death, they are doing their duty. We can distinguish between the marching and the sedentary battalion from the former's firmer and prouder air, from the sadness on the serious faces. No, I have never seen anything as beautiful as these companies going to the battle, companies made up of men and the elderly, of young men who yesterday were only boys. Reverent and resolute they follow the flame of the red flag; they are silent or speak little, but the strident and sonorous brass fill the air with the tune of the sacred hymn, "Le Chant du Départ":

    The Republic calls on you!"
    O people of Paris, how I love you!

Tuesday, May 16

I saw it fall, the twice imperishable monument, made of glory and iron. I saw it fall, the Vendôme column, symbol of the Bonapartist dynasty, glorification of the Empire, bauble of chauvinism.

How proud we are to be French when we look at the column! Now that there will no longer be a column to see, the Frenchman will no longer be so proud, and how much better that will be!

The Commune said: "Given that the presence of the Vendôme column is a perpetual insult to humanity and the negation of the brotherhood of peoples, the column will be demolished." Posed in these terms the Commune's decree is unarguable; the column had to fall when confronted by the universal republic.

The Commune has spoken; it drew up its decree in the name of universal brotherhood, a new principle in the face of old history, a principle superior to that of punishment and expiation. Let the column fall, then! Let the idol of the greatest malefactor of the century fall! Let us sweep it up, clean it up.

The crowd was enormous; it was parked on and around the square for several days waiting for the event. The column had been sawed obliquely at the level of the pedestal, and the men had dug up the earth in front of it, replacing the dirt with struts. Cords passed around the neck of the false gentleman of bronze were wrapped around the capstan. At 5:35 p.m. to the simple blow of a whistle, with no blow of a cannon, the capstans turn, the struts fall, the statue gently moves as if stupefied, it tilts back looking at the blue sky. Boom! It lies in the manure twenty to thirty feet deep. It fell deeper than the manure and buried itself in the blacktop. While still in the air the column had broken and the head of the perjurer had separated from the trunk, the murderer's arm was cut, the hand that held Victory was smashed.

"Long Live the universal republic!" the people cry on all sides. They approach; they enter the dust cloud. "What? The bronze crust was so thin? What? This false Roman Emperor that we thought so big was as small as that?" And up close, how hideous and ugly his face is. Was it really worth his trouble to take off his green frock coat, his boots and his little hat and dress himself in a shirt and leggings in order to indicate that he was entering his apotheosis and that he didn't deign to remain simple emperor of the French, but that he wanted to be, if not God, at least emperor of the whole world. This is what he lost, this is why they trample on him, and this is how they spit in his face!

Saturday, May 20

The question of hostages to be executed is now posed with a terrible clarity, with a horrible insistence. After the executions of the regular soldiers, which never stopped, after the executions of National Guardsmen, which are starting again, after the rape and murder spoken of everywhere of an ambulance worker of the 105th battalion, after the explosion of the powder works and the cataclysm of the Gros Caillou, the population demands reprisals. *Le Rappel* publishes that all of Paris is frightened. *Le Salut Public* claims that at the Commune Amourroux has demanded that the hostages be executed, "beginning with the priests, since all evil comes from them." A month ago M. Thiers didn't consent to have M. Darboy and consorts released, confident that the Commune would never dare carry out the threats against them. M. Thiers has again refused the Darboy-Blanqui exchange because there exists but one law in the world, that of war. Thiers is a heartless man, for the laws of war permit the exchange of prisoners, and it is precisely this horrible law of war that the Commune can invoke to execute the hostages.

Saturday, May 20

We come, we go, we see to our daily affairs, we sign our names in registers. A little further away, comrades are in combat, friends are shot. The day before yesterday the National Guardsmen were invaded at the convent of the Oiseaux by a superior force of Versaillais. They didn't want to surrender and they perished to the last man. And in the dormitory where once, under the wings of Jesuit mothers, the aristocracy of the girls of France slept, there is blood up to the ankles.

In the evening after the fatigue of the day, people walk on the balcony, breathing in the fresh air, gazing at the stars: Algol, Altair, Aldebaran, the inflexible Polar Star which holds up the axis of the world. And from time to time the heavens shiver with palpitations of light. It is the lightning flash of batteries that speak to and answer each other from Versailles to Paris.

At night we go to sleep as usual, doubtless supposing that tomorrow we will get up as usual. We stretch out under the sheets, we sleep well or badly. And several times our sleep is interrupted either by a detonation stronger than the others or by the drumbeats of the National Guard. While we sleep, 150,000 men prowl and are on the alert around our walls, with ladders and explosives. During the night 20,000 men here, 20,000 men there make an assault, and if they pierce the walls, if our brave National Guardsmen, surprised in one way or another, disconcerted by one of the thousand accidents of war don't manage to repel the invading hordes, then the city is massacred, the revolution is lost, and the world is delivered to the horrors of a reaction whose end can't be foreseen.

Sunday, May 21

Yet another attack has just been repelled. It is said that it's the sixth major attempt by the Versaillais. The week that was supposed to put an end to it all, according to M. Thiers, is over; after a seventh, an eight, or a ninth attack the army of Versailles will probably consider itself satisfied. As for the Parisian army, it is not yet at the end of its courage, not in the least. It seems to me that it is more firm and resolute, more certain of victory than ever. I have always had my reservations about the final success. I always counseled the Commune to hold out and to continue to hold out, to never offer any negotiations in the face of the incessant provocations of Versailles. Nevertheless, my hope has always resided in the intervention of the big cities, speaking severely to the Assembly and reconciling Paris with the rest of France. But today I begin to believe in a victory for Paris gained in combat, and I feel gay and in good form.

I am in no way among the most confident, far from it, in fact. But there are those who are more difficult to reassure, those who six weeks ago, declared it impossible that Paris hold out one week more. They haven't ceased telling us that every evening, with the arrivals from Germany and the provinces, "the most noble army in the world" grows by at least one regiment of excellent troops; that it is by hundreds and hundreds that the large caliber cannons brought against Paris can be counted; that piled in front of the weakest points in the walls is an impressive amount of powder and bombs, of explosives and incendiary devices; that there is no fort in the world, no fortification capable of resisting batteries firing 4,000 shots an hour, when an army of 200,000 men is ready by day and especially by night, to rush through one of these breaches. And if we answer yes, these fearsome batteries fired 4,000 shots an hour, and the bravest troops in the world already attempted an attack several times, then the prudent don't want to listen to anything; they want to remain frightened.

I am not unworried, but it seems to me that the battle cannot be more terrible than it has already been. Several times already the Versaillais have smashed themselves against our walls. It's true that they demolished a fort, virtually demolished two others, but everywhere in the past three weeks that there was hand-to-hand combat, in Neuilly, Asnières, in Colombe, we have advanced on one side, retreated on another, won elsewhere, and in the end we are in just as good a position as before. I don't think there is any great strategy in this; I don't think that any of our generals has risen to a strategy superior to that of remaining in place and not retreating in good order as in the time of Trochu. But it's already been two months that this has lasted, and "lasting is what matters," as the Normans say.

Monday, May 22

We had gone to sleep in the joy of the repelling of the sixth attack; even the pessimists believed that because of this triumphant resistance the provinces would finally intervene to impose reasonable negotiations on Versailles. The optimists already saw…. Alas, it would be too painful to speak now of their faith. Today we are awakened to the cry that: "The Versaillais have entered the city! They're on the Champs de Mars, the Trocadero; they're at the Arc de Triomphe, the Champs Elysées and are still advancing. They are arriving en masse. Treason opened the gates wide to them. They themselves say that they have passed through the walls without firing a shot. The reactionaries are going to deliver the rest of the city to them. Another powder works has just exploded. The smoke of an enormous fire blackens the sky. No one knows what is burning."

Is it true? Has the end arrived?

On the streets there is a singular silence. Here and there several groups speak softly among themselves. In the middle of one of these groups I notice a young liberal, someone very liberal, who in the past chased after me to speak to me amiably. I approach him" "So what's the news?" He answers, negligently offering me the tip of his finger, "Oh, what you already know. The army of Versailles effected its entry yesterday evening. It marched all night. It occupies an entire side of Paris. It is now just outside the Place de la Concorde. It's moving quickly, as you can see."

I bid him good bye. That fingertip offered me by this very liberal young man sufficiently indicated to me possibility of success left to the party of the revolution.

With a friend we explored the quarter. We went down the Rue des Saints-Pères with the intention of crossing the bridge. When we arrived on the quay, a bullet whistled by our ears. Where did this messenger of death come from? We look in the direction indicated by the noise. Nothing can be seen. But entrenched behind closed curtains some good bourgeois is "establishing order," like those brave Marseillais who shoot down sparrows from deep within their fortresses.

We continue on through the hills of the Rues de l'Université, Lille, Varennes, Dominique, and Grenelle-Saint-Germain. We would have liked to enter the ministries of war or public instruction, but we are stopped by National Guard barricades. "No one goes through." We understand that these ministries are already occupied by the Versaillais. We go back in the same direction from which we came. At several corners people are putting up pretenses of barricades, but the men working on them have worried, somber, and careworn faces. On the contrary, it isn't difficult to discern the secret jubilation of all those concierges, shopkeepers, merchants of objects of piety, and believers who compose the heart of this population. They already look at you as if preparing to denounce you to a future gendarme or the first policeman. They snicker at the consternation of their neighbor; a hateful and triumphant sarcasm pierces their contrite air and their mask of beatific and comfortable humility.

The attempts at resistance are carried out haphazardly; those who don't want to come don't, those who want to come come where they want and as they want. There is no order. There is an absence of general leadership; the surprise is complete. The enemy penetrated the camp unexpectedly. It is impossible to deny the evidence; the Left Bank was not defendable against the Versaillais. The areas around the military school and the Invalides have always been Bonapartist. From there you pass to the private homes and gardens of the noble faubourg Saint Germain, a nest of legitimists. There then come the Jesuit centers of Saint-Sulpice, of the Abbaye, of Saint-Etienne, of Sainte-Geneviève, and the Rue Lhomond, not to mention the academics of the Sorbonne and the Jardin des Plantes, rallied today around the clerical banner. And the students of the Latin Quarter? They are budding academics. These future lawyers and magistrates, professors of medicine and certified doctors are not, cannot be, except for some exceptions, anything but future bourgeois. And so we saw them refuse to join the Commune, which offered them the Federation of Schools and the reorganization of higher education however they wished and saw fit to do it. As soon as the bullets scrape the paving stones the lion of the Latin Quarter will cease shaking his golden mane; he won't let out his fearsome roar, but instead will seek refuge in the cool grotto of the café Le Source, at the beer fountain, where the doe come to quench their thirst. To be sure, the Versaillais this morning can set out unhindered from the military school and the Gare de Montparnasse up to the Gare d'Orleans station and on this side join up with the Prussians, their new friends.

And on the Right Bank? There is less confusion on the Right Bank. The fortresses of the Tuileries, the Louvre and city hall, the Bastille, the Prince Eugène Barracks are solid points of resistance for the National Guard. Doubtless the population of all these wealthy and commercial quarters is at the very most republican, and not in the least revolutionary. But the terrain isn't mined from below as on the other side of the Seine. And then, people here feel themselves to breathe the fire of the reds of Batignolles and Montmartre, of Belleville and Menilmontant.

The physiognomy of the inhabitants differs noticeably according to the neighborhood, and one must be Parisian to find some interest in a politico-geographic description of the various arrondissements. In general, one can say that in Paris the republican and revolutionary thermometer rises and falls according to the altitude above sea level. The map of the sewers could, with slight modifications, serve as a political map. The great line of depression is the Seine and the center of the Tuileries.

A legend is spreading about that the National Guard is executing a turning movement, has retaken the entry gates and that the Versaillais, having their retreat cut off, are now caught between two fires. It is a legend like too many that we heard during the siege.

Nevertheless, it is true that the Versaillais either weren't able or didn't want to take advantage of the enormous advantage of a surprise that handed Paris over to them almost without a shot being fired. Bypassing the Place de la Concorde and the Madeleine they seized the Gare Saint-Lazare and followed the railroad to the new Chaptal College, which was turned over to them by a battalion of National Guardsmen who are friends of order. This battalion fired from the windows on their comrades of yesterday. The soldiers of Versailles have advanced as far as the

Église de la Trinité, which commands the Chaussée d'Antin, but they don't hold the block of interior houses. A friend tells me with enthusiastic admiration that he saw National Guardsmen raise a barricade on the Rue Ferme des Mathurins under enemy fire. Laying across the street was a line of paving stones, one on top of another, three sandstones and not a single one more. Lying flat, the men had organized a chain of paving stones which they raised about their fragile shelter, while comrades exchanged fire with the Versaillais. And all of this was performed peacefully, with no fine words, without even singing. "To die for the fatherland... calmly...soberly." All day I kept an eye out for drunks, and in my travels, on both the Right and Left Banks, I only saw two men taken with wine and one who pretended to be.

From the Boulevard des Capucines I heard fired from the very streets, from within the sacred walls of the city, the cannon of civil war. It was right nearby; bullets struck against the opera house. With the first shot I was gripped by emotion. One felt a physical pain, as at the fusillade of January 22, which was ordered on the Place de l'Hôtel de Ville by M. Chaudey acting on behalf of Messrs. Favre and Trochu, the cannon thundering within our walls bearing messages from Frenchmen to Frenchmen!

The entire length of my walk from the Madeleine to the Chateau d'Eau, on the boulevards, more deserted of passersby than in the old days at 2:00 or 3:00 in the morning, a few National Guardsmen of good will improvised barricades. There was no sign of activity up to the Saint-Denis and Saint-Martin gates, which serve as the line of demarcation between the wealthy and popular quarters. We went willingly to the Saint-Martin gate, where citizens formed a chain of paving stones while others stopped passersby exclaiming, "Citizen, citizen, to work!" What children accomplished at work was truly amazing: boys set themselves in twos and threes to loosen a paving stone that a kid of five or six then took away, bent under the weight of his burden. Children perched on the walls filled the role of masons and even architects. All of these escapees from school were happy and proud to play—and "play" is the word—their role in the civil war.

At night I go back up the Faubourg du Temple. With feverish activity people accomplished immense labors. The men dig, the women stand guard off to the side, armed with a rifle and bayonet.

Tuesday, May 23

At the barricade on the Rue Lafayette I was placed under arrest by a group of brave National Guards who, with reason, found that my pass was insufficient. People had seen me carrying paving stones to several barricades and they perhaps asked if my appearance of good will wasn't hiding espionage. I didn't protest my affection for the Commune, nor did I get angry, limiting myself to responding simply and politely to the two or three officers who came to examine my case. It seemed to be worthy of being referred to the police superintendent of the arrondissement. Two National Guardsmen placed themselves at my side and we marched, I remaining silent, they not posing any indiscreet questions. One of them offered to follow us so that I wouldn't look like I was under arrest. I thanked him, but why hide the truth? "Let's go; they requisitioned us to carry paving stones to a barricade under construction." I had already carried too many. My acolytes were thirsty; they stopped at a wine merchant who was a friend of theirs and offered me a drink. I refuse, but they are insistent and I accept sugar water while they take watered down wine. We toasted without saying a word, and they didn't allow me to pay.

When the turn for my affair presented itself at the police commissariat it is briefly recounted in low voice by my companions. The citizen superintendent furrowed his brow and asked me a few questions which I discretely answered, and the decision is announced: "Given that no fact is articulated against the citizen holding insufficient papers, the citizen can continue along his way. He is released." I salute, thank them with a gesture, and go on my way without saying a word. My captivity lasted a little more than an hour.

I don't relate this incident because of its biographic importance, but as a detail that serves to fix the physiognomy of the whole. Everyone can speak of what he's seen.

I head up the boulevards towards the stock exchange. The expressions were somber. Nevertheless I met a group of reactionaries who were laughing uproariously at some Chinese joke. In the newsstands there were three reactionary newspapers for sale telling how our valiant army had already exterminated the horde of bandits at all points. And *La Vérité* which, were it not for its dislike for the brothers Picard, would have been totally reactionary, called down on the heads of the members of the Commune the just punishment they won't escape. Finally, there is *Le Rappel* which, in this critical moment, declared itself against the Assembly but not for the Commune, and reprinted in big letters an old almost incomprehensible page of Victor Hugo. A week later *Le Rappel* and *La Vérité*, more daring than they thought themselves to be, were punished for their criminal audacity, and all the editors that could be taken were imprisoned.

And yet I could only advance with difficulty. At every barricade I had to show my pass, and fearing that the lack of an identity card would end up by doing me harm I decided to end my voyage of exploration from quarter to quarter, from barricade to barricade.

How lovely the setting sun is in the evening, seen from the Bercy Bridge. The green waters flow slowly and move gently. The buoys, the masts, the arched arcs are clearly reflected in their tranquil mirror. Above the immeasurable depths of a calm and luminous sky there fall on the river, there fall on the city a dew or gold and silver, a rain of opaline and iridescent pearls, an orange dust; the monuments are silhouetted in the slightly violet vapors, the massive towers of Notre Dame, the proud colonnade of the Pantheon still topped by a red flag, the bell tower of Saint-Etienne du Mont, the belfry of Saint-Jacques.

Mixed in with these fogs, with these gentle plays of nuance, with these grandiose harmonies of light and color, here and there are thick black vapors, the smoke from fires, here, there, a bit further away, almost everywhere.

And in this august and deep calm, if you open wide your ears you can distinguish distant noises floating through the vast extent of the luminous skies, the song of the bugle, the call of the drum, the whistling of the fusillade and the staccato of the machine guns. But these noises are weak, so weak that you could almost confuse them with the buzzing of flies, the gentle murmur of the breeze and the river, which half-heartedly collides with the bank, and complains of its slight effort.

Saturday, May 27

From time to time we hear from the Gare de Lyon and the Gare de Orleans and the construction sites the rolling of the gunfire of a firing squad; about a dozen, two dozen shots. It is the prisoners being executed: the men swept up in the cellars and the attics and who three soldiers and their corporal believed suspect; passersby whose face displeases the policemen and squealers swarming about the streets, revolver in their belt, blackjack in their pocket, tricolor armband on the sleeve, friends of order who found a way not to serve the Commune by seeking refuge in their concierge's lodge or some other hideout. They take vengeance on the National Guardsmen of disorder who went into battle and paid with their persons. They denounce former soldiers who had the clumsiness to allow themselves to be seen in bright red pants or military cap, and consequently were guilty of treason or at least desertion in the face of the enemy. Executed, executed!

From behind our curtains we saw these unarmed unfortunates passing, bourgeois and workers, in street clothes or some piece of uniform. They march erect, with a firm and proud step, but their faces are pale. In an hour they will be dead.

The Bastille taken, the popular neighborhoods of the Temple, of Saint Antoine, of Belleville, and Père Lachaise remain to be forced.

Under a sky heavy with rain, the gusts of wind carry the screaming of the machine guns, the bullets dig into the barricade with the sound of hail. Over there the combatants are killed in the ardor and excitement of struggle; they aren't assassinated as they are here.

The people of the quarter begin to go out; they are trying to learn what is going on outside. They retire with frightful tales. The banks of the river are scattered with corpses, the streets as well. In certain courtyards the dead bodies are piled up. Carcasses are taken away in cartloads to be buried in deep ditches that are covered with quicklime. Elsewhere they are sprinkled with petroleum and burned. We saw a convoy of ten to twelve buses full of human debris.

A friend who brings us information shows us his boot heels, soaked with blood.

From both sides of the Seine a red thread flows along the shore. In several spots there are piles of smashed weapons, of equipment, of kepis, of uniform jackets, of torn effects, of papers and registered that have been burned, or are still smoking.

May 28, in the evening

Surrounded, attacked on all sides, Père Lachaise cemetery was invaded by the rural troops. The last defenders of the Commune were massacred.

An historical period has likely just closed. A new one begins. It's all over for our generation, destined no doubt to be the powerless spectator, the pitiful victim of a stupid and furious reaction.

Poor France. If you are really condemned to death, you were never in so much danger. How low you fell after the Favre-Trochu capitulation. And now how far will you fall? The best of your sons, the bravest, the most intelligent, the hope of their race are no more. The leagued wastrels and exploiters have killed the workers; how ruined will we be? The Bonapartist corruption was followed by cowardice towards the Prussians; after the cowardice comes the terrible cruelty towards the revolutionaries. What will follow? How gloomy are the visions that unfurl before our eyes.

But let whatever happens happen. We don't surrender. We are mortal, but our cause is immortal. If we don't triumph, our children will be victorious, and if our children fail too, our grandchildren will succeed. It is more likely that civilization will perish than that our social ideal will. The old world is built on the privileges of idleness; the new is established and will be established on the rights of labor. In the past labor was a slave. He became a serf and now he is still exploited, but he will be free, with all due respect to the bombardiers and murderers.

And even if France were to perish, its glory would be to have perished along with the social idea, the highest, the most comprehensive, the most fertile ever formulated by human society. And even if they were to cut down the trunk of the beautiful fruit tree that is called France, even so, from its strong subterranean roots new offshoots would grow. We are the children of our earth, and they will take away neither our heaven nor our sun!

---

[1] Reference to the June revolution of 1848 and December 2, 1851, the date of Napoleon III's coup d'état

Men and Things
from the Time of the Commune

The book *Hommes et Choses du Temps de la Commune* (Men and Things from the Time of the Commune) was the collective work of three men involved at varying levels in the Commune.

Léon Massenet de Marancourt was the son of a wealthy manufacturer and the brother of the famous composer Jules Massenet. Though he was a monarchist until his mid-twenties (and a gambler heavily in debt) during the siege he was a lieutenant in the National Guard, and under the Commune was named chief of his cavalry battalion. He apparently joined the International in 1871, which didn't prevent him from having 500,000 francs from the Bank of France turned over to him during the Bloody week.

After the defeat of the Commune he fled Paris for Brussels and Geneva, and by 1879—the same year he was pardoned after having been sentenced in absentia to deportation—was editor of a newspaper in Rio de Janeiro.

Henry Bellenger was one of the most active journalists during the period of the Commune, writing for Félix Pyat's *Le Vengeur*, Valles's *Le Cri du Peuple*, as well as the Commune's *Journal Officiel*. His revolutionary fervor was evidenced by an article he wrote after the failed sortie of April 3: "I hope that once and for all we are going to break with the magnanimous and merciful traditions of the past. We must prune the tree, sweep clear, clear the place in order to establish on a solid base the glorious edifice of our young revolution."

He was able to escape Paris along with his fellow journalist Maxime Vuillaume, and though stopped by the Versaillais authorities, the police superintendent who captured him was unaware of his role during the Commune and he was able to flee France for Switzerland and later England.

The third author of *Men and Things...* was Maxime Vuillaume (1844-1926). Vuillaume was from a modest background, and under the Empire he wrote for a number of republican newspapers, which he writes of in the chapter here about "Père Duchêne." During the Commune, after writing for the Blanquist newspaper *La Patrie en Danger* he was a lieutenant in the National Guard, participating in the revolutionary events of October 31, 1870 and January 22, 1871.

His journalistic activity during the Commune was immense, as he either edited or wrote for his own *Père Duchêne*, which was founded just before the proclamation of the Commune and ceased publication ten days before its crushing, as well as for *La Sociale*, *L'Estafette*, and the *Bonnet Rouge*. Beside these papers he also wrote for the *Journal Officiel* until its final issue on May 24. In his newspaper *Père Duchêne* he revived the gruff-speaking man of the people of that name who had been created by the sans-culotte leader of the first French Revolution, Jacques Hébert, and it was in his voice that Vuillaume expressed the great anger of the people.

The account of Vuillaume's escape is even stranger that that of his collaborator Bellenger: when he was stopped by the police, the arresting officer apparently forgot him in the train wagon in which he'd been found.

Though sentenced to death in absentia in 1872, by that time he was already in Geneva where he joined the "Socialist Section for Revolutionary Propaganda and Action," and it was while in Geneva that he began the publication of *Men and Things from the Time of the Commune*.

Vuillaume remained in exile until 1887, where he was engaged in various industrial and engineering activities in Italy and Switzerland, including the digging of the tunnel through the St. Gothard pass in Switzerland. When he finally returned to France he wrote for various republican—but not revolutionary—publications, and during World War I was the author of a number of patriotic pamphlets.

Men and Things… contains remarkably vivid first-hand accounts of the founding of the commune, of the disastrous sortie of April 3, and of the life of a journal and journalist during those heady days. It also puts forth the thesis that the Commune was actually the result of a provocation by the bourgeois government. The theory, outlined below, was that the only way to put an end to the working class as a threat was to push it to rash action that would provide a pretext for a bloodbath.

March 18
Léon Massenet de Marancour

When two irreconcilable adversaries come to blows, victory almost always goes to the one who delivers the first blows; and the one who delivers them only decides to start the fight because he thinks his enemy's defense ill prepared.

And so, let us calmly examine the conditions for the combat between Versailles and Paris.

On one side was the Assembly, which felt that its place was in the capital but which refused to legislate in the presence of 400,000 bayonets. It was conscious that any law voted for it would be an attack on the rights of those who, for the moment, had the greater numbers and the greater strength.

Five billion francs to pay, new taxes to levy—this was the economic situation, along with the rents that were overdue and the debts whose terms had been reached and hadn't been paid.

Where was this money to be obtained if not from the pockets of the poor? Our good deputies didn't seem inclined to strike out at capital and it was yet again labor, and labor alone, that would pay the price of the Empire.

To decree is simple; plucking the fruits, therein lies the skill, especially when the person to be robbed holds a rifle.

How to disarm Paris—this was the entire question.

What practical and peaceful means could M. Thiers use to arrive at this disarmament, the sole measure that would calm the fearful apprehensions of the Chamber? Various proposals were put forward. The slyest individuals proposed the opening of the cash boxes of the national pawn shop. They said, "Loan fifteen francs per rifle and tomorrow the Hotel des Blancs Manteaux will be transformed into an arsenal." This was a pitiful measure, and one that would merely have served to rid the National Guard of 150,000 of the undecided or fearful who, through their inertia at the most important moments, hinder the march of the true citizens. The latter, strong in their rights, remained nevertheless armed.

As a palliative, others issued a plan for the reorganization of the army, mandatory service, a *levée en masse*, a kind of Prussian Landwehr. But before the law could be discussed, promulgated, and executed there were six more months of the status quo.

In the end, and in the opinion of the most moderate conservatives, it was decided that the best way to take the rifle from a National Guardsman was to provide him with a pretext to use it so as to be able to snatch it from him by a military surprise. In order to do this, the Guard must be killed. But that didn't matter: the principle and society would be saved.

The Government was not unaware that the Federation [of the National Guard], still in its infancy, was lacking in cohesion since, when it gave them a signal, 210 commanders of the 215 who signed the federative pact shamefully fled to Versailles. Nevertheless, if the government had procrastinated, if they hadn't precipitated the crisis of March 18, there is no doubt that the federated battalions, having had the time to choose their leaders and to organize, would have been able to act purposefully when the moment arrived.

Six months later, the reimbursed Prussians withdrew to a position forty leagues from Paris. The departments, having recovered from their stupor, reawakened to political life. At that point there would then have been an exchange of delegations, a communion of ideas between Paris and the provinces, and the armed citizens of the entire nation would have formed one immense federation: the French National Guard.

The inevitable result? The dissolution of the Chamber, the election of a Convention.

France would enter its final revolutionary phase. It would be up to the workers to speak up and dictate a program in conformity with their duties, their rights, and their needs.

Now let us see, on the eve of March 18, what group it was that the semi-official papers called "that secret association," and which was already known as the Central Committee. Let us speak of its origin, its existence, its strength.

On a certain day in November, a brave young man named Finet, of the 230th battalion, set up a meeting at the Café Hollandais at the Palais Royale for all the color bearers to discuss the matter of wages, as these officers had been excluded by decree of the marching companies.

The presidency of the group was voted to Commander Raoul du Bisson, a presidency well deserved in a republican assembly, as much by the regulatory cut of his moustache as by the cross of a Commander of the Order of Saint-Janvier that shone on his breast. If M. Raoul de Buisson was on the best of terms with His Former Majesty François II, M. Vrignault, one of the standard bearers of the meeting, was a friend of General Vinoy. He took it upon himself to obtain the moneys claimed.

Nothing more was heard of this affair. No one went to the strongbox. And yet this meeting was not a waste for all concerned, and the future editor of the *Bien Public* laid down the foundations for a federative organization which he hoped to benefit from at the right moment.

Two months passed. They starve Paris, exasperate it, mislead it. Long live the armistice!

Long live Peace! Despairing but not defeated, Paris consoled itself by gazing at its weapons. At least Jules Favre didn't dare touch them. Like

M. Thiers, M. Favre knew that you can only take a rifle from a worker's hands by killing him. Events had only been postponed.

Growing impatient, M. Vrignault laid down his cards and, conveniently remembering the meeting at the Café Hollandais, exclaimed in his newspaper: Federate the National Guard! All the battalion chiefs joined in this appeal, for during the siege they had seen through a crack in the door the sweet gaiety, the succulent repasts of headquarters. The editor of the *Bien Public* allowed them a glimpse of the possibility of becoming, by the votes of the ragged, the comrades of Nivière and Luppé. Over there it rains stuffed pheasant and crosses of the Legion of Honor. What glory and what profit!

All swore to earn the honor of dining at the table of power through the duly carried out surrender of their battalions' rifles. M. Vrignault, who knew how much the promises of this society were worth, took care to place one of his accomplices behind each naïf. These accomplices, Montaud and the others, will later be found as witnesses for the prosecution at Versailles's military tribunals.

As for the simple Guardsmen, of whom experience has taught to be suspicious, they had the presentiment of another betrayal and the majority took the helm by creating the Central Committee, alongside Vrignault's Federation (which was still under the presidency of Brisson),.

It was a solemn rendezvous at the Vaux Hall, with 2,000 men attending. Vrignault and his men were invited. A unanimous vote brings together the Federation and the Central Committee into one group. Time passed, and it was imperative to name leaders. The members of the Central Committee were elected by acclamation. It was understood that their powers were provisional and, in conformity with the statutes of the Federation, would end the day when the members of the Committee would pass through the triple elections of the companies, battalions, and legions. In several arrondissements they set to work the next day. Nevertheless, the elections were not completely finished, since on March 17 the Central Committee only had twenty-three members whose powers were verified. And it was only at 1:00 a.m. on March 18th that Bergeret was elected a member of the Central Committee and promoted chief of the 18th legion from Montmartre. He so little expected this that three hours later Bergeret left the Rue des Rosiers, the site of his headquarters, to return to his home behind the Luxembourg.

It was no small task to reorganize the National Guard. During the armistice the government had applied itself to breaking it up. One day it would take its camp equipment from it, the next its wages. And every day brought new vexations. Let's not forget the rents and terms due, burning questions that kept the public mood in a state of turmoil. People thought little about politics. M. Thiers knew all of this; he knew that on March 18 it would have been folly for the revolutionaries to attempt social reform.

As for the International, which people see everywhere, we deny its role in the Committee. It was represented there by only a dozen members, intelligent individuals, but they lacked a precise mandate.

The watchwords were *patience* and *reorganization*. No one thought of an attack. In order to understand what was behind this, we must turn back to February 28. The Government of National Defense had sworn that the enemy would not step foot in the capital, and so Paris, knowing its masters to be dishonest, consequently prepared an appropriate entrance for the victors of Montretout.

That evening, the officers of General Clément Thomas's general staff were already discussing the order of march of the Prussians in Paris. Each spoke about the ravishing mourning attire of their wives and sought out the most gallant way to hang crepe from the pommel of his sword. The Marquis de Chanaleilles had his apartment dusted and he garnished his flower boxes with the rarest of flowers in honor of His Royal Highness, the Duke of Weimar.

And yet one thing worried him. The starving of the faubourgs—the canaille—having neither horses nor mistresses to show off, would perhaps want to defend their arms and homes.

Everything was in place for the festival!

Belfort had been thrown to the people as an attenuation of the ignominy. The Parisian is a good child; right or wrong, he thought he had won Belfort through his submission, but he couldn't bear that his rifles and cannons be added to the deal, like so many pins. Our diplomats of Versailles had foreseen this and they whispered smilingly into each other's ears, "Let them take the cannons, pillage the powder works and arsenals, construct barricades. All the better! These cannons and rifles that they take piecemeal, we'll get them back wholesale."

We are still to learn these men's method for victory.

The stolen cannons had to be guarded. Parks were created in Montmartre, Belleville, and on the Place d'Italie. Based on the Committee's plans, Commander Poulizac constructed the redoubt on the Buttes. This same Poulizac, in order to win back the military medal that he'd lost in a card game, deserted on March 18. Versailles counts him among its dead; he was killed May 23 on these same works that he constructed.

Clearly establishing its antagonism with the command staff, the Committee issued orders daily. Its rights grew from popular suffrage, while the colonels of the Elysée held their ranks at the pleasure of the minister.

The battle was imminent. Deputies and journalists joined together to incite M. Thiers, who wanted to give the appearance of having his hand forced. The violent suppression of six newspapers hadn't been able to cause an explosion. The taking of the cannons, which they knew couldn't be wrested from the hands of those who held them without conflict, remained as a pretext for military action.

What were the probable chances of this *coup d'état?* Who prepared it? The guilty party is the sole individual with an interest in the success of the enterprise.

The die was cast. At 4:00 a.m. on March 18 General Susbielle seized the Monmartre position hardly firing a shot. A federal Guardsman was the only one to fall; the others, at most fifty, were taken prisoner. The cannons were seized, but there were no horses with which to take them away. The hours passed in an inactivity that appears premeditated. A few hastily assembled guardsmen assaulted the Buttes, seized General Lecomte, and fraternized with the troops. Susbielle and his general staff fled the square, leaving in the hands of the insurrection—their handiwork—a hostage who, by the force of circumstances, would inevitably become a victim.

Just as reaction had brought about the June days, the prologue to the Empire, March 18 was to bring a Pretender, a new Savior of the Nation.

To those who are unable to believe in this daring resolve to surrender Paris to the revolution, we reply that the author of the peace treaty, feeling himself powerless to preserve Paris through justice, preferred to brave the hazards of a battle at a chosen moment, when he knew his enemy was disarmed.

The flight to Versailles had been decided upon since March 15. Everything was ready to be moved—strongboxes and archives. At the Ministry of War copies of letters and papers were found tied up to be taken away. The last date on these letters was March 15. The departure had been resolved upon since that date and on March 18 Paris was to be surrendered to all the dangers of an improvised government.

The objection to this plan was that an army would be needed in order to retake this city that was being abandoned. Why not the army of Sedan and Metz? Would this not be the way to again earn, in an easy and brilliant campaign, the ranks so generously given to the armies of Gambetta and Trochu? The government knew full well that while it was reorganizing its troops in Versailles, nothing similar could be done in Paris. Thanks to the disorder it had created, the government knew that the Parisians would discuss and would elect before they would unite and act.

At the same time, the government briefly thought that Versailles and Montmartre would come together. The dissident battalions had counted themselves; not all of Paris belonged to the Central Committee.

Despite the machinations of Versailles, the dissidents and the Federals refused to kill each other. Finally, Vice-Admiral Saisset, speaking in the name of the executive power, spoke words of reconciliation: the laws on debts due, rents, municipal freedoms, the federation of the National Guard with all its leaders named by election, even generals, all was granted. Even M. Saisset posed his candidacy. Who could doubt the sincerity of the poster he had put up? Was it not signed by the mayors, solemnly convoking the citizens to elect the Commune?

At this call, Paris lay down its arms. The Place de la Bourse fraternized with the Place St. Pierre, the Chausée d'Antin with Belleville. The dissidents handed over their posts, the town halls their doors.

It was only that night that the Central Committee met uncontested at the Hôtel de Ville. Paris belonged to it by the right, by the force, by the grace of Versailles. Alas, that poster was a new trap laid for republican loyalty. Admiral Saisset was disavowed; negotiations were broken off; the gates of Paris were closed.

The Central Committee, carrying out its patriotic task to the final degree, a few days later placed Paris in the hands of the freely elected Commune. It was a broken and demoralized Paris, without finances, without a government and, it must be said, without an army.

The Sortie of April 3
Henri Bellenger

In the first chapter of this book, entitled "March 18" we established why and how M. Thiers decided to play his trump card by abandoning to itself an armed Paris that he feared. In acting this way, he hoped to provoke general confusion and disorder in the great city, abruptly cut off from police and government – even the most urgent services—which would soon be translated into bloody anarchy through scenes of violence and pillage.

A pompous man seasoned with a touch of Machiavelli, M. Thiers, in an obvious sign of senile debility after forty years of public life, had come to believe his own lies. Possessed of a limited intelligence, he was a short-sighted politician having no other quality than an intuition that was at times correct; one for whom parliamentary tightrope walking, which had once served as a springboard to attain power, now seemed the be all and end all of governmental science. There was nothing more to him. What is more, he was profoundly selfish, refusing to admit that human acts could have any motive other than immediate and brute personal interest. He judged the people based on those in his entourage and thought that the starving people of the siege would hasten to pillage as soon as they knew that the iron fist of the gendarme was far away.

And so he confidently awaited the flowering of the chaff he had sown, of the discord he spread in handfuls. In the meanwhile he hastily organized a praetorian army made up of prisoners embittered by the shame of the defeat and the sufferings of captivity. "Paris, tired of the excesses of the low multitude," said the son of the dock worker from Marseilles, "will soon recall me. A country cannot do without a government for any extended period of time. In the meanwhile let us forge the ring, prepare the yoke, and make supple the strap that we will place over the horns of the bull as soon as he lowers his head."

But time was passing and none of the little man's predictions were being fulfilled. There was no disorder; the streets of the capital were never safer than they were after March 18. As was the case in '48, it didn't hold responsible the republic that it instinctively loved as the promise of a new era for its poverty. The affair of the Rue de la Paix—a clumsy attempt at civil war—had miserably failed. And finally, in what was a cause for serious concern for Versailles, the major cities of France were becoming agitated, one after the other pronouncing itself in favor of the

Communal revolution. The red flag already flew in Lyon, Marseilles, and Saint Etienne.

Everything was working to confound the rural dictator. Frightened by the extent of the movement he had provoked, the old trickster furiously sought in his box of evil tricks a new application of the monarchical axiom: *divide et imperas*. It was of the utmost urgency that he take a decisive step. Every day of additional existence of what they called in the Seine et Oise the "insurrectionary power" undermined the already-contested authority of the Versailles Assembly, elected with the defined mandate of making peace in conditions of general fear.

It is then that M. Thiers imagined the well-conceived plan the first act of which we recounted in our previous chapter. To attack the lion in his den, to attempt to enter by force the Paris they had so hastily fled would have been sheer folly. But by exasperating the Federals through summary executions they pushed them to a premature sortie, a poorly conceived, angry reaction. They drew the Parisians onto terrain plotted in advance, where the regular and disciplined army would easily win the day over an armed crowd, guided by inexperienced chiefs, a verbose, nervous militia incapable of patience, acting on impulse.

The Commune, issued from the elections of March 26 and proclaimed on March 29 found itself, at the moment the Versaillais attacked it, master of Paris. Entirely absorbed in the enormous labor of reorganization, it had broken up into commissions that one can't help thinking weren't lacking for work. Everything had to be made anew or be created.

When the news of the murder of the prisoners in Courbevoie reached the Hôtel de Ville , it was like a thunderbolt. Under the risk of losing the support of the National Guard, the communal power had to act, and act quickly. A war council was immediately convoked.

Flourens, Duval, Ranvier, Bergeret, Eudes, and Chardon participated in this council. They discussed the need for a sortie the next day and for a march on Versailles in order to have done with the Assembly once and for all. As we can see, the Commune was falling into M. Thiers' trap.

And yet a serious difficulty stopped it. One of the wisest of them asked the question: what would be Mont-Valérien's attitude?

In order to fully understand what will follow, it is necessary to open a parenthesis. The fortress whose name we just wrote, a name that will often return throughout this book, this Mont-Valerién, which was established more to master Paris than to defend it—as we saw during the siege—had until then remained strictly neutral. And yet the regular army still occupied it as the result of a compromise ridiculously concluded under the following conditions:

Immediately after March 18, several officers of the federated National Guard, understanding the importance for the victorious revolution of the possession of the fortified works that dominate Paris, hastily assembled their companies and, without a mandate and without precise orders from the Central Committee, occupied the forts of the Left Bank, which were surrendered to them without resistance by the demoralized soldiers. It is thus that Captain B..., followed by only fifty seven men, successively took control of Issy, Vanves, and Montrouge on March 21. This was an admirably successful feat of daring. In each fort he left fifteen National Guardsmen as a garrison. His task completed, the red flag flying over the three fortresses, the heroic daredevil sent an orderly to the *Cri du Peuple* charged with bringing back an editor.

"I am not used to handling the pen," he said on a piece of paper that the Federal took from his cap, "and I'd prefer that you tell the story... Just a few words printed in the newspaper. When I return home I don't want to be treated like I made this up."

In the confusion of the first days, a man of this stripe, granted sufficient power and followed by determined volunteers of his choosing, would surely have taken control of Mont-Valérien. But through unbelievable negligence, the Central Committee didn't even think of putting this dedication to use.

It was only on March 29, the day of the proclamation of the Commune, that Lullier received the mission to occupy the colossal fortress. This was a terrible choice: the former navy lieutenant was the least-appropriate man for this undertaking. An officer of a certain value, well read and educated, possessing an unquestionable military education, Lullier offers us the strange phenomenon of a gifted, well-bred, brilliant, brave, young man, who knew much, but whose rare qualities only amplify his faults. Gifted with an unheard of vanity, infantile, ridiculous, he will forever allow himself to be duped by whoever flatters him. However vulgar the incense, he inhales it deeply and grows intoxicated on it, like the god he thinks himself to be. What is more, he frequently—too frequently, alas—gets drunk on alcohol. In less than an hour I've seen him drink nearly a half-liter of cognac. Intoxication, far from making him sleepy, increases his exalted conceit to a paroxysm. He becomes mad as a hatter.

And under this influence, he only says or does foolish things. And this is what happened to him at Mont-Valérin.

Leaving Paris with three battalions, he neglected to supply himself with ladders, mining powder, and the devices necessary for a possible attack. Nevertheless, he ably deployed his 1500 men and presented himself, followed by a small escort, at the foot of the drawbridge and called on the fort to surrender.

Commander Solichon, governor of Mont-Valérien, had only eighty discouraged men with him. If they had attacked him, climbed the ramparts at three different points, blown up a part of the wall with dynamite, caused a breach, Mont-Valérien was taken.

The commander of the fort saw this at a glance and thought all was lost. But as soon as he learned that the National Guardsmen were commanded by Lullier he regained hope. Knowing the man, he resolved to trick him. He immediately lowered the drawbridge, offering to negotiate with the general. When Lullier, braided from head to toe, passed through the outer wall, the drums beat and Solichon advanced with a humble look, saluting with his sword.

They sat at the table and the corks popped. Lullier, whose mania the commander set out to flatter, readily consented to be satisfied with his host's word. It was verbally agreed that in case of armed fight, Mont-Valérien would support neither Paris nor Versailles. In this way, Solichon's military honor remained safe.

They separated on the best of terms, the drums rolled again, the drawbridge was lowered, and Lullier returned to Paris leading the Federals, who were torn between disappointment and anger, for they vaguely understood that they had just been mocked.

This point clarified, let us now return to the war council held the afternoon of April 2 at the Hôtel de Ville . We are at the moment when Duval is taking the floor and asking what Mont-Valérien's attitude will be in the fight.

Bergeret answered that he would bypass the fortress. And in any event, didn't they have the formal promise of neutrality that Solichon had made to Lullier?

"And if Solichon is no longer there? And anyway, Lullier doesn't inspire much confidence. Didn't we have him arrested precisely because of that shameful failure?"

Despite these considerations, the sortie was decided on. It was agreed that they would divide the communal army into four principal corps with the following itinerary:

1st corps—Bergeret, the Nanterre Road

2nd Corps—Flourens, the Asnières Road

3rd Corps—Duval, the Chatillon Road

4th Corps—Eudes, the Bas-Meudon Road, going simultaneously to Versailles

Twenty general staff officers were immediately delegated to the twenty arrondissements. They carried to the legion chiefs the order to form columns of at least 5,000 men and to have them followed by a sufficient number of wagons filled with munitions and supplies. In order to do this, they were granted full power to carry out requisitions.

Despite the activity deployed to execute these orders, it was with great difficulty that they managed to assemble an army of 30,000 men in all of Paris: 12,000 on the Right Bank, 18,000 on the Left Bank. The army was assembled in two hours. The difficulty, and it was one that was not overcome, was to procure sufficient provisions quickly to begin a campaign and especially that of accurately distributing munitions by battalion.

The artillery was dragged by horses from the bus companies, mounted by impromptu drivers. We can affirm that of the eighty pieces of artillery that followed the army, most had half-empty caissons and the army considered itself lucky if the artillery had projectiles of the correct caliber.

There was no cavalry and, consequently, no scouts.

The assembly points designated for 5:00 p.m. were, for the battalions of Montmartre-Belleville on the Right Bank forming the Bergeret column, the Place de la Concorde; the assembly point for the Flourens column was the Place Wagram. For the battalions of the Left Bank, the Duval Column, the point was the Place d'Italie; for the Eudes Column, the Champ de Mars.

Mont-Valérien
Léon Massenet de Marancour

At 5:00 p.m. on April 2 eleven battalions of the twenty two of Montmartre, forming an effective unit of a bit more than 3,000 men, are lined up for battle on the Boulevards Rochechouart, Pigalle, and Clichy.

The marching orders don't arrive until 11:00. The losses: 1,500 men who, worn out by the wait, return home or get drunk.

From 11:00 until midnight, the Belleville battalions join with the artillery on the Rue Royale. Long lines of Guardsmen head to the Champ de Mars to join the Eudes division. There is an extremely tiring wait on the Place de la Concorde. It's cold; the men lay down on the street where the drizzle penetrates and freezes them. Finally, at about 1:00 a.m. the Bergeret column, of which I am a member, sets out, preceded by cannons of various calibers and three or four machineguns. The horse teams are of poor quality, and the artillerymen inexperienced. Three or four kids are seated astride each piece of artillery.

We note with concern that the munitions carts and the supply wagons aren't there. We have another wait, from 2:00 until 4:00 a.m., just before the Neuilly Bridge. The worn out men demand to eat and drink. They have had nothing since the morning, the assembling of the companies having taken place at around 2:00 p.m.

With great difficulty they manage to wake up a wine merchant, whose cellar is promptly emptied. Colonel Bourgoin, Bergeret's aide-de-camp, finally arrives and gives the order to advance. The artillery sets out and the column follows. No order of the day has been read to the troops. Most of the Federals, fooled by the memories of March 18, the excessive confidence of their officers, and the optimistic language of certain newspapers, imagine that all they'll have is a military stroll to Versailles. Many pouches contain not a single cartridge.

As we pass over the Courbevoie Bridge, which we cross in a tight column, my adjutant-major pulls me aside and says: "If Mont-Valérien isn't ours, imagine the butchery it could carry out. The Versaillais must be hidden in ambush somewhere and, I don't know why, but I'd rather we were already being fired on by the cannons. At least that would be a warning. That would shut up the singers and we'd hear better. One man on the alert is worth two."

At the Courbevoie roundabout Bergeret finally arrives in a carriage pulled by two horses. I approach his car to shake his hand. At his side I glimpse two individuals, the father and brother of Colonel Henry, his headquarters chief. I exchange a few words with Henry junior, lieutenant of the mounted chasseurs, who had arrived the day before from Leipzig where he had been a prisoner. This brave young man had hastened to offer his services to the Commune, thus putting an end to his career.

Bergeret gives the order to advance. I insist that he tell me the truth about Mont-Valérien so that in case of danger I can give my battalion the order to march in two rows on each side of the road with three meters between each man, the practice on a road exposed to fire.

I am unable to draw a categorical response from Bergeret: he is so busy! So much so that my battalion, along with those that follow and precede it, continue their march by sections in line, and this on an open, uncovered road, a rifle's shot from the fort. As we can see, this hardly constituted "bypassing Mont-Valérien."

My adjutant observes that he sees a suspicious movement in the lower batteries of the fort, as well as in those called the Gibet batteries. And since the men had heard his observation: "It's nothing," they said. "Those are National Guardsmen. We can clearly make out the uniforms from here. The fort is ours."

For a quarter of an hour we marched in wide open country. There was not a house, not a tree for shelter. The artillery, as well as nearly 2,000 men, have already begun their descent towards Nanterre. And Mont-Valérien still remains silent.

I thought: "Of course they got it right. If not, in an instant we could be cut up in Rueil by the fire from the fort crossing with that from the field pieces and the machineguns placed on the hills of Jonchère. Add a thousand gendarmes as *tirailleurs* and the trap would be complete.

At the moment we reached the point called the Bergères roundabout, the lower batteries of the fort are illuminated with lightning and disappear behind the smoke. We receive a volley of cannonballs. Unspeakable surprise, general terror. The Federals throw themselves flat on the ground and then get up, furious, believing, as usual, in a betrayal. Most of them flee, some to take shelter in the roadside ditches, others to hide behind the nearest houses, which are a few hundred meters away.

An exploding cannonball disemboweled one of the horses of Bergeret's cart. The other reared and a National Guardsman killed him with a rifle shot. The Guard general leaps onto the road, followed by his two companions. Henry's brother wants to bring back those who were fleeing and cries "Forward!" when the fort is again enveloped in a white cloud. A cannonball cuts the brave young man in two; only his abdomen holds the two pieces together. His father, devastated, rushes forward despite the cannonballs that continue to rain down. He wraps his child's corpse in two blankets that Captain Malardier of the 215th has hastily taken from the backs of the dead horses by cutting the straps that hold them on.

An incident occurs that increases the disorder and adds to the alarm. Two cannons, quickly lined up as a battery by overly zealous soldiers, respond from the Bergères plateau to the fire from Mont-Valérien. Those guardsmen still climbing, understanding nothing of the din of the artillery exploding so close to them, think that a Versaillais battery, placed on the plateau, is taking them on the flank. Instead of advancing, they break ranks and spread across the countryside towards Puteaux.

Bergeret doesn't lose hope, though, and managing to rally a few men, continues to Nanterre. There he meets Flourens. But what a disappointment! Instead of 1,000 men, Flourens has barely 800. Bergeret isn't followed by many more.

It is 9:00 a.m. The general staff officers will probably bring more men. Bergeret stops there to eat, as do his troops. There isn't much to eat, only canned preserves and hard bread from a supply wagon that was fortunately able to pass through the fight. Flourens heads to Rueil and Chatou where his column preceded him. But when he rejoins them, there are barely 300 of them. Damn! What do you expect? The men, who hadn't eaten since the previous day, were spread out along the road.

It is only at 11:00 a.m. that Bergeret, despairing of everything and fearing an offensive, gives the order to retreat. This retreat is greeted, of course, by a large number of cannon shots and a heavy fusillade coming from the area around Mont-Valérien. With great difficulty we finally manage to reach Neuilly, where the defense works have already begun. An impressive barricade rises up from the bridgehead.

In all, a deplorable day.

The Death of Flourens
Henry Bellenger

In the pages we just read, we told of the rout of the Bergeret and Flourens columns, and we explained its causes. Taken by surprise by the fire from Mont-Valérien—which they thought to be friendly or at least neutral—the troops of the Commune, holding their weapons any which way, singing gaily, music in the lead, broke in disorder at the first cannonballs. Their leaders, as surprised as their soldiers and lacking in military experience, were unable to rally them. They would have had to work together quickly, make a clear choice: either retreat or continue to march forward. They had neither the time nor even the thought. Each went his own way.

Nevertheless, we saw that in the general confusion Bergeret was fortunate enough to be able to rally most of his men and bring them back to Paris.

The Flourens column, on the contrary, already in the depths of Reuil, spread out in every direction, placing them at the mercy of the cavalrymen of Versailles. Lost in a country they didn't know, for no one knows the area around Paris less than a Parisian, the Federals, dying of hunger, hunted like wild beasts, were quickly picked up by the gendarmes. Many were denounced by peasants they'd been naïve enough to ask for clothing so they could change and flee. We shouldn't see the proof of ignoble political sentiments in this act, not in the least. Always the friend of the strongest, the good villagers would just as willingly have handed over the Versaillais, had they been defeated.

And so, woe on the vanquished! The nooks and crannies, the farms, the copses are carefully searched through. "Throw away your arms," the gendarmes shout at the National Guardsmen. The latter, thinking their lives are secure, quickly obey.

It is here that we see, in all its horror, the system of pitiless repression that was coldly conceived before the attack by the Thiers government in order to render any attempts at reconciliation impossible, and to drown the Parisian insurrection in a sea of blood. As soon as they are disarmed, the unfortunate Guardsmen are surrounded and, without the pretext of battle, of any resistance, have their heads smashed with a pistol blow. This was in execution of the formal orders given to the Versaillais troops by the generals of the Empire, capitulators freshly returned from Germany. What is more, in the course of this book we will see these systematic massacres by those of Versailles continue without interruption until the taking of Paris, until the well-known week of carnage and pillage. But what we want to note here is the order given before the combat by Versailles to murder the prisoners. If the defeated are spared, it's because the soldier refused to obey; he didn't want to become an executioner. The hands of the Federal are tied behind his back, he's stripped of his best effects, his pockets are emptied, and he's pushed with rifle blows towards Versailles, where the deserters of the siege, sitting in the cafes, will strike him with their canes and spit in his face.

Even though thirty Federals were summarily executed on April 3-4 in the villages of Nanterre and Rueil-Chateau, the Marquis de Gallifet published the following proclamation, marked as we will see with the purest tradition and the clearest memories of December 2:

> "War was declared by the gangs of Paris.
>
> "Yesterday, the day before yesterday, today they have assassinated my soldiers(?).
>
> "It is a war without truce or pity that I declare on these assassins. I had to set an example this morning; let it be salutary. I don't want to again be reduced to such an extremity.
>
> "Don't forget that the country, the law, and that consequently the right are with Versailles and the National Assembly, and not with the grotesque assembly in Paris that calls itself the Commune.
>
> "The Brigadier General
> Gallifet"

While they hunted down the remains of the Flourens division in this way, what had become of the commander? Abandoned by his troops, he had declared that he wanted to continue on the way to Versailles. Several National Guardsmen and Pisani, his aide-de-camp, accompanied him.

Near the Chatou station, the small, famished troops stopped at an inn. While three National Guardsmen, a captain, a sergeant major, and a guardsman from the 172nd battalion prepared an omelet in the kitchen, Flourens and Pisani went up to the second floor.

Suddenly the gendarmes surround the house. The three cooks are seized, dragged into the courtyard and executed, though they had surrendered with no resistance. Pisani manages to go to the cellar and hide under a pile of straw. As for Flourens, he quickly puts on civilian clothes and goes down the stairs. A gendarme sees him, grabs him, and drags him into the courtyard. In an effort to escape, at the doorway Flourens puts up a struggle, takes out his revolver, and fires. The bullet glides over the leather belt and at the same moment the gendarme captain, a butcher the size of a Hercules, rising on his spurs delivers a furious saber blow to Flourens' head, splitting skull open and spilling his brains on the ground.

The gendarme didn't know the name of the man he'd just killed. Nevertheless, his clothing, his linen, and the whiteness of his hands, led him to suspect he was a leader.

The corpse was picked up, tossed into a wheelbarrow, and transported to Versailles. It was only there that he was recognized.

This explains the contradictory versions that circulated around Paris concerning the news of his death. The Commune itself didn't believe it. A *turco*—an Algerian soldier who was his batman—who had fled from the inn at Chatou pursued by a hail of bullets, one of which had smashed his teeth and wounded his tongue, had even said, "Good, good, Flourens caught."

The poor boy thought his leader was safe and took joy in having deflected from him the anger of the gendarmes. After a more or less superficial search, the gendarmes hadn't uncovered anything and didn't want to take the trouble to turn over the pile of straw, but it occurred to them to feel it out with their sabers. Five or six times they sank their naked blades into the straw; nothing moved. The gendarmes were leaving when one of them, on replacing his saber in its sheath, noticed that it was stained with blood.

This time they turned over the straw from top to bottom and found Pisani, covered in blood. The unfortunate man had had the terrifying courage to be able not to shout, not to make any movement, though the blade had entered his thigh three times.

This is how Flourens, this elite individual, this generous heart, this soul of a poet and artist, met his end. A poor general, he had neither the calm nor the overall view necessary to successfully lead a military operation. But he had considerable hold over the crowd. His strange face, with its largely bald forehead, its prominent nose, dark and piercing eye, and profound gaze, his great beard, his emphatic and feverish speech, his staccato gestures, all of this gave him the air of one of those preaching monks, socialist militants of the Middle Ages or the Renaissance who aroused the populace in the name of the idea of reform and virtue. Savonarola must have been like him.

His dominant character trait was a heroic obstinacy. His death is explained by this. Upon leaving in the morning, he had sworn to sleep in Versailles. Like the others he could have returned to Paris by following the flood of the rout. But he had promised, and he wanted to keep this mad word, upon which he staked his life. He was, in fact, to sleep in Versailles, but as Maroteau said, "On a slab in the morgue."

Père Duchêne
Maxime Vuillaume

The *Père Duchêne* (of 1871) was founded in the beginning of March (16 Ventose, year 79) a few days after the publication of *Le Cri du Peuple* by Jules Vallès, who later became a member of the Paris Commune.

To be sure, the era into which it was born didn't hold presage for a long life, a brilliant career. The times were stormy and the skies were dark over the Buttes Montmartre; all of the eyes of Paris were turned toward the Buttes. It was at this moment that *Père Duchêne* was founded.

On 16 Ventose, year 79 (March 1871) the walls were decorated with red rectangular posters bearing this slogan:

ONE SOU!
Tomorrow at 6 in the evening
It's
Père Duchêne
Who'll be really fucking angry
And there's reason to be!!!!!!!!!

The next morning *Père Duchêne* was publishing 60,000 copies!

This lasted five issues, after which *Père Duchêne*, using rude language "recalling the darkest days of our history" and knowing how to strike its target, was caught up in General Vinoy's razzia of journalists hostile to the coup d'état that was in preparation: Jules Vallès's *Le Cri du Peuple*, Félix Pyat's *Le Vengeur*, Paschal Grousset's *La Bouche de Fer*, Pilotell's *La Caricature*, and finally *Père Duchêne*.

Because of their low price—one sou—these newspapers were read by the people, to whom they daily preached resistance to the coup d'état that was being prepared against the republic. This was what our rulers, tired of a status quo that they would have liked to quickly change to monarchism, called "preaching revolt, spreading subversive ideas, inciting hatred and contempt for the government."

Père Duchêne courageously received its suspension order, though it was never cited before any tribunal. On passing we would ask why articles that are today PUNISHED WITH DEATH OR FORCED LABOR FOR LIFE were not, at that time, even cause for lawsuits; why were they satisfied with simple suppression? The reason is simple—the only goal of the government was to incite the people, by all means possible, to take up arms. The suppression of the newspapers that represented its principles was one means of doing this. They used it, though they didn't concern themselves with the editors, who were in no way troubled.

A simple excerpt from issue number 5 of *Père Duchêne* will allow us to judge these famous "incitements to civil war, etc." We shouldn't forget that we are on the eve of March 18; *Père Duchêne* is addressing the soldiers who were recalled in great numbers in Paris:

If you were to find yourselves side-by-side with the people, the friends, the brothers you would see that they are seeking to learn, that they want happiness for all through work for all, and not the happiness of a few fat men through the poverty of all.

You would understand, by frequenting the workers, that we aren't full of the hatred and contempt that they seek to convince you of to our reciprocal detriment in order to separate us.

You would rejoin the great family from which you are issued. By shaking the hands of comrades and family members you will shed yourselves of those evil thoughts, of those ideas of esprit de corps against true right and the interests of your people, and you will re-immerse yourselves in the generous and loyal friendship of the people.

Could you obey if you were told to fire at your fathers, your brothers, your uncles, your comrades who want to reconquer the rights that were stolen from them and to live and work?

You can rest assured that *Père Duchêne* who on that day, like all others, will be with the patriots, will not fire the first cartridge.

It is to its honor that *Père Duchêne* didn't recognize the capricious act that banned it, though the printer Sornet, who was at the time in the newspaper's office, pinned the official notice to the wall and then peacefully prepared its issue number 6. The rebellious issue was laid out and completed. It was going to be put on the presses when the police, who had been given word of the paper's suppression, came to warn the printer that he was either to prevent its publication or they would oppose it forcibly.

And so the mock-up was put in the corner, though something told us that the day of the paper's reappearance wasn't far away. And in fact, six days later, issue number 6 was finally set on the printer. It was March 18. Vinoy wouldn't have dared to oppose its publication by force.

Since we find ourselves forced to place a period here in the history of a newspaper that will continue from March 18 and end with the horrible battle, we will take advantage of this to paint a portrait of each of its editors.

The public long sought to discover who it was that was hidden behind the famous pseudonym of the old furnace merchant. There was no shortage of guesses. A newspaper in Lyon cited the names of Félix Pyat and Millière, who were entirely innocent. The anonymity was successful and indispensable: it increased our success.

The three of us together were 80 years old. And so we laughed heartily when we heard it asked in public places: so what is the old *Père Duchêne* up to? He could only be an old man, one man said. And it's always the same one, a second one said, who claimed expertise in the field of literature and closed the discussion with an air of authority. But since everyone in the world of Parisian journalism rubs shoulders, all journalistic secrets are eventually revealed. So one day the newspapers wrote our names, or rather the name of Vermersch, who was better known that the other two editors and who was to truly assume first place in the newspaper.

Today Vermersch is known to all. Every paper, every book that has appeared since the fall of the Commune has told his life story. I have nothing to add to them. Everyone knows that he is blond, that he has a delicate and penetrating gaze and a skeptical smile. Those who have read and spent time with him know that he is a man of wit, a delicate litterateur, that he writes verses, which is one of the most common of things, and that he writes them about some of the rarest of things.) Proof of this is the poem "Les Incendiaires." I can't say enough good things about him for fear that I would be accused of being his friend. I can't say anything bad about him, for that would mean lying. At this moment he is in London, where he is editor in chief of *Qui Vive!* with Leon Sornet, the printer of *Père Duchêne*, his friend and mine.

The two other editors, who took a less considerable part, were Alphonse Humbert and Maxime Vuillaume. Humbert had collaborated in *La Marseillaise*, *Le Journal du Peuple*, and *Le Vengeur*. He had particularly made himself known at public gatherings in 1869 for his famous campaign against Jules Favre and in favor of Henri Rochefort, who was then in Brussels. We all remember Jules Favre's shameful failure, when he was forced to accept the votes of the official candidate in the second round of the election so as not be defeated. Jules Favre maintained a horrifying hatred for Humbert, which perhaps had something to do with the frightful sentence our friend just received.

Humbert, as is clearly affirmed in the letter addressed to Vermersch at the third military tribunal, didn't really work at the newspaper. His collaboration was virtually nonexistent. His columns that were printed in the newspaper were prepared by Vermersch. The role he played was more that of secretary than of editor, and so the sentence against him was unjust. In his entire political life it is certainly the act for which he is the least responsible. It is our duty to render homage to the letter our friend Vermersch sent to the judges of Versailles.

Vuillaume was little known before the founding of *Père Duchêne*. He had had a few articles in *Le Journal du Peuple*, in Jules Vallès's *La Rue*, in *Le Vengeur*, and in the newspapers of the final days of the Empire, newspapers which lived just long enough to have their editors placed on the road to Sainte Pélagie prison, and nothing more.

For Léon Sornet, our manger and friend, this was not his first political sentencing. He had already become known through the famous trial of "the Renaissance,"[1] in which Rigault (who was then entering politics for the first time), Protot and Tridon (who were later members of the Commune), and others, were implicated. In 1869 Sornet was again sentenced to prison as editor and manager of a small paper, *La Misère*, founded by Passedouet, Vuillaume, and himself. Today he is editor of *Qu Vive!* in London.

Since we have just spoken in passing of that multitude of small papers that appeared around 1869, papers that died after seven issues only to reappear a week later under another name, it would be of some interest to write their history and to discover the names of their editors. *Père Duchêne* is one example among many. *Père Duchêne* had its predecessor in 1869 in that of Maroteau. Leafing through the seven issues we find the following names, almost all of them condemned to terrible sentences today:

> Maroteau, Vermersch, Vuillaume—the death penalty
> Mourot (manager)—deportation
> Passedouet—prisoner in Versailles

If we consult a collection of these little papers, so old today, *Père Duchêne* of 1869, *La Misère*, *Le Faubourg*, *La Rue Quotidienne*, etc, we always find the same names: Maroteau, Vermersch, Vuillaume, Sornet, Bellenger, Passedouet, Cavalier, Puissant, Francis Enne, and Mourot. Count how many of them are free!

One fine morning the clouds broke and the weather cleared up above the Buttes. It was over. In the evening the red flag floated over the Hôtel de Ville . I was alone in Paris at that time. Vermersch had left for Lyon after Vinoy's suppression of the newspaper. Suppressed in Paris, we intended to reappear in Lyon, even if for only one issue, just to make a show of resistance. Vermersch had left, along with an administrator; I remained in Paris with the other salesman, ready on the propitious day to publish issue number 6, which was still waiting to come out.

On March 19 the *Père Duchêne* reappeared, still with the printer Sornet. Vermersch soon arrived and told me that in Lyon the prefect Valentin had been quite surprised by the aplomb of the *Père Duchêne*, which he had threatened with seizure even before its appearance. Despite all this, the advertising posters had been printed. They were going to be posted and the *Père Duchêne* was going to try its luck when March 18 arrived and opened wide the doors of the printing shop on the Rue du Croissant.

That was when the adventure began. We must follow this terrible drama step by step, just as revolutionary journalists tracked the history of the drama every day.

At the same time as the *Père Duchêne* other newspapers, *Le Cri du Peuple*, *Le Vengeur*, and *Le Mot d'Ordre*, reappeared within a few days of each other. The fever gripped everyone and new ideas burst on the scene. Never before was such an affluence of newspapers and journalists seen.

We will follow the march of events in this article which, given its framework, must be brief. It would be of particular interest to take each key point of the revolution and to set against it the articles of the *Père Duchêne*.

The elections to the Commune were held on March 26 (8 Germinal, year 79). The *Père Duchêne* did not want to adopt the official list. It made up its own lists and put the name of Blanqui, who was imprisoned since March 19, at the head of each list:

Elect those you love, O! Patriots, but name them with prudence, with circumspection.

As you know, the good bugger who under the Empire wrote "Les propos de Labienus," Citizen Rogeard, said to you not so long ago: "Mistrust is a republican virtue, and Marat's eyes must always be open."

So name people you are sure of and whom you have known for a long time; it matters not if celebrity surrounds them or if they are shrouded in darkness.

And above all, O! Patriots, name Blanqui to the head of your lists, the patriot who never retreated before danger, who never despaired of the fatherland, and who always placed at the service of the revolution all the force of his being, his mind, and his heart.

Long live the Social!

April 3, after the unfortunate sortie of Mont-Valérien, there was "The great mourning of *Père Duchêne* for the patriots who died for the social revolution."

> I salute you, our dead!
> O you who died for the social revolution!
> O you who fell for the cause of right and justice!
> O you who, wanting reconciliation and peace, were the victims of rioting and war!
> I salute you, you who died!
> I salute you just as I loved you, with my soul, with all I gave to the Republic, to the social and to the future, my life and my ideas!
> Ah, your graves, your sons will make them bloom!
> They will make them bloom with forget-me-nots on July 14!
> For they will be at the Bastille!

We will only quote the headlines of those articles having some relation to the measures decreed by the Commune: "The great joy of *Père Duchêne* because they're going to knock the fuck down the [statue of the] son of a bitch Bonaparte I and they're going to make money for the patriots; with his great motion that we destroy everything that sustains international hatred, since for us people are brothers."

At a given moment there was fear of a second siege and a second famine; shopkeepers increased the costs of goods.

Père Duchêne cried out his great anger: "The great anger of *Père Duchêne* against the sons of bitches butchers who raise the price of meat so that the patriots will die of hunger, and against all the merchants who speculate on the misery of the people; with his great motion, presented to the Paris Commune, so that they take measures against the infamous monopolists."

As is known, *Père Duchêne* was the official organ of no one; it struck out at both friends and enemies, at the Commune and Versailles. It was concerned with one thing alone: the goal to be reached, the organization of victory, testified to by the issue of 17 Floréal (no. 52).

The great anger of *Père Duchêne* against the citizen members of the Committee of Public Safety who warm their mitts instead of working; with his great motion that they press military organization by all means in their power.

Number 56, of May 9, one of the most interesting, contains Rossel's resignation addressed to the Commune. I will speak later of our relations with Rossel, relations that earned the three editors the threat of arrest.

From this point on we advanced towards defeat. No, the Commune didn't grow weaker; it was powerless. The wound was too deep and too wide; the Commune had to fall.

And then nothing until the final hour, until the declaration of the minority and the tearing down of the Vendôme column, which was the occasion for a violent attack on the part of *Père Duchêne* against the minority of the Commune:

"The trial demanded by *Père Duchêne* of the bastards who are fleeing the Commune; with his great motion that they purely and simply be put before a court martial as traitors to the city."

And concerning the column: "The great procession of patriots led by *Père Duchêne* around the Place Vendôme, and his great joy because he saw on the ground the bastard Badinguet I and because the people gave him a piece of it, along with a damn patriotic proposal.

As I recall, the final issue of *Père Duchêne* was a great anger against Raoul Rigault and Ferré.

The *Père Duchêne* energetically supported Rossel, as did *La Sociale*, which was put out by the three of us, with the collaboration of Mme. André Léo.

One evening the news reached us that it was strongly possible that we would be shut down, if not worse, arrested. It was 10:00 p.m. I only had the time to take a coach and run to see Vaillant, who gave me a note for Eudes, who I already knew, and who was at the time a member of the Committee of Public Safety. In the end, nothing happened. Later, during the battle, Rigault confirmed our suppression, and Da Costa confirmed this during our trial.

Along with our personal friendships, it was claimed that we had daily relations with the men at the Hôtel de Ville , that we received our marching orders from a fraction of the Commune. This is completely false. I don't think that the three of us together set foot ten times in the Hôtel de Ville during the whole lifetime of the Commune.

On the Rue du Croissant we had a small shop where we sold *La Sociale* and *Père Duchêne*. How may visits we received during those two months! Everyone came to the *Père Duchêne*, the women came to work while the husbands fought. We placed some of them in hospitals to take care of the sick, others in munitions workshops wherever we could.

But we didn't only receive visits by those with an interest in our paper. In the newspaper office one day we found, carefully wrapped, a magnificent copy of the Bible. It had been left by "a well-dressed lady," according to one of our sellers. A letter was attached.

I took the Bible and the letter, which I attached to the first page as a souvenir. The Bible and the letter were taken from me, along with many other things, during one of the five or six searches that were carried out in my house after the debacle.

On the other hand, there were occasionally amusing episodes. I don't know in regard to what, but one of us said in an article that *Père Duchêne*, after having felt great satisfaction concerning a decree of the Commune (or something else, I don't remember) had gone for a drink and a plate of tripe on Rue Montorgueil. The next day a gray pot of respectable mien was left at the office for *Père Duchêne*. We opened it. Tripe from Jouanne's on the Rue Montorgueil! It was a gracious present in response to our article, which hadn't been intended as an advertisement. We ate the tripe, of course, and in order to even things up, the next day we sent him a collection of the complete *Père Duchêne*, with this dedication: "To Jouanne, Tripe merchant, from Père Duchêne, furnace merchant."

This collection would later be of some interest.

One day another person sent us a box of jewelry, asking us to dispose of it for the benefit of the orphans of Federals killed in combat. There was a gold chain and a vermillion spoon, I seem to recall. We locked them in the cash box, hoping to one day have the donor accept them back, for we had refused them in vain. What became of them? We'll never know. Perhaps they ended up with some second-hand dealer, sold by a drunken soldier.

Père Duchêne's end was sad. The issue came out on Monday morning. In the afternoon I went to the Rue du Croissant, determined to publish the next day, in spite of everything. *Le Salut Public* had come out, *Le*

Vengeur was going to come out and we didn't want to be left behind. At the Rue du Croissant we found no one. I was with my friend Bellenger, the editorial secretary of *Le Vengeur*.

When we arrived everything was in a state of disarray; one of the sellers had broken open the cash box which held the day's receipts. Even more, he had sold the paper that remained and taken with him a few thousand copies of the collection of the newspaper. There was nothing to be done; the issue didn't come out. Later on, the same seller sold this collection, which he had safely stored, at a fabulous price. That day he was the least foolish of all of us, which was not usually the case.

I ran to *Le Vengeur* and remained there while they hastily wrote their final issue. The battalions were marching up the Boulevard Sebastopol; in the distance you could hear the shots as they approached. Rogeard, the famous author of *Les Propos de Labienus* was at the editorial office. It was he, I think, who wrote the call to arms that appeared the following morning, signed by him and several other editors.

For some time already we had broken with our former best friends, Félix Pyat and Rogeard. Dragged into the immense maelstrom, personal friendships and respect for our professors of revolution no longer existed. At the printing shop one fine evening, a lively discussion about an article erupted between Félix Pyat and one of us. Were we right or wrong? I can't even recall what it was about. From that day on, we never saw Pyat. The regrettable and envenomed polemic concerning Vermorel ended our relationship for good. Since then hatred has fallen with full force on Pyat, our former teacher and friend. This was reason enough to forget our former disagreement. We will soon say what we think of his conduct during those two months; what we know today is that no one else accumulated so much hostility around his person.

I had come to know Rogeard upon his return from Stuttgart, where he had lived in poverty the five years of exile his famous pamphlet *Les Propos de Labienus* had earned him. Though separated from each other by our respective ages, we lived as the closest of friends. How many happy evenings we spent together, Rogeard, Longuet and other old friends, all of them today under sentence or proscribed.

It was the *Père Duchêne* that again caused trouble, this time in regard to Rogeard's refusal to take a seat on the Commune. He objected to the insufficient number of votes, citing the law of August 1849. Right or wrong, for us this constituted pure legalism at a revolutionary movement.

The evening before, while dining with him, I had laughingly said: "Watch out tomorrow for the great anger of *Père Duchêne*."

And in fact, the next day I wrote a great anger against Citizens Rogeard and Pyat. Rogeard was insulted and we no longer saw each other after that day. He even wrote a column in response to me in *Le Vengeur*. A propos of this article, since I am speaking of it, something quite strange occurred. I had attributed to Danton the famous phrase: "May my memory perish!" Rogeard harshly criticized me in his article. The phrase is more commonly attributed to the Girondins. Though I don't want to offend anyone, it is also from Danton in his speech at the Champ de Mars, November (?) 1792 (see Michelet, *History of the Revolution*).

The battle alone reconciled me with Rogeard. That day discussions were closed and hatreds extinguished. Friends worthy of trust have assured me that at the final instant, at one of the horrible moments of the supreme struggle, Pyat and Vermorel shook hands. Today, when we are defeated, hatred is something that is useless, and in my opinion base, because it is often derived from jealousy, which is always harmful. "Our great ill," said a historian, "is constantly studying the causes our defeat, which prevents us from preparing the future."

Let us break off here, at these more-or-less interesting episodes; we would need a volume to tell them all.

In a short while we will enter the dark days. No more red flags fringed with gold floating gaily in the wind, proud under the machineguns, marching into combat under the great April sun.

It is on a heap of paving stones that they will plant the flag of the Commune; it is behind the barricades that they will await the enemy, eyes on the alert, amidst piles of shells and steaming black kettles. The hand-to-hand combat in the alleyways where defeat puts your back against the wall will replace the great battles on the plains, where you can fall asleep at night, hand on the still-warm rifle, eyes closed to the stars.

We are in full rout, with the sinister crackling of the machineguns and the popping of rifle fire around us. The palaces collapse under the thick, heavy black smoke of the flames; the courts-martial function.

The Commune is defeated.

---

[1] Site of the arrest of 42 Blanquists by the Empire's police on November 7, 1866.

Benoît Malon: The Third Defeat of the French Working Class

Benoît Malon was born to a poor provincial family and was forced to start working at age seven, tending chickens and sheep, among other things. He learned to read while living with an older brother who was a school teacher.

Malon moved to Paris in 1863 and in 1865 was among the founding members of the Paris branch of the International Workingmen's Association. He was a French delegate to the International's first congress in Geneva in September 1866.

His work for the International included travelling throughout France establishing sections, for which he was arrested numerous times; his final release from prison coincided with the proclamation of the republic in 1870.

During the siege of Paris he was deputy mayor of the 17th arrondissement, and was among the signatories of the famous "red poster" issued by the International which proclaimed, "Make way for the people; make way for the Commune."

Malon was elected to the Commune on March 26 and sat on the Commune's Labor Commission. He was a member of the so-called "minority" on the Commune, made up primarily of members of the International, and was among those who signed the controversial letter of May 16 condemning the Committee of Public safety. "The Paris Commune," the letter stated, "has abdicated its power into the hands of a dictatorship to which it gave the name of Public Safety."

Malon was among the organizers of the final defense of the Commune and was saved during the Bloody Week when he was hidden in the home of the concierge of a Protestant chapel. He later fled to Switzerland and was sentenced in absentia by a military tribunal to deportation.

In the years immediately following the Commune he lived a peripatetic existence, and while living in Italy he became a Freemason. By 1872 he was already developing disagreements with his former comrades in the International who attempted to expel him from the organization in 1872. He grew close to the anarchists, particularly Bakunin and James Guillaume, but he broke with them in 1876.

Upon his return to France after the amnesty, he joined Paul Guesde's Parti Ouvrier, and though he continued to define himself as a socialist, he definitively broke with Marxism in 1882. He defined his beliefs as "let us be revolutionaries when the circumstances demand it and reformists always."

This account of the politics and policies of the Commune is drawn from his *La Troisième Défaite du Prolétariat Français*. For Malon, the Commune was the direct continuator of the revolt in Lyon's Croix Rousse quarter in 1834 by the weavers known as "les Canuts." Like the Paris Commune, the third in the series of Malon's defeats, this was one brutally crushed by the then Minister of the Interior, Adolphe Thiers. The second defeat was that of the crushing of the revolution of 1848.

As a member of the International, Malon's account stresses the socialist character of the Commune, as opposed to the Blanquist Gaston Da Costa's insistence on its Jacobin nature. Even more, and in clear keeping with the ideas of the International, and again in opposition to the Blanquist position which stressed the patriotic nature of the Commune, Malon reminds us of its internationalism.

The Third Defeat of the French Working Class

It would be of some interest to examine the composition of the Commune. The International had seventeen representatives, the Central Committee had thirteen, the Blanquist group had seven, the radical press and the revolutionary party had nine, the clubs had twenty-one representatives, and the moderate or bourgeois party had fifteen. For the most part the latter group never sat, and after a few days they all resigned.

In the first ten days of April there were six new resignations. The resignations of the bourgeois representatives were foreseen: they didn't accept the Commune and even less the socialist tendencies of the representatives from the working-class faubourgs. The resignation of the final six was less explicable. The Commune considered this retreat in the face of combat to be flight. Looking at this retreat in the light of the events that followed, it can be judged even more severely. It was often the case that the measures with the most serious consequences were passed by a majority of only a few votes. For example, the formation of a Committee of Public Safety was only decreed by a majority of six votes. It can be maintained that had Ranc, Goupil, Fruneau, Lefévre, and Ulysse Parent (the final six to resign) been less fearful about accepting responsibility, the socialist minority would have become the majority, and the consequences of this fact would have been immeasurable.

Among the remaining members, the Internationals were those best known to the working population. Varlin and Malon had fought for the cause of the working class since 1865. In 1869, the period when the International went through its moment of crisis, these two citizens, assisted by Combault and other devoted men, fruitfully continued the propaganda of the International. These men, and in particular Varlin, were not without influence in the sections of the International and the working-class societies, and they succeeded in founding numerous groups in Paris and in the departments. Theisz, Avrial, Langevin, and Pindy were the main representatives of the Federal Chamber of Worker's Societies. Assi was known since the Creuzot strike. Frankel (an Austrian citizen) founded a German section of the International in Paris. Eugène Gérardin, Clémence, Chalain, Victor Clément, and Dereure were also well known in the worker's societies. Lefrançais, less exclusively International, was especially known for his active socialist propaganda in the clubs. It goes without saying that all had been condemned by the Empire's tribunals. All of these workers knew each other; they had fought together and lived together in the Imperial prisons—they were a group of friends. Their federalist tendencies, their socialist convictions, and their organizational and administrative practice distanced them from the empirical terrorism of 1793. From the first day—with the exception of Dereure and Chalain, who went over to the majority—they formed a compact group that sat on the left and called itself socialist, and who were to be reinforced by Jules Vallès, Vermorel, Ostyn, Arthur Arnoud, Tridon, Beslay, Jourde, Verdure, and Babick.

The socialist minority first wanted a manifesto to be addressed to France and an ultimatum sent to Versailles to lay out the limits of the Communal revolution and, if possible, to arrive at France's recognition of the communal freedoms of Paris. It generally voted against the measures it qualified as arbitrary, among others the suppression of newspapers, and protested against various arrests it considered pointless. Vermorel, Jourde, Lefrançais, and Theisz were its most listened-to orators.

The other representatives constituted the majority, whose chiefs were Félix Pyat, Miot, Grousset, and Gambon, all well-known members of the republican party. Ferré, Rigault, Billioray, Chalain, Amouroux, Chardon, Urbain, Ledroit, Parisel, Ranvier, Fortuné Henry, and Blanchet were its most frequent spokesmen.

Jacobinism dominated this side of the Commune due to the influence of a few men of 1848 who were members, as well as from the fact that the young revolutionaries who followed them had passed through the secret societies. However, the preponderance of Jacobinism was felt only in policies, its authoritarian side being the only one the members of the majority saw. It in no way excluded socialism, whose legitimacy was contested by only two or three members. It should be noted that socialist measures were generally voted for unanimously.

It would be useful to briefly characterize several notable individuals whose influence was particularly felt during the deliberations of the Commune.

Vermorel was still a young journalist (he was born in 1841) but already a veteran of the militant press. He was the first in the Empire, in the *Courrier Français*, to raise the banner of socialism. Persecuted and slandered by all the political parties, but especially by those of the Left whose treasons he had revealed, he had also earned the esteem of the socialist workers, who knew his talent and uprightness of character. Elected to the Commune without having sought to be a candidate, he left his village in the Lyon area, where he had gone to stay after the siege, to go to Paris and occupy a place he felt he was called to by a sacred duty. Nevertheless, he had a foreboding of defeat and from the beginning, despairing of the revolution, he only thought to keep it on the path of justice and to die for it with dignity.

Though throughout his past, Delescluze belonged to the generation of 1848, a period during which he distinguished himself by his valiant republican propaganda under the presidency and his deportation to Cayenne by the Empire, he didn't limit himself to within a narrow Jacobinism and showed himself to be open to the most advanced ideas. As far as possible he held himself outside the two parties. He sometimes voted with the majority, at other times with the minority, and he preserved an influence over the two fractions of the Commune, both of which demonstrated their recognition of his total devotion to the revolution, his courage, and his austere integrity.

Protot, known from his participation at the Liège conference, from the argument he sustained at the Geneva Congress in 1866 against Fribourg and the Parisian mutualists, from his condemnation at the trial of the secret society of the Café de la Renaissance, and from his defense of Mégy, during the two months of the Commune, expended a great effort to implement judicial reform, which he had conscientiously studied.

Tridon had been one of the organizers of the Liège congress (1865), a veritable wake-up call for the youth of the Latin Quarter, the original idea for which belonged to Blanqui, and in which, among others, Longuet, Jaclard, Arisitde Rey, G. Casse, Villeneuve, Protot, Alph. Humbert, Hector Denis, and Arnould all participated. In a book written with remarkable verve that was prosecuted by the Empire, Tridon rehabilitated the Hébertists, men he correctly called "the great damned of history." From that point on he became—in a restricted circle to be sure—a veritable party leader, under the suzerainty of Blanqui.

Vallès has a powerful and noble nature and was able to turn aside the political disappointments of our generation. The success of the Empire, which he combated at the barricades on December 3rd, made him despondent and he became a rebel. As such he delivered vigorous blows against the enemies of the revolution. In 1869 he posed his candidacy in the eighth circumscription under the title of the "candidate of poverty." He always had a word in defense of the poor and a curse for the oppressor, but the revolution could have received more from this true talent. He was very popular in Belleville.

If any man of our time was able to study the march of the revolutions in France it was Charles Beslay, the elder of the Commune, who so lightly wore his seventy-seven years. Born to political life under the white terror of 1815, he was elected deputy after 1830 and was a participant in the constituent assembly of 1848. He said of himself, "Starting from the Bonapartist opposition under the Restoration, I passed through liberalism and republicanism to arrive at socialism." And indeed, after 1848 he attached himself to Proudhon, whose friend and disciple he remained. A capitalist by position, as a mutualist he is nevertheless partisan of the abolition of the interests of capital. An industrialist, he made several attempts at forming associations among his workers. He was the first bourgeois to go over to the International. Beginning in 1865 he frequented the meetings on the Rue des Gravilliers, and he has remained a member of the great Association, where he was well liked.

Paschal Grousset, a professor of Corsican origin, former editor of *La Marseillaise*, made himself known by a pamphlet called "The Dream of an Irreconcilable," in which the most advanced socialist ideas found a place. With some talent he defended Jacobin ideas in the Commune.

Rigault, known for many years in the Latin Quarter, made his presence felt in the faubourgs by becoming one of the most assiduous orators at public gatherings, where Lefrançais, Flourens, Mme Paule Mink, Longuet, Lissagaray, Gaillard, Ranvier, Tolain, Peyrouton, Chemalé, G. Casse, F. Ducasse, Héligon, Jaclard, Amouroux, Briosne, Poirier, etc, spoke as well, but with less brilliance. The Blanquists, who admitted him to their meetings, said of him that he had the abilities of a police prefect. And he was, in fact, along with Ferré, the leader of this group of young people, among whom were Dacosta, Chalain, and Le Moussu, who also thought themselves born to be in the police. All of them threw themselves on the prefecture of police as if it were their prey, and in that place they conducted the affairs of the Commune poorly.

Much better known, and much better loved, was the good and brave Flourens. Son of the famous scholar of the same name, and having taught in the same place as his father, he made himself known in the faubourgs upon his return from the island of Crete, whose independence from the Turks he had long fought for. An orator much applauded at public meetings, editor of *La Marseillaise*, extremely popular in the faubourgs, he was at the head of all the attempted uprisings against the empire. During the demonstration of January 10 (the burial of Victor Noir) he wanted the people to march on Paris, and barely forgave Rochefort for having made the opposing opinion prevail. In order to win over Belleville, the men of September 4 named him major of ramparts, but Flourens didn't follow a wait-and-see policy for very long; on October 6 he came down from Belleville at the head of five battalions. The members of the government owed their lives to his generosity on October 31, and in thanks for his generosity they imprisoned him. Freed by the people, he took no part in January 22, but was nevertheless sentenced to death in absentia on March 10. His silence was remarked upon at the Commune. This ordinarily so expansive man was constantly preoccupied. Did he see the terrible reality of the situation? Did he have a foreboding of the imminent death that was to repay his indefatigable devotion to the people's cause?

The opposite remark can be applied to the foundry worker Duval, General of the Third Communal army. He was known to be quiet, but in the Commune he often spoke and submitted several proposals until he was assassinated by order of Vinoy after the defeat of April 4.

Miot, the former representative of the people, is particularly known for the so-called Opera Comique trial (1862), in which he was the principal guilty party (three years of prison). Everyone recalls the agitation caused by Gambon's refusal to pay the Empire's taxes in 1869. This former people's representative, deported in 1851, the most socialist and amiable of the Jacobins of 1848, is well known to French democracy.

One of the men of the Commune who most occupied public opinion is Félix Pyat, socialist littérateur before 1848, deputy in the legislature later on, exiled by the Empire in 1851, and one of the founders of the revolutionary commune of proscribed Frenchmen of London. Having returned to France after the amnesty of 1869, he wrote brilliantly for the *Rappel* and returned to London after being sentenced to six months in prison. After September 4 he successively founded *Le Combat* and *Le Vengeur*. In these two journals he furiously waged a war which events showed to be only too justified against the men of the national defense, whom he regularly and rightly accused of incompetence, duplicity, and cowardice. In the Commune he was the spokesman for neo-Jacobinism, which rendered him frankly antipathetic to his socialist colleagues.

At the same time as Flourens was sentenced, the military tribunal of March 10 also sentenced to death the old champion of radical revolution, Blanqui. Arrested in the south of France on March 17, Blanqui was unable to take his seat on the Commune, to which the voters of two arrondissements had elected him. His colleagues, sensing how useful this organizer of so many conspiracies would be to the Commune, did all they could to free him. As ransom they offered the Archbishop of Paris and as many priests as they'd like. But Thiers refused this exchange, and Blanqui, buried in some dungeon, perhaps dying, certainly was unaware of the terrible events that washed Paris in blood.

We can say that from its beginning the members of the Commune generally tended to let themselves go in a typically French fashion and either deal with events with speeches or aim at immediate results instead of seeking causes. For the most part young in years, they could not in any case have the necessary calm that commands over terrible situations. This vivacity was the main reproach made against them by Delescluze, Vermorel, and others, who often and rightly complained of the abundance of personal concerns and attacks. The members of the Commune had acquired this tendency toward violent recriminations at public gatherings under the Empire and in the clubs after September 4. During those sad days the indignity of the rulers was such that criticism of governmental acts, however violent it was, was always justified by the facts. The people became used to this and the most ardent orators were the most applauded. These same orators, elected by the people, naturally brought this same language to the discussions in the Commune. But even if the attacks were lively, there were never base insults, thanks to the unfailing respect for any gathering of men demonstrated by French workers. Those who saw the Parisian clubs in action know that in the most tumultuous of its assemblies a certain dignity, unknown among other peoples, was never absent.

Many representatives were lacking in the education and experience needed by politicians. But it should not be forgotten that this was the first time that the working class held power. Aside from a few littérateurs, all had had a life of labor and fatigue, and it was only by stealing from their needed rest that they were able to learn the little that they knew. The greatest misfortune was that the majority, too imbued with the Jacobin and theatrical side of the great Revolution, was naturally disposed to ignore realities, to fail to take obstacles sufficiently into account, and to sacrifice to the sovereignty of their goal—dear to the authoritarian school—the principles imported into politics by the new socialist school. It was this particular tendency within the majority that the socialist minority combated without truce.

But what almost all of these men possessed were a great love for the oppressed and that vigorous hatred for injustice that the entire working-class population of Paris possesses to such a high degree. They could feel that in representing the rebellious Parisian proletarians they represented the great cause of all those who suffer from the oppression and exploitation of our unjust society. And so even if they differed in their methods, in general they showed themselves ready to give their lives to hasten the arrival of the new world that they glimpsed in the universal social republic.

In fact, one of the distinctive traits of the Commune was its realizing the internationality that it proclaimed and which until then had never been consecrated in any governmental representation. They did this by declaring that it would receive any elected representatives sent by the people of Paris, of whatever nationality they might be. And so it accepted the Hungarian citizen Frankel, elected by the 13th arrondissement.

The sessions were always held in the so-called hall of the municipal council, a low, poorly ventilated room whose suffocating atmosphere rendered its sessions difficult and nerve-wracking. They often took place at night, the day being dedicated to the administration and carrying out of affairs.

The most urgent measures that had to be dealt with were the settling of rents and debts due; the re-establishment of the administration of Paris, which had been completely disorganized by the fugitive Versailles government; the legal consecration of the universally formulated revolutionary aspirations; and, after the Versaillais aggression, the leadership of military operations. And so the first measures of the Commune were the following:

A general postponement of rents due for quarterly in October 1870, and January and April 1871.

Suppression of the sale of objects deposited at the national pawn shop.

Abolition of conscription.

Separation of church and state and suppression of the religious budget. Confiscation to the profit of the Commune of property passed on to lords at the death of their tenants.

A decree according a pension of 300-1200 francs to any National Guardsman wounded while fighting for Communal freedom.

A decree according a pension of 600 francs to the legal or common-law wife of any Federal killed by the enemy, and a pension of 365 francs for every child, recognized or not, until the age of 18.

Establishment of a military tribunal in each legion.

Creation of a court martial under the presidency of Rossel.

Preferring charges against the members of the Versailles government after the aggression against Paris.

Convocation of the worker's syndical chambers and the chambers of commerce and industry, invited to present proposals for a law on debts that were reaching their due date.

Decree on debts due permitting payments starting July 15 and spread across three years.

Decree giving the administrative leadership of their respective arrondissements to the members of the Commune.

Prohibition of the holding of multiple offices simultaneously; fixing of a maximum income of 6,000 francs.

Fixing of the emoluments of the members of the Commune at 15 francs per diem.

Adoption of the families of the victims of January 22 and March 18.

Decree ordering that notification of any arrest carried out by the security forces must be made to the delegate for justice, who will decide on the sustaining of the arrest. Prohibition of searches without warrants.

If appropriate, allocation of alimony to any woman demanding separation.

Decree ordering the organization of a civil tribunal of the Paris Commune. Abolition of the *procedure ordinaire*. The parties are authorized to defend themselves. If lawyers are lacking, bailiffs can represent the parties.

Organization of a jury to ensure citizens involved in judicial matters judgment by their peers, election of magistrates, and freedom of defense.

Attribution of a fixed salary for bailiffs, notaries, appraisers, and trial clerks, who are dispensed from having to pay an advance but who must pay to the delegate for finance the sums received for acts within their competence.

After investigation, and the amounts due the employer being held in reserve, attribution of abandoned workshops to worker's associations.

Decree raising the salaries for schoolteachers of both sexes to 2000 francs and the salaries of assistants of both sexes to 1500 francs.

Decree ordering the tearing down of the Vendôme column. "Considering that the Imperial column is a monument to barbarism, a symbol of brute force and false glory, an affirmation of militarism, a negation of international law, a permanent insult to the victors and the vanquished, a perpetual attack on one of the three great principles of the French republic: fraternity."

Decree ordering that, in order to put an end to the execution of prisoners taken by the Versaillais, hostages can be taken from among the supporters of Versailles.

Prohibition of fines and withholding of wages in workshops and government offices.

Abolition of political and professional oaths.

Institution of doctors for the newborn charged with the saving of newborns through officially registering births.

Opening in every town hall of a register of those seeking and offering work, with the conditions of the search and offering.

Naming of an initiative commission for social reforms. In its turn, this commission appealed to the delegates of the International, the worker's societies, the democratic committees, industrial and scientific groups, to engineers and architects, and all initiatives of good will.

Reform of the service for the verification of weights and measures.

Introduction of a charge book fixing the salary of manual labor in all negotiations concluded or to be concluded by the Commune. This measure had as its goal the reducing of competition to its scientific principle, i.e., to circumscribe it within the sole limits of profit, the honesty of quality and fabrication being guaranteed to the purchaser and a reasonable salary remaining guaranteed to the worker. This is a way of proceeding that is radically different from what is done now, where competition takes place at the expense of quality and wages, misleading the purchaser and exploiting the worker.

Remission with an indemnity to the administration of the National Pawn Shop of objects deposited there for a sum not greater than 25 francs.

Suppression of night work in bakeries. Abolition of the government placement office.

The two decrees for which the Commune has been attacked are those relating to hostages and to the Vendôme column. The first was rendered necessary by the execution of prisoners that the Versaillais publicly allowed: the assassination of Duval and two officers of the general staff; the assassination of Flourens; the assassination of National Guardsmen taken by surprise by the cavalrymen of the Marquis de Gallifet, an act which the latter bragged of in a public proclamation; the systematic slaughter of all soldiers who had gone over to the Commune, according to a note in the *Journal Officiel* of Versailles; and the proposed establishment of provost courts in Versailles. The taking of hostages was not able to prevent the ill treatment the Versaillais inflicted on their prisoners, but it put a brake on their ardor for slaughter after battle. It is, however, true that they took revenge by inaugurating a war of surprise and nocturnal massacres. The law of hostages was thus imposed on the Commune in order to safeguard the lives of its people.

The tearing down of the Vendôme column was perhaps inopportune. It nevertheless expressed a generous and just idea: the reprobation of wars among peoples and the defense of international fraternity.

Gaston Da Costa: The Commune Lived

Few revolutionary figures have been as revered as Louis Auguste Blanqui, the tireless revolutionary conspirator who spent thirty-seven years of his life in various French prisons. Blanqui's goal was to overthrow the existing order through small, well-organized groups of conspirators, and neither he nor his followers had any set design for the society that would follow their successful revolution.

It's undying hatred for the bourgeois order earned Blanquism a not-insignificant following in the working class quarters of Paris, and though it only had seven members on the Commune, its ideas had an influence far out of proportion with their numbers.

Blanqui himself was unable to participate in the Commune, having been arrested and sentenced to death for his part in the seizing of the Hôtel de Ville on October 31, 1870, but his followers occupied key posts in the Commune.

La Commune Vecue is the account of the life of the Commune from the Blanquist point of view. Written by Gaston Da Costa, its four volumes are an organizational jumble, but they are a fascinating record of the thought of a vital revolutionary trend.

Gaston Da Costa (1850-1909) was the son of an atheist republican father and a religious mother, a marriage that was far from happy. Da Costa studied law, and during the siege he was chief of staff for Raoul Rigault, who was police prefect. His relationship with Rigault, and his life-long bachelorhood, led to rumors of homosexual relations between the two men. A firm Blanquist, when Rigault was named the Commune's procurator the 21-year-old Da Costa was made one of his assistants, as a result of which he was accused of a role in 45 arrests and the execution of a police informant after the Commune's fall. As well as having played a role in the burning down of the Palais de Justice and the prefecture of police.

He fled Paris on May 28, the last day of the Commune, but was denounced and arrested in July. He cracked under interrogation, giving away what he thought to be the hiding places of several Blanquists, though all had been able to find other shelter in the interim. Despite his having provided information he was sentenced to death, a sentence commuted to forced labor for life. He was pardoned in 1880, and was placed in shackles on the ship taking him back to France for refusing to uncover his head during prayers on the ship.

After Blanqui's death, Blanquism was a form of political action in which the extreme right and left could join hands, and upon his return to France Da Costa was given a job by the great propagandist Henri Rochefort on his newspaper *L'Intransigeant*. During the Boulangist agitation Da Costa was a key figure in that movement's Blanquist left.

The Events of January 22, 1871

The government led by Trochu and Favre (for it is these two rhetoricians who best personify it) would be forgiven everything, even its betrayal, if after failing to keep its word, it had been inspired by the patriotic wishes of Paris; if it had used its thousands of sailors, its 80,000 men of the active army, and its 300,000 National Guardsmen and, ceaselessly harassing the enemy, prepared and led the sortie that was possible, hoped for, necessary, and useful.

But instead of doing any of this, Trochu, who on October 31 only asked for two weeks to surrender Paris, until January 19 committed every possible military mistake. At the same time, the civil power, compounding its inertia with administrative negligence, sped up the moment of famine. Finally, on January 19, a stupidly conceived attempt at a sortie, miserably led by its chiefs—with the exception of Bellemare—pitifully failed. This occurred despite the bravery demonstrated at Buzenval by the disdained marching battalions of the National Guard.

This failed attempt awakened the patriotic anger of the Parisians, an anger more threatening than that of October 31 because it was even more justified, and because everyone understood that we had either to die of hunger, surrender, or smash the circle that was choking us.

*

This time the indignation was general. Bourgeois republicans and revolutionaries appeared to have agreed through insurrection to put an end to a harmful government that played Bismarck's pitiless game by maintaining Paris in a state of inaction and driving it to famine[1].

While the Government of National Defense was busying itself with the capitulation, the people of Paris, convinced that the failure of January 19 was strictly attributable to the failings of the commanders, became ever bolder at the idea of a sortie en masse, an action it still considered possible.

The days of January 20 and 21 were extremely feverish, notably in the 10th, 11th, 13th, 14th, 18th, 19th, and 20th arrondissements.

On January 20, it was learned that Trochu had renounced the military command of the garrison but remained president of the government, naming Vinoy the governor of Paris. The latter, no longer concerning himself with the Prussians[2], hastened to affirm his determination to prevent the imminent popular uprising:

"Internally the party of disorder is stirring things up, while at the same moment the cannons thunder. I will be a soldier to the end. I accept this danger, convinced that the collaboration between the good citizens, the army, and the National Guard will not be lacking and will maintain order and public safety."

There was not a mention of the enemy in the entire proclamation.

Under these conditions, the accession of the soldiers to supreme military power of coups d'état could only increase popular exasperation to its highest point. And this is precisely what happened.

During the night of January 21, National Guardsmen of the faubourgs went to the Mazas prison and freed Flourens, as well as all the prisoners arrested after the events of October 31.

Flourens immediately went to Belleville, where he had been elected mayor during his detention. He took control of the town hall, which had been occupied by a governmental commission, and ordered the battalions of the legion to go to the town hall. This order was only partially executed because Flourens, ever hot headed, hadn't clearly stated what he wanted done, not knowing this himself. The National Guardsmen of the neighborhood hesitated before following a man whose bravery they, of course, admired, but whose confusions demonstrated on October 31 had worn them out.

*

In the meantime, all across the city, revolutionary militants were active, and secret meetings were held at various locations, particularly in Montmartre and in the 13th and 14th arrondissements. A meeting was set for the next day at the Place de l'Hôtel de Ville .

*

The government for its part, foreseeing a tempestuous day, wasn't inactive: the battalions of the Breton Mobile Guard, sailors, and Municipal Guards occupied the Hôtel de Ville . At the same time, Clément Thomas posted the following proclamation:

> To the National Guard
>
> Last night a handful of agitators forced the gates of Mazas prison and freed several detainees, among them M. Flourens.
>
> These same men attempted to occupy the town hall of the 20th arrondissement and install the insurrection there.
>
> Your commander-in-chief counts on your patriotism to repress this culpable sedition.
>
> The city's salvation depends on this.
>
> While the enemy bombards it, the seditious unite with them to annihilate the defensive forces.
>
> In the name of public salvation, in the name of the laws, in the name of the sacred duty that commands us to unite to defend Paris, be ready to have done with this criminal enterprise.
>
> At the first call, let the entire National Guard arise and the troublemakers will be struck powerless.
>
> The Commander of the National Guard,
>
> Clément Thomas
> Paris, January 22, 1871"

It required a certain aplomb to write in this way at the very moment that the government was concerned only with deciding on the terms of the capitulation.

And so they accused us of wanting to annihilate the defense at the very moment when they were surrendering. It was clear that this accursed government, which had put in place an inert dictatorship, would never stop lying from its first moment to its last.

Whatever the case, this poster had the effect of hindering, or at the very least considerably diminishing, the next day's attempted revolt.

Many said that we had to continue to wait and that the government would still make one last effort. Led by revolutionary chiefs, only a few battalions went the next day to the Hôtel de Ville.

*

On the foggy morning of January 22, between 11:00 and noon, groups of demonstrators, most of them without weapons, began to form on the square. From time to time armed citizens, their rifles slung over their shoulders, joined them. This crowd was quite noisy, more threatening than that of October 31, but just as undecided about the action to be taken. People commented on the failed sortie of January 19, they spoke against their leaders, and they spoke of treason. The naming of Vinoy as governor exasperated them and the demonstrators took the general's proclamation as a threat. They awaited the arrival of the people from the faubourgs to put an end to the traitors of the Government of National Defense.

*

For such an undertaking to succeed, the Alliance Républicaine, the spokesmen for the overwhelming majority of the discontented battalions, would have had to summon the discontented. In that case, the few revolutionary battalions, having brought the masses along with them and easily invaded the Hôtel de Ville despite Chaudey and his Bretons, would have determined the outcome of the day, as they did on September 4.

Such was not the case. After the events of the previous night, the Alliance Républicaine was inclined to reconciliation for fear of the revolutionary element that would have ensured its victory. It limited itself to sending a delegation which, after having preached for calm on the square, entered the Hôtel de Ville and was taken to Gustave Chaudey, deputy mayor of Paris.

Chaudey, made arrogant by the reinforcements he had received during the night, was disdainful of the crowd. Had he seen them at the head of a great mass of demonstrators, he would have been concerned about the revolutionaries. With reason he felt that with his Mobile and Municipal Guards solidly sheltered, he would easily be able to handle their small numbers if the need arose.

Chaudey responded to the delegation which, summing up its mission, demanded the predominance of civil over military power and the immediate election of the Commune.

On the first point, the government shared the ideas of the Alliance Républicaine, but the government was absolutely opposed to the election of a Commune and resolved to repel, any violent attempt to impose it, with arms if needed.

The good Tony Réveillon, gentle spokesman of the delegation, withdrew after this threatening response and gave an account of his failure to the people on the square.

If at that moment Réveillon would have transmitted Chaudey's response to the many battalions that his friends had foolishly kept at a distance from the Hôtel de Ville , the government's threat would have brought the invasion of the square in its wake. It's true that, under this hypothesis, the threat would probably not have been made.

*

At that hour, under the orders of the young, former commander Sapia, fragments of various battalions of the 14th arrondissement were lined up in battle ranks across from the fences, violently arguing with the officers of the Mobile Guard and the famous Colonel Vabre, future organizer of the executions of the Place St Jacques.

In addition, several companies of battalions from Batignolles entered the square through the Rue de Rivoli, while a battalion from the 10th arrondissement arrived through the Rue du Temple, and the 101st battalion from the 13th arrondissement entered through the Arcole Bridge, all to vehement cries of "Long Live the Commune! Down with Trochu!"

*

Several times already Mobile Guards had opened the windows on the ground floor and aimed at the crowd. An immense clamor answered these threats. And then, with the Mobile Guards quickly closing the windows and doors, Sapia and his men tried to pass through the fence that protected the building.

One or two shots rang out from the square, but were aimed at the walls of the palace and not at the men who defended it, since at this key moment all its door and windows were closed[3].

Behind these 200-300 armed National Guardsmen, there amassed crowd of a few hundred men and women, passersby who didn't think there was any imminent danger. The other National Guardsmen were at the quay and on the Rue de Rivoli.

Suddenly, without any warning, the windows and doors opened. The crowd and the National Guard received the fire of a squadron, which instantaneously produced panic and confusion.

The Mobile Guards, coming out of the building, charged the square, turned to the right and pushed the guardsmen towards the Rue de Rivoli and the Rue du Temple.

With the first shots, Sapia fell along the fence, his head shattered. A few men fell around him, but it was on the square itself, in the crowd of passersby and women, that the bullets of the Mobile and Municipal Guards—who fired from the second floor windows—hit the most victims, around fifty in all.

The armed citizens had taken refuge in the buildings of the bureaus of public assistance, taxes, and the labor service, the Café of the National Guard, in other shops on the Rue de Rivoli, on the square itself, behind the streetlamps, and on the quay. From all these locations, they fired back on the Municipals Guards who, sheltered behind the windows, continued the fusillade.

The drama lasted barely a half an hour.

During this time Chaudey telegraphed Jules Ferry to request reinforcements in order to "complete the clean-up of the square."

And, in fact, shortly afterwards, two battalions of Mobile Guard and two squadrons of Municipals answered the call.

It was all over.

Gustave Chaudey's friends have claimed that this telegram did not render him responsible. It was a pointless effort, since before his implacable revolutionary judges, Ferry's deputy accepted responsibility for his own acts.

*

During the course of the evening, in the mad agitation caused by the pitiful victory, Jules Ferry wrote this unbelievable dispatch:

> Paris, January 22, 1871 4:52 p.m.
>
> Mayor of Paris to the commanders of the nine sectors:
>
> A handful of seditious National Guardsmen, members of the 101st of the March, attempted to seize the Hôtel de Ville . They fired on the officers and seriously wounded an adjutant major of the Mobile Guard[4].
>
> The Hôtel de Ville was fired on from the windows that look out on it from the other side of the square, which had been occupied in advance. Bombs were thrown at us and shots fired at us.
>
> The aggression was at its most cowardly and odious at the beginning, since they fired one hundred rifle shots on the colonel[5] and his officers at the moment they were dismissing a delegation that had just been admitted to the Hôtel de Ville.
>
> It was no less cowardly afterwards when, after the first shots, after the square had been emptied and our fire had ceased, we were fired on from the facing windows.
>
> Tell all of this to the National Guard and inform me if order has been restored.

Jules Ferry

We rendered homage to Jules Ferry for his personal courage on March 18, but we must here render him this justice and say that on this occasion he deployed as much daring in falsehood as he did in action.

*

The undertaking of January 22 failed for the following two reasons: the lack of decisiveness of the Alliance Républicaine, which didn't want to lead the unarmed crowd to the Hôtel de Ville , and the lack of organization of the revolutionary party.

We cannot say this often enough: since the besieging of Paris by the Prussians, the Blanquist party had sent its men into the battalions of the National Guard, and in doing so lost all cohesion.

And then we must admit that Blanqui's cry of "the fatherland in danger," as meritorious as it was, was also a disintegrating factor for the revolutionary forces it disposed of until then. The great revolutionary, in granting credit to the evil men of September 4 was absolutely in the wrong. And so, when after these pointless concessions he wanted to take in hand and bring together his dispersed forces, he failed. Not because these forces had ceased to be absolutely devoted to him, but he failed because they had lost all enthusiasm.

*

And later, when the great insurrection of March 18 broke out, the Blanquist party, remaining dispersed, had great difficulty in reconstituting itself on the battlefield, if we can use the expression. But it is precisely here that the merits of this political organization appear. With Blanqui absent and amidst general confusion, the Blanquist party was able to affirm its strength to such a point that everything that was truly revolutionary between March 18 and May 28 bears its imprint.

And from this I draw the conclusion that a thousand revolutionaries, solidly organized with action in mind, will always be necessary in order to win out over the indecisiveness of 100,000 demonstrators and then to lead them, whatever their hopes, indignation, or even their rage.

The Commune and Socialism

All parties have grown accustomed to considering the insurrection of March 18 to be a socialist insurrection.

This is a serious error.

It doesn't in the least bit follow that since most of the leaders of the Communalist government were either revolutionary socialists, like the Blanquists, or reformist socialists, like the dreamers and phonies (both kinds could be found there) of the International Workingmen's Association; or that since the National Guard was almost entirely proletarian (workers, employees, petit-bourgeois) that the civil war of the time was a social war.

Yet one must recognize that the victorious Commune would have established the social republic in place of the oligarchic republic which the bloodthirsty Thiers founded, the realization of a dream long held by this Machiavelli of the bourgeoisie.

It is only if we look at events in this light that we can say, along with Benoît Malon, that "the revolution of March 18 marked, with a terrible gradation, the third bloody phase of the French proletariat, starting with the Croix-Rousse uprising" (April 1834, June 1848, March 1871).

*

But if the Commune wasn't a social war, then what was it?

This is an historical question to which we will attempt to give an historical solution.

*

To start with, what would be the characteristics of a socialist uprising?

It is the revolt, either instinctive or considered, either spontaneous or thought out, of the oppressed masses, despairing of their wages or threatened in their right to work.

So anyone who coldly and impartially studies the insurrection of 1871, either in its origins or in its acts, will recognize that it is impossible to reasonably grant it the character of social revolt.

Antiquity's triple slave wars, the Jacquerie, the formidable uprising of the English agricultural masses under Wat Tyler, the great peasant war in Germany, the starvation riots of 1789, Babeuf's brave attempt, the proletarian insurrections of Lyon in 1831 and 1834, that of the workers of Silesia that inspired Hauptmann's noble drama "The Weavers," and finally the insurrection of 1848: these were all socialist revolts and episodes of the great social struggle which has certainly not ended and risks fighting its final battle on the shifting, terrible, and troubling terrain of the class struggle, where the sectarian, reactionary, and profoundly inhuman theories of Karl Marx have sprouted.

All of these tragic events had their origin in a legitimate feeling of revulsion by the workers against those who exploit and starve them.

Look as closely as you'd like; you won't find this sentiment among the insurgents of 1871.

*

No. The insurrection of March 18 was essentially political, republican, patriotic, and, to qualify it with just one epithet, exclusively Jacobin.

*

The Franco-German War broke out like a thunderbolt, the sorry consequence of a diplomatic machination that at the time was unknown to the masses. In addition, it was begun without the consent of the nation, and we can even say against its will.

What is more, the Empire, driven to carnage as a last resort of its internal policy, was in no way prepared for the fight: our first disasters occurred successively and inevitably, despite the valor, not to mention the heroism, of many units.

Then came September 4 and the collapse of the regime of December 2, which we suffered under for twenty years. Then came Gambetta's grand effort for the final fight. Then, with Paris under siege, came the arming of all healthy citizens and the organization of an army of 300,000 National Guardsmen in the capital. The Guardsmen have been much criticized by those who didn't know how to utilize them as an excuse for their own acts. Then came the events of the siege, the republican and patriotic enthusiasm of the first days, the stupidly culpable inaction of the Government of National Defense, the ceaseless agitation of the revolutionary groups, and Blanqui's gloriously energetic appeals in *La Patrie en Danger*.

Then came the famine, the ensuing physiological and psychological misery, the growing anger, the indignation against the lying leaders, blowhards like Ducrot or the inert like Trochu. Then came the insurrectionary attempts of October 31, 1870 and of January 22, 1871. And finally came the capitulation.

There then followed the elections and the usurpations of the Bordeaux Assembly, which was elected to decide on war or peace and which voted for a disastrous peace – which Paris, right or wrong, did not want – and which already insolently manifested its determination to give this unfortunate, amputated, ruined, and demoralized country a monarchical constitution.

And then came the supreme insult to Garibaldi, the resignations of Victor Hugo, Rochefort, Gambetta, and Tridon; the threat to decapitalize Paris, the postponing of the municipal elections, the suppression of the republican newspapers by the *Decembriseur* Vinoy, the stupid and iniquitous law on debts due, and the arrest of Blanqui; finally, Thiers' decision to disarm the population when each citizen rightly considered his rifle a guarantee of the vitality of the nascent republic.

Truly, is anything else needed to explain the inevitability of that formidable insurrection, its legitimacy, and its character?

*

In good faith, where can one find in these circumstances, driven by necessity, the characteristics of a social uprising?

Was the question of salaries posed? Was there a strike? Was there some social reform that was in question? Among this great people of Paris, always generous in its insouciance, was there the least concern about a worrisome future? At the end of that pitifully conducted war, disastrous for France, ruinous for its capital, were the poor of Paris concerned with the fight for their life? They thought about it a good deal. And one must truly not know the carefree character –the too-carefree character – of the inhabitants of our working class faubourgs to sustain such a thesis.

*

We must insist: the error in judgment comes above all from the fact that the insurgents, almost all of them salaried workers, counted among their leaders many socialist and revolutionary militants from the final days of the Empire. But those who lived those hours of distress and obsidian fever know full well that Paris, with the good sense and clear-sightedness of its great days, rose solely against those it considered enemies of the nascent republic and who it considered resigned in the face of the mutilated fatherland.

*

Read the proclamations of the Central Committee and the Commune: are they not all, or almost all of them, impregnated with the sentiment—vaguely socialist because humanitarian, but above all Jacobin—of the Montagnards of the Convention and the Commune of 1793, a revolutionary sentiment that Delescluze personified in his fashion, and the disciples of Blanqui in theirs.

From our current perspective, this is truly the way the essential character of the great and praiseworthy revolt of 1871 appears.

*

It is nevertheless impossible to argue that socialist ideas, if not doctrines, were not spoken of within the assembled Commune, but these affirmations remained verbal, platonic, and in any case foreign to the 200,000 rebels who on March 18, 1871 slid cartridges into their rifles in indignation. If they had truly been socialist revolutionaries, which our good bourgeois like to believe, and not indignant Jacobin and patriotic revolutionaries, they would have acted completely differently. For example, instead of lingering over the harmful tragedy of the hostages, they would have attacked property itself. Instead of a hundred priests, gendarmes, and secret agents they would have taken hostage the 3,000,000 francs guarded in the middle of a rebellious Paris by a feeble reactionary troop at the Bank of France.

The priest survived, the gendarme survived, and the secret agent survived. Would it have been the same for the capitalist fortune of France if they had carried out the seizing of the great safe?

If the Commune had surrendered to the concerns of social revolution, it would have immediately accomplished this truly revolutionary act. It didn't even consider it, and if some of us thought of taking this precious hostage, it was with the strictly political intention of forcing Thiers to negotiate.

*

What is more, how could revolutionary socialism, the only one in my eyes of any worth, have affirmed itself then when today's socialists are still manifestly unable to give us a truly positive explanation of their social concepts?

The internationalists of the time, embarked on the raft of a utopia that was Napoleonic in its origins[6], in the end were anything but revolutionaries. It was they who made up the minority of the Commune, and during the sessions of that assembly their theories were affirmed only through timid decrees lacking sanction concerning the payment of debts due, on night work for bakers, and on the reorganization of the national pawn shop.

It was time childishly wasted to Thiers's profit and at the expense of the organization of the battle!

*

As for the socialist revolutionaries of the Blanquist school, they had very clear ideas on this matter which they had formulated many times under the Empire, but which they had no thought of applying. Their sole concerns were the defeat Versailles and preventing Thiers from organizing the republic that he created and whose goal, today more obvious than ever, was delaying the coming of a democratic, communal, and social revolution.

No one can reasonably contest the following statement: it was the Blanquist party that dominated the insurrection. And so, if this party thought that this insurrection could immediately result in a social revolution, it would have manifested its socialism. It didn't do so. Why? Because it had a precise concept of the only sentiments that had produced the insurrection: republicanism and patriotism.

*

Adversaries of Blanquism have given another reason for this. They claimed, and they still claim, that if the Blanquists failed to show proof of socialism, it's because in reality they weren't and never were anything but political revolutionaries, without a defined socialist idea.

This is yet another legend that must be destroyed.

*

Blanqui and his disciples never were and never will be socialist *doctrinaires*. Does this mean that they are not socialists, in the truly revolutionary meaning of the word? I will establish the contrary by demonstrating that what constitutes the revolutionary socialist character of Blanquism is precisely its contempt, in the past and the present – if not in the future, beyond our sociological vision—of any form of "doctrinairism", if I can be forgiven the expression.

The Blanquists have no POSITIVE social *doctrine*, but they have a revolutionary socialist *theory*, unlike the socialist *believers* who claim to have a positive social doctrine and who have no revolutionary *theory*. What is the Blanquist *theory*? I will attempt to briefly summarize it.

*

In 1789 the bourgeoisie made its revolution. It was the result of a class struggle. It definitively freed itself and took possession of public power. Its revolution was thus simultaneously social and political. A new social order was established and consolidated as a new political order. Thus was organized a new society based on property, the family, and religion.

From that point forward, these three social elements – family, property, and religion – formed the fearsome trilogy that would enslave all the governmental regimes issued from the Revolution, including the most gendarme-like of all of them: Caesarism.

Whatever the governments were that succeeded each other after 1789, for the truly sovereign bourgeoisie there was but one reason to arrive and to hold on: the duty to be the conservative gendarme of the three social pillars—family, property, and religion.

Two revolutionaries understood this perfectly – Proudhon and Blanqui.

> From this flows two aphorisms that are essentially identical:
> "God is evil; property is theft." (Proudhon)
> "Neither God nor master." (Blanqui)

*

As for the trilogy, "Liberty, Equality, Fraternity," which is basically banal and contradictory, it was conceived by the triumphant bourgeoisie in order to hide from the eyes of the naïve crowd its selfish goal of social preservation.

*

But from the naïve crowd, there also sprang men avid for *social* justice: Marat and Hébert during the revolutionary storm; Babeuf, Fourier, Saint Simon, Pierre Leroux, Victor Considérant, Cabet, Louis Blanc, Proudhon, and Blanqui under the parliamentary regime. These men thought that everything was not for the best in the best of all possible worlds; they attacked the three pillars.

It is these men who, by their writings and acts, established the contemporary and, let us say in passing, *French* principle of the social revolution, which must continue the completed bourgeois revolution.

*

And so the Blanquists only grant the title of socialist to those who want simultaneously to destroy and transform the family, property, and religion. For them, any socialism that is not revolutionary remains a doctrinal and vain utopia, the socialist task being above all destruction before construction.

And so as concerns socialism, Blanquist theory can be summed up as follows: first nihilism, and then on to the grace of evolution.

So while non-revolutionary socialists imagine that the social revolution must be the consequence of the successive transformations first of property, then of religion, and finally that of the family, the Blanquists think that the family, a natural social organism, was modified in a reactionary fashion by the addition of private property, which was imposed as a stimulating necessity on one hand and, by religion, imposed as a moral necessity, on the other. They conclude from this that the communal family, freed from proprietary and religious ties, must be substituted for the bourgeois family.

The property registry and the church steeple: these are two monuments incompatible with the emancipated Commune.

*

In conclusion, the Blanquists claim that human evolution must first be preceded by a social revolution which will organize the family as an element of that other organism, the commune, which they consider the sole natural political and social government of individuals living in society.

They say that a social order resulting from the social revolution will have the family and the commune as its sole rational basis, subject to the utilitarian morality of the common interest. This affirmed, they have no positive doctrine and *they don't want to have one* as long as the revolution—violent, obviously—has not placed the social individual in his two natural environments. For the Blanquists, the words collectivism and communism remain poorly defined. Though the first appears to be a euphemism for the second, a euphemism imagined by politicians, no sociologist can say how a society brutally placed in an environment that we know nothing about would evolve. As revolutionaries, we wish for this environment because for us it is the sole terrain for the cultivating, if we can speak in these terms, of human equity, but that's all. From a negative point of view, what we claim is that any society organized on any other foundation will inevitably return us to some kind of oligarchy.

*

In summary, the Blanquists think that one cannot be socialist without being revolutionary, because socialism, unless one plays with words, is the necessarily violent substitution of a new social organization for that founded by the French Revolution, which was essentially bourgeois. Secondly, they reject any positive preconceived doctrine because they believe that human evolution towards equity and the total liberation of man can only be the result of the placing of associated units in an environment that is yet to be created, and whose conditions of development it is impossible to formulate a priori.

*

Neither Blanqui, if he would have led us, nor his disciples dreamed of creating this environment in 1871. At that time the Blanquists were the only thing that they could be: Jacobin revolutionaries rising up to defend the threatened republic. The idealist socialists assembled in the minority were nothing but dreamers, without a defined socialist program, and their unfortunate tactics consisted in making the people of Paris and the communes of France believe that they had one.

On which side was truth? Contemporary socialism is sufficiently proving its emptiness for us to continue to believe that the truth was on ours.

*

Whatever the case, the Commune has been presented by the historians of the reactionary vogue of the time, Maxime Ducamp and Claretie in particular, as nothing but a horde of bandits and imbeciles. And the Commune, as the *arrivé* radicals and so-called socialists—beneficiaries today of its republican valor—represent it was an unthinking uprising of proletarians thirsty for social justice and guided by incompetent idealists. This is a double fiction that must be destroyed. We believe we have established that the insurrection was above all republican and patriotic, and that despite the socialist philosophy of its leaders, the republican and patriotic will of the people was the supreme law at the time.

In addition, whatever admiration we might have for the revolutionary works of Élisée Reclus, that persuasive apostle of libertarian philosophy, we cannot accept this powerfully phrased judgment he bears on the character of the insurrection of 1871:

"The Commune raised up for the future, not by its rulers but by its defenders, an ideal far superior to that of all the revolutions that preceded it. It commits in advance all those who want to continue it, in France and throughout the world, to fight for a new society in which there will be neither masters by birth, title, or money, nor slaves by origin, caste, or salary. The word 'Commune' has everywhere been understood in the broadest sense, as having to do with a new idea, formed of free and equal companions, knowing nothing of the existence of ancient borders and mutually and peacefully assisting each other from one end of the world to the other."

Élisée Reclus obviously marched with this idea in his head as he went to attack the Châtillon redoubt, where he was gloriously taken, his weapon in hand. But Duval and his soldiers had no other objective in marching on Versailles than that of saving the nascent republic sold by Thiers to the Orléanists, just as he sold France to the Prussians.

---

[1] The proclamations of the Alliance Républicaine (radicals) and the Union Républicaine (moderates) which confirm, after the battle of Buzenval, the previous declarations of the delegates of the twenty arrondissements. — Authors' Note.

[2] We know that in a sadly famous poster, Trochu declared that the governor of Paris would never capitulate. This is why, like the good Jesuit he is, Trochu passed the act on to Vinoy! — Authors' Note.

[3] The reader will note that I accept the reactionary's version, though it is not supported by any certain testimony. — Authors' Note.

[4] This is false. The name of the officer could not be given. — Authors' Note.

[5] This colonel was the famous Vabre, the executioner and gravedigger of the Place Saint Jacques. — Authors' Note.

[6] We know that the French delegates of 1862 to the London exposition were for the most part Bonapartists; we also know that Messrs. Jules Simon, Guéroult, Henri Martin, etc., were early members of the International Workingmen's Association — Authors' Note.

Debate on the Hostages and the Committee of Public Safety

Like any good French government, the Commune had its *Journal Officiel*, in which were published government decrees, notices, foreign news, financial reports, death notices, and starting with the issue of April 15, minutes of the meetings of the Commune. Many of the most important revolutionary propagandists of the time participated in its publication, including Pierre Vésinier and Maxime Vuillaume, a feat all the more astounding because along with the *Journal Officiel* they also published their own newspapers during the same period.

After the death of the Commune, many survivors mocked the journal's excessive parliamentarism and, given the circumstances, the discussions there are a mix of the ridiculous and the sublime. We find discussions of the delegates to be sent to attend a funeral as well as the debate on the postponing of the payment of debts due; discussions of the changing of place names and of the legitimacy of elections with insufficient participants. The minutes are frequently cut off abruptly as the Commune entered into secret session.

On May 17 one of the stormiest of the Commune's sessions revolved around two principle subjects: the executions of the hostages held by the Commune and a letter of the minority of the Commune, largely members of the International, protesting against the extraordinary powers granted the Committee of Public Safety. The discussion was so lengthy that its publication required two issues.

Below is the contents of the minority's letter, followed by the minutes of this session.

Letter from the minority

At the session that was to have taken place Monday, May 15, the members belonging to the minority of the Commune had resolved to read a declaration that would doubtless have made the political misunderstandings that existed in the assembly disappear.

The absence of almost all the members of the majority did not permit the opening of the session.

It is thus our duty to enlighten public opinion concerning our attitude and to make known the points that separate us from the majority.

The members present: Arthur Arnould, Ostyn, Longuet, Arnold, Lefrançais, Serraillier, Jules Vallès, Courbet, Victor Clément, Jourde, Varlin.

DECLARATION

By a special and precise vote, the Paris Commune has abdicated its power into the hands of a dictatorship to which it has given the name of Public Safety.

The majority of the Paris Commune declared itself irresponsible by its vote and abandoned all responsibility in our current situation to this committee.

The minority to which we belong on the contrary affirms this idea, that the Commune at the politically and socially revolutionary moment must accept all responsibilities and decline none, however worthy might be the hands into which they will be abandoned.

For our part, we, like the majority, desire the carrying out of social and political renewal, but contrary to their ideas we demand, in the name of the suffrage we represent, the right to respond for ourselves for our acts before our voters, without hiding behind a supreme dictatorship that our mandate permits us neither to accept nor recognize.

And so we will only attend the assembly on the day it constitutes itself as a court of justice to judge one of its members.

Devoted to our great communal cause for which so many citizens die each day, we retire to our too neglected arrondissements. Convinced in any case that the question of war is more important than all others, we will pass the time our municipal functions allow us among our brothers of the National Guard and we will play our part in the decisive struggle carried out in the name of the people's rights.

Here too we will usefully serve our convictions and will avoid creating the splits in the Commune that we all condemn, persuaded that, majority or minority, despite our political divergences, we are all pursuing the same goals: political freedom and the emancipation of the workers.

Long Live the Social Republic!

Long Live the Commune!

Ch. Beslay, Jourde, Theisz, Lefrançais, Eugène Girardin, Vermorel, Clémence, Andrieu, Seraillier, Longuet, Arthur Arnould, Victor Clément, Avrail, Ostyn, Frankel, Pindy, Arnold, J. Vallès, Tridon, Varlin, Courbet.

Journal Officiel
Session of May 17, 1871

Presided over by Citizen Leo Meillet,
Assistant, Citizen Dr. Pillot

The session is opened at 2:30 p.m.

In conformity with the notice inserted in this morning's *Journal Officiel* a roll call by name is proceeded to by Citizen Amouroux, one of the secretaries and a member of the Commune. Sixty-six members are present.

Citizen President: There will be reading of the minutes of the session of May 12.

The minutes are read and adopted without observations.

Citizen President gives a reading of a letter from Citizen Sicard, resigning as member of the war commission.

The assembly gathers as a secret committee to hear a communication from Citizen Ferré, delegate for general security.

The open session begins again at 3:15 p.m.

Citizen Urbain communicates to the assembly a report by Lieutenant Butin, denouncing the rape and massacre of a female ambulance assistant while she was taking care of the wounded.

Citizen Urbain: This report is certified by Lieutenant Urbain of the 3rd Company of the 105th Battalion. I demand that either the Commune or the Committee of Public Safety decide that ten of the hostages we have in our hands be executed within 24 hours as reprisals for the murders of the nurse and of our parliamentarian who was greeted by a fusillade in contempt of the laws of men. I demand that five of these hostages be solemnly executed inside Paris before a delegation of all the battalions, and that the other five be executed at the advanced positions in front of the guardsmen who witnessed the murder.

Citizen J.-B. Clément: I support Citizen Urbain's proposal. I have information from a relative who has returned from Versailles where he was a prisoner. Our men who are detained in Versailles are badly mistreated; they are given very little bread, they are insulted, and they are struck with rifles butts. This must end. On this subject I will address a question to Citizen Parisel, head of the scientific delegation.

Citizen Parisel: I demand the floor.

> Several members: A secret committee!
>
> The assembly meets as a secret committee.
>
> The public session resumes.

Citizen Rigault, procurator of the Commune: I present the following proposal. Given its urgency the Commune decrees:

> Article 1. For those accused of political crimes and misdemeanors, the jury of accusation can provisionally pronounce sentence immediately after having pronounced on the guilt of the accused.
>
> Article 2. The sentences shall be pronounced by a majority of votes.
>
> Article 3. These sentences shall be carried out within 24 hours.
>
> Raoult Rigault, Urbain, L. Chalaine

In my opinion we should answer the murders by the Versaillais in the most energetic fashion by striking the guilty and not the first people we see. And yet, I must say that I'd rather allow guilty men to escape than to strike a single innocent man. Among the people we've detained there are true criminals who deserve to be considered as more than hostages. Well then, chance can very well designate the least guilty, and those who are the guiltiest might be spared. While waiting for justice to be completely established I have thought it useful to establish a tribunal charged with examining the crimes in question. What is more, I declare that I will request that the prescriptions for crimes of this kind not be taken into account. And I put on the same level both the men who are in agreement with Versailles and Bonaparte's accomplices.

Citizen President: There is a proposal formulated by Citizen Urbain.

Citizen Urbain: If the assembly decides that the reprisals will take place within a short time...

Citizen Raoul Rigault, procurator of the Commune: The jury of accusation is assigned for the day after tomorrow.

Citizen Urbain: If we are given the means to carry out the reprisals legally, and in an appropriate and prompt fashion, then I will be satisfied.

Citizen President: Here is the Urbain proposal:

Given the urgency of the situation, the Commune decrees that ten individuals designated by the jury of accusation shall be executed as punishment for the murders committed by the Versaillais, and in particular the murder of a nurse, executed by them in contempt of all human laws.

Five of these hostages shall be executed inside Paris in the presence of the National Guard.

The other five shall be executed at the advanced positions, as close as possible to the place where the crimes were committed.

Urbain

Citizen Protot: On the subject of the proposal presented by Citizen Rigault, I declare that the jury of accusation can only decide on questions of fact, that there are no punishments for the crimes that Citizen Rigault is speaking of. We must thus determine the punishment they are subject to.

Citizen Amouroux: It is my opinion that we must carry out reprisals. A month ago we announced the carrying out of a proposal that put an end to the crimes committed by the Versaillais for a certain period. But since in the end we did nothing, the Versaillais have once again started killing our people. Before what is occurring, I ask what use we are making of the law on the hostages. Should we condemn those held as such? But do the Versaillais judge our National Guardsmen? They take them and kill them on the open road. Let us act! And for each of our murdered brothers, let us answer with a triple execution. We have hostages, and among them priests; let's strike these first, for these matter to them more than do soldiers.

Citizen Vaillant: I am, I must confess, in a difficult situation when I, incompetent in the serious question that occupies us, see the only two individuals in this assembly who are competent in this matter in complete disagreement. Would it not be good if Citizens Protot and Rigault were to come to an agreement and bring this to some kind of resolution?

Citizen Protot, delegate for justice: There is no resolution to take. The procurator of the Commune can bring before the first two sections of the jury of accusation the people to be judged.

Citizen Rigault, procurator of the Commune: Given the nature of the events, these means do not suffice.

Citizen Pillot, president: Let us not lose sight of what is under discussion, that is, Urbain's proposal. The great question of the moment is that of annihilating our enemies. We are in a revolution and we must act as revolutionaries. We must establish a tribunal which judges and which has its decrees executed.

Citizen Urbain: Will the jury of accusation which we just spoke of function? If it must function then my proposal stands; if not, we would do better to vote on Rigault's proposal.

Citizen Philippe, delegate of the 12th arrondissement: We are exposed to a terrible reactionary force. We must take energetic measures. We must let it be known that we are determined to smash all the obstacles they put up against the triumphant march of the revolution.

Citizen Urbain: If we vote on the Rigault proposal, I withdraw mine.

Citizen Vaillant: If your jury of accusation functions as it should there is no need for a special proposal. You only have to apply the Commune's decree relating to reprisals, declaring that Citizens Rigault and Protot are charged with its execution.

Citizen Protot, delegate for justice: If I could have spoken with the procurator of the Commune I would have shown him that it would take at least two weeks to put on trial all those accused of complicity with Versailles. Those tried in absentia should already be sentenced.

Citizen Raoul Rigault, procurator of the Commune: According to the criminal code, juries are not competent to judge those tried in absentia. It is necessary that your juries be a true revolutionary tribunal.

Citizen President again reads the proposal of Citizen Raoul Rigault: I am going to put this proposal to a vote.

Citizen Protot, delegate for justice: I request the postponement of the vote until tomorrow.

Citizen Regère: Yes! Until tomorrow!

Citizen Leo Frankel: Yes! Until tomorrow!

Citizen President: It is proposed to submit the different proposals to a commission composed of Citizens Protot and Rigault.

Citizen Régère: With a third party; I propose Citizen Paschal Grousset. (Various movements)

Citizen Protot: A decree of the Commune says that a chamber composed of twelve jurors will decide on the fate of those accused of complicity with Versailles. I demand that this decree be carried out.

Citizen Urbain: I demand that my proposal be put to a vote.

Citizen Protot, delegate for justice: The notices have been given to have the detainees brought before the jury of accusation.

Citizen Urbain: In that case, I go along with the motion, but I declare that if the decree isn't carried out, I will resubmit my motion in two days.

Citizen Amouroux, one of the secretaries, gives a reading of the following decree:

> The Paris Commune
>
> Considering that the government of Versailles openly tramples upon both the rights of humanity and of war; that it has rendered itself guilty of horrors which didn't even sully those who invaded French soil;
>
> Considering that the representatives of the Paris Commune have the pressing duty of defending the honor and lives of two million inhabitants who have placed the protection of their fates in their hands; that it is essential that all measures called for by the situation be immediately taken;
>
> Considering that politicians and magistrates must reconcile public safety with the respect for freedoms:

Decrees

Article 1. Any person accused of complicity with the government of Versailles shall immediately have a warrant issued and be arrested.

Article 2. A jury of accusation shall be established within 24-hours to learn of the crimes for which he is accused.

Article 3. The jury shall decide within 24 hours.

Article 4. Any accused held as a result of the verdict of the jury of accusation shall be a hostage of the people of Paris.

Article 5. Any execution of a prisoner of war or supporter of the government of the Paris Commune will immediately be followed by the execution of triple that number of hostages held by virtue of Article 4, who will be designated by lot.

Article 6. Every prisoner of war shall be brought before the jury of accusation, which will decide if he will be immediately freed or held as a hostage.

Citizen President: Here is the motion that I am putting to a vote: "The Commune, referring to its decree of April 7, demands its immediate execution and passes to the motion."

The motion is adopted.

Citizen Paschal Grousset makes the following motion: Citizens, at the opening of the session we noted with pleasure, but not without surprise, that several members of this assembly can be found at their benches whose names are found at the bottom of a manifesto published yesterday by certain newspapers. Their manifesto announced that they would no longer participate in our sessions. I would first like to know if their presence among us is a rejection of the harmful act of which they are guilty. I don't accept that certain members of the Commune can fill the papers with a manifesto in which they announce a split, in which these new Girondins declare that they are withdrawing, not to the departments—which they can't do—but to the arrondissements. ...that they should then come, without explanation, without justification, take their seats in their regular places....

Voice: This is not a motion! (Noise, interruptions from different sides)

Citizen Paschal Grousset: This is a motion, a motion of a higher order. After having asked the minority for the reason for this conduct I request the right to present a few observations on the subject of its manifesto. The minority accuses the Commune of having abdicated its power into the hands of the Committee of Public Safety. It accuses us of evading the responsibilities that weigh upon us. And yet it knows full well that in concentrating power in the hands of five men who have its confidence to decide on the terrible necessities of the situation, the Commune in no way intended to abdicate. For our part at least, we accept full responsibility. We are united with the committee that we named, are accountable for its acts, are ready to support it to the bitter end, as long as it marches on the revolutionary road, and ready to strike and smash it if it deviates from it.

It is thus false that we abdicated.

It is even more false that the minority's manifesto was provoked by this so-called abdication. The proof of this is that this same minority took part in the vote on the naming of the second Committee of Public Safety; that Article 3, conferring plenary powers to the Committee of Public Safety already existed at the time of the vote; that the very definition of these plenary powers had at that time been adopted on the proposal of one of the members of the minority.

We thus have the right to say that Article 3 is not the real reason for the manifesto. We thus have the right to say that the real reason is the failure suffered by the minority in the choice of members of the committee and the revocation of the military commission that issued from its ranks. If the reasons it alleges were sincere, the minority should have formulated its protest before the renewal of the Committee of Public Safety, and not after having participated in the vote, which meant recognizing the principle.

Finally, the minority declares that it wants to move from the parliamentary role to action by entirely dedicating itself to the administration of the arrondissements. Of course, they will not reproach those of us here for not being supporters of this system.

Who opposed the parliamentary tendencies that came to light in this assembly? Who has always demanded brief and rare sessions, closed to the public, without speeches—action sessions? Who, if not this minority that noisily announces its withdrawal on the pretext that it can't act; who constantly, as much as it could, prevented us from acting?

Citizens, I conclude. If the members of the Commune who announced their withdrawal really intend to dedicate themselves to the arrondissements, I would say: all the better. That would be better than coming here and preventing courageous and resolute men from taking the measure that the situation demands and the responsibility for which they accept.

If, instead of keeping their promises, these members attempt maneuvers that might compromise the safety of the Commune they are deserting, we will seize and strike them.

As for us, we will do our duty. Until victory or death, we will remain at the combat post that the people entrusted us with.

Citizen Jules Vallès: We came here yesterday to declare to the assembly that we were ready to enter into discussions on the political differences that seem to divide us. Our sentiments are contrary to those Citizen Grousset seems to suppose we hold. I declare, for myself and my friends, that what we want in the Commune is the most perfect harmony.

Citizen P. Grousset, in reminding us that we voted the establishment of the Committee of Public Safety, forces us to say that we sacrificed our sentiments in the face of a bombarded Paris.

We saw a danger in Article 3 of the Commune's decree. We ask that all of us together investigate whether instead of creating a weapon, you haven't created a threat. We ask that this be calmly discussed. In a word, we want all forces to come together to ensure our salvation.

For my part, I declared that it was necessary to come to an agreement with the Central Committee and the majority, but the minority must also be respected, which is also a force. In all sincerity, we declare to you that we want harmony within the Commune and that our withdrawal to the arrondissements is not a threat.

We ask that you place on the agenda for tomorrow a discussion in which we can examine the facts and ensure the gathering of all forces to march against the enemy.

Citizen Langevin: I completely agree with the words of Citizen J. Vallès, but I protest against those of Citizen Paschal Grousset. I voted against the Committee of Public Safety, but the majority having established it, I accepted it. Nevertheless, I think I have the right to say that there is a serious danger in Article 3 of the decree, which places in its hands the nomination and removal of delegates. (Noise)

Citizen Miot: Yesterday the minority carried out an act that was clearly hostile to the majority. Why did it not give and ask for explanations before making a decision? A serious accusation was made against us: they dare to say that we renounced the exercising of the mandate that was entrusted to us. This is not the case. Isn't absolute control reserved to the Commune in the decree that establishes the Committee of Public Safety? As author of the proposal I did all I could so that the authority of the Commune not be absorbed. Can you not revoke this Committee at your will when you come to think that its authority might be dangerous? I repeat: the minority carried out a regrettable act yesterday that the public severely judges and which it will have to account for to its voters.

Citizen Arnould: I request a correction to the minutes of the last session published in the *Journal Officiel*; it has to do with this question that is stirring us up. The *Officiel* has me say: "If one of the motions proposed to you is adopted, the Commune will serve only to incriminate the members of the Committee of Public Safety when it judges this convenient, and it could very well never hold another session." This is as far from my thoughts as possible. What I said and mean is: "I will not fight the Billioray and Ferré amendments. I will vote for them, for they are the inevitable deduction from Article 3, establishing the Committee of Public Safety, and I will ask that the Commune, understanding the logic of its acts, cease its periodic meetings."

In my opinion the Commune should only meet to question the Committee of Public Safety concerning its acts or to judge a member of the Commune. This is what I said. It was a formal affirmation and not an incrimination of the consequences of Article 3. I ask that this fundamental rectification be made to the *Officiel*.

Citizen President: Rectification shall be made to the *Officiel*.

Citizen Arnould: I made a formal affirmation and not an incrimination of Article 3. The Commune should assist the Committee of Public Safety, and if need be revoke it if it doesn't carry out its mandate, but it must stop discussing. We must meet in our arrondissements, follow our battalions when they march on the enemy, and avoid sterile discussions. I do not see in this either separation or hostility.

Citizen Paschal Grousset: You should have said this instead of publicly accusing us.

Citizen Arnould: We came here last Monday to explain ourselves, but there was no session. (Interruptions)

Citizen Régère: The publication of the separation signed by the minority is a regrettable act. But really, if that declaration went further than our colleagues' ideas, let them withdraw it. Their goal is the same as ours. We only differ on the means, and as soon as they return to us we should receive them fraternally so that we can all work together toward the goal we are pursuing. In any case, it was the minority that supported Citizen Lefrançais when he demanded that the broadest powers over the delegations be given to the Committee of Public Safety. (Noise)

It was the minority that wanted the latter to be able to strike the delegations. (Interruptions, noise)

A large number of voices: That isn't correct!

Citizen Régère: Come citizens; you have returned and you will remain among us.

Citizen Courbet: But we are all here for the safety of the public.

Citizen Jules Andrieux: It was said that the minority separated from the majority because it didn't want to accept a defeat in the election of the Committee of Public Safety. If that were correct then the minority would have been in the wrong. But this reproach is unfounded. The minority proposed its resolution because a motion was placed on the desk by the Committee of Public Safety, though everyone was in agreement that the Committee of Public Safety didn't have to consult us but rather should act. It seemed to us that there was only one thing to do, and that was to withdraw to our arrondissements and delegations as long as we weren't relieved. And I never participated more actively than I have since these events. I understood the economy of the proposal submitted by Citizen Miot. It was said that you would abdicate your authority as long as the Committee of Public Safety would meet. (Interruptions and prolonged noise)

Citizen Félix Pyat: I demand the reading of the minority's manifesto.

Citizen Jules Andrieu: Please allow me to finish. We didn't come to discuss. We came to tell you that the day when you will want a discussion we will explain everything, not to judges, but to the Commune, without either passion or splits.

Several members: The motion!

Citizen Raoul Rigault: I requested the floor for a motion. The signers of the manifesto have declared that they will only present themselves to this assembly when the Commune will have set itself up as a court of justice. And so I don't understand either the presence of some of them among us or the discussion that is occurring at this moment. (Approbation)

Citizen Vaillant: On the question we are dealing with, I feel that I am so impartial that I can make observations that others here cannot make. I am a member of neither the majority nor the minority, since I was unable to find any group of men with whom I can march. Given what has happened, I ask that the assembly act like an assembly charged with saving Paris. We don't need internecine quarrels. This manifesto has delivered a serious blow to the Commune by placing before the public questions that should only be brought up in secret committee. But when these members, disavowing their manifesto, return here, we shouldn't wave it in their faces, forcing them to persevere in their error.

I spoke of the minority. But note this well, citizens: there was an act that provided if not the excuse, then at least the explanation for the error committed by several members of this assembly, and that was the change in the military commission. And so there is only one thing to do now: let the minority tear up its program and let the majority tell it: "Let's unite our efforts for the salvation of all. Be with us, for if you are against us we will smash you."

Citizen Billioray: I will answer Citizen Vaillant by saying that we changed the military commission because that commission, charged with arresting Rossel, allowed him to escape. We couldn't keep men in place who didn't obey the orders of the Commune. If the members who signed the manifesto withdraw their signatures and tear up their declaration I think that the discussion on this question should be closed.

Citizen Amouroux: As concerns the manifesto, I will say that the members who signed it did great harm to the majority by seeking to make them look like parliamentarians. (Noise)

I declare that it was the majority that was the first to demand that there be only two sessions per week. The proof is that it was Citizens Delescluze, Vésinier, and Amouroux who made this proposal: Considering that all efforts should be focused on the war and the organization of the defense, the Commune decrees:

> Article 1. All members of the Commune shall be at the head of their arrondissements and legions.
>
> Article 2. The war commission will centralize all reports and will make them known at the sessions of the Commune.
>
> Article 3. The sessions of the commune will take place on Sundays and Mondays at exactly 1:00 p.m.
>
> Article 4. The Commune can be convoked on an emergency basis upon the request of five members.

This proposal is dated May 5.

You cannot grant yourselves the monopoly of everything in your arrondissements and legions, because we revolutionaries are the ones who demanded it. You did everything, you attempted everything to become the majority, and when you saw that it escaped you abdicated through a manifesto in your papers.

We too ask to be in our arrondissements and on the ramparts, and it's for this reason that we named a Committee of Public Safety, so as to avoid sterile discussions. But far from abdicating, we asked for two sessions weekly to examine the conduct of the Committee and to reverse its decisions at its first error.

Citizen Frankel: I feel that I am in the same situation as my friend Vaillant. I don't belong to any fraction of the Commune, and yet I signed the conclusions of the manifesto and will defend it before you and my voters.

The Committee of Public Safety smashed the war commission because it included men who had voted against it. It surrounds itself with more or less capable men, as long as they go along with it. If the manifesto was published, it is your fault; we came here and you weren't here.

As long as you haven't relieved me, I will remain in my delegation and I will continue to concern myself with the interests of the workers, which I've done until now. I will send the decisions taken in accordance with the labor commission of the Committee of Public Safety. But I declare to you that I will only come here under the conditions indicated in the manifesto.

Citizen Urbain, the President: The minority should accept the actions of the Committee of Public Safety and not put stumbling blocks before it.

In acting in this way it fails to do its duty. What is the minority going to do in its arrondissements? You only have one duty to fulfill, and that is that of withdrawing your manifesto and remaining here to watch over the safety of the revolution.

Citizen Viard: In order to summarize and terminate the question, I request that the minority not only disavow its manifesto, but that it no longer put the Committee of Public Safety in question. It is doubtless because it is afraid that the minority acts as it does, but for my part I declare that the Committee of Public Safety cannot harm me and that it doesn't want to do so. In any case, don't we have the right to control it, and can't we strip it of power if need be? What we need more than anything is not only our devotion to the people's interests and our abnegation, but also our political unity.

Citizen President: I will now give a reading of a first motion, signed by Vaillant: "The so-called declaration of the minority not having been directly produced in the Commune, and the presence of several members of that minority at today's session de facto annulling the declaration made by a portion of the assembly, the Commune passes to the motion."

This motion is not taken under consideration.

Here then is a second motion, signed by Miot:

> "Considering that the Committee of Public Safety is responsible for its acts, that it is at every moment at the orders and disposal of the Commune, whose sovereignty has never been nor could be contested, the majority of the Commune declares:
>
> "That it is ready to forget the conduct of those members of the minority who will withdraw their signature from the manifesto.
>
> "That it condemns the latter and passes to the motion."

Citizen Courbet: I request to make a motion. It is impossible for me to remain at the head of the town hall of my arrondissement. I am unable to obtain information from the delegation for war, especially since my municipal council has resigned.

Several voices: That's not a motion!

Citizen Courbet: Being responsible for my administration, I can no longer remain in this situation.

Several voices: That's not the question!

Citizen Serrailler: I signed the manifesto while reserving to myself the right to come to the session. There is only one thing we can be attacked for, and that's the publicity that was given it. We came Sunday and Monday to participate in the session and there was no one. (Various calls) So we then wrote the manifesto and I will not renounce it. Doing so would be a culpable act. (The motion! Cloture!)

Citizen Langevin: I request the floor to speak against cloture. I have something personal that I want to speak about.

Citizens Victor Clément and J.-B. Clément request the floor to speak against cloture.

Several members: To a vote! To a vote!

Citizen President: I put cloture to a vote.

Cloture is put to a vote and pronounced.

Citizen Langevin: Citizen Urbain said that the minority had supported Lefrançais's proposal, which conferred the Committee of Public Safety with plenary powers over the commissions and delegations. I am proud to have voted with the minority in many circumstances, but I reject Citizen Urbain's assertion. I voted against the Committee of Public Safety's motion, which gave it plenary powers.

Citizen Urbain, president: I maintain my assertion.

Citizen J.-B. Clément: I don't accept despotism, and I protest against the cloture vote. Conspiracies were spoken of and I want to defend myself. (Interruptions) We are told to run to our neglected municipalities; many among those of the minority have never gone to their town halls.

Citizen Dereure: That's true!

Citizen President: Cloture was voted and I must sustain it.

Citizen Ostyn: You didn't sustain it when you let people speak.

Citizen J.-B. Clément: I ask to respond as well.

Citizen Régère: I request that we vote on the motion of Citizen Vaillant. This motion, all of whose terms I don't accept—since I believe Citizen Vaillant has gone beyond his ideas—nevertheless gives satisfaction to the majority and the main interests of the Commune, because it states that the minority, by resuming its seats here, tacitly disavows its regrettable manifesto.

Citizen President: I gave readings of the two motions put forth by Citizens Miot and Vaillant. I am going to put them to a vote.

Citizen Victor Clément: I will not vote. Given that I don't recognize a majority's right to commit a minority, I don't recognize our right to commit our colleagues.

Citizen Pyat: You declared that the Commune had abdicated.

Citizen Victor Clément: Will Citizen Pyat permit me to speak only of the motion? I think that if there is someone who has never stirred up passions in a debate, it is I.

Citizen J. Miot pronounces a few words that don't reach us.

Citizen Victor Clément: I will answer Citizen Miot by saying that if he wants to descend to the realm of intentions we'll never finish. For my part, I would never insult a member of the Commune by believing that outside his acts he has evil intentions. It's your right to condemn our manifesto, but what I call for is an act of justice. We can't vote the motion because that would mean committing colleagues who are not here.

Citizen Arnould: In response to an interruption, I will say that if I wasn't at my town hall it's because I had an important delegation that took up my time.

Citizen Dereure: You had no need to say that the municipal administrations were neglected.

Citizen President: I put to a vote the two motions that have been proposed.
  The motion proposed by Citizen Vaillant is voted on and rejected. The motion proposed by Citizen Miot is then put to a vote and adopted.

Citizen Billioray (returning): The cartridge depot on the Rue Rapp has just exploded and it's still burning. This is treason and yet you talk! They've arrested the traitor who set the fire. (Movement)

Citizen President: I will no longer cede the floor on the question of the manifesto.

Citizen Vaillant: I ask the members who are in charge of the municipalities to please listen to me. The Commune gave me a delegation in which I often find myself in conflict with certain municipalities, while with others everything is for the best. Education doesn't function as it should. Today I will speak to you about the Jesuits. They are intervening everywhere and in every way. The enthusiastic municipalities were done with them in two days; in others they weren't able to be driven out. It is urgent that two months after March 18 we should see no more of these people. It would be good if the municipalities were to be a bit more zealous…

Citizen Régère: Be precise!

Citizen Vaillant: …and make them completely disappear within forty-eight hours. Here is what I propose: "On the proposal of the delegation for education the Commune decides: Given the many warnings given to the arrondissement municipalities to substitute secular education for religious education;

Within forty-eight hours a list shall be compiled of all the schools still held by the congregations. This list shall be published every day in the *Officiel*, including the names of the members of the Commune delegated to the municipal government of the arrondissement where the orders of the Commune on the subject of the establishment of strictly secular education have nor been executed."

Citizen Vaillant's proposal, put to a vote, is adopted.

Citizen Ostyn: I request that I be allowed to place on the desk the list of the religious communities that exist within Paris.

Citizen Mortier: I have an important question to address. A police superintendent came to our arrondissement to evacuate and close the church. This operation was carried out in such a way that it caused a riot in the neighborhood. Why weren't we notified in advance?

Citizen Courbet: In the presence of serious acts that are occurring at various points General Safety had to take exceptional measure and execute them without delay. It believes it has done its duty. (Yes!)

Citizen Gambon: At a time like this we should exclusively concern ourselves with the war and all the questions that go with it. (Agreement)

Citizen Urbain, president: Citizen Vésinier proposes the following decrees:

> Titles of nobility, coats of arms, liveries, noble privileges and honorific distinctions are abolished. Pensions, rents, prerogatives, and all that go along with these are suppressed.
>
> Increases of all kinds are abolished, and the rents, pensions, and privileges that flow from them are suppressed.
>
> The Legion of Honor and all honorific orders are abolished. A subsequent decree will determine which legionnaire pensions should be maintained; the rest shall be suppressed.

Another proposal:

> "The law of May 8, 1816 is annulled. The decree of March 21, 1803 promulgated the 31st of that month is once again in effect.
>
> All recognized children are legitimate and will enjoy all the rights of legitimate children.
>
> All so-called natural children who are not recognized are recognized by the Commune as legitimate.
>
> All male citizens aged eighteen and female citizens aged sixteen who declare before a municipal magistrate that they want to unite in the ties of marriage shall be united, on the condition that they also declare that they are not married and that they have neither father nor mother nor relatives up to the degree that in the eyes of the law is a hindrance to marriage.
>
> They are dispensed from any other legal formality.
>
> Their children, if they have any, will be recognized as legitimate on their simple declaration."

And another proposal of Citizen Durand's:

I propose to the Commune that it decree that in the future no move can take place until a customs officer or some other agent of the Commune has checked the packaging.

Citizen J.-B. Clément's proposal is put to a vote and urgently adopted.

Citizen President: Here is a proposal made by Citizen Miot: "I ask the commission of justice if it is ready to make its report on my proposal relating to the reform of the prisons."

Upon the request of Citizen Ledroit a reading is given of the following proposal, made by the council of the Fifth Legion:

> "Considering that every honest citizen has the right to fight for his country's freedom in whatever camp chance has placed him,
>
> Decrees:
>
> Article 1. Any citizen who will have taken part in the defense of communal freedoms and the republic will have the right to a pension of 300 francs, the first quarterly amount of which will be paid three months after the day when total victory is carried off by the defenders of the republic over the Versaillais royalists.
>
> Article 2. Any soldier from the Versaillais army, whatever corps he might belong to, who lines up under the banner of the Commune and the republic will have the right to the same pension.
>
> Article 3. Any citizen from the provinces who takes up arms to defend the republic and the communal institutions will also have a right to the same pension.
>
> Article 4. Any officer or non-commissioned officer of the Versailles army who comes to defend the flag of freedom will have right to a pension in proportion to his rank."

Citizen Billioray: I request that I be allowed to read you a dispatch that I just received on the subject of the explosion that just occurred on the Avenue Rapp. (Movement of lively interest)

A reading of the dispatch is made.

Citizen President: In the face of all that is happening we should show less hesitation in voting for the repressive measures that are proposed to us. (Yes)

A member: I ask that a war contribution be voted against the shopkeepers who left Paris to escape service in the National Guard. (Supported)

Citizen President: This proposal will be discussed at a later time. Citizens, I inform you that our next session will be the day after tomorrow.

Citizen Léo Frankel: Given the events that are currently taking place I declare that I will participate in the sessions.

Citizen President: The minutes will state that Citizen Léo Frankel has withdrawn his signature from the manifesto.

The session is adjourned at 7:00 p.m.

The secretaries,

Amouroux, Vésinier

The Sessions of the International in Paris During the Commune

Though the International only had seventeen members on the Commune it was a considerable force there (though it was commonly referred to as "the minority"). Frederick Engels, in his introduction to Marx's *The Civil War in France* debatably characterized them as being "chiefly adherents of the Proudhon school of socialism," but he also credits these "Proudhonists" with being "chiefly responsible for the economic decrees of the Commune, both for their praiseworthy and their unpraiseworthy aspects."

What we see in these minutes is a group struggling with financial troubles, with the inability to put out a newspaper, with difficulties gathering members together because they're at the front lines, while others stray (or are excluded from) from their ranks. But its meeting place on the Place de la Corderie was the center of working-class political organization in France, and the great Jules Vallès wrote in his newspaper *Le Cri du Peuple* that it "was the equal of any forum of Antiquity."

And so in these minutes we get to hear the voices of some of the most important men of the period. For example, Eugène Varlin, "tall, thin, with hair once black that was now gray," according to a contemporary, a bookbinder by profession who was among the founding members of the International's French section January 1865, was elected to the Commune by three different arrondissements, and was killed on the last day of the Commune, fighting to the bitter end. Varlin was shot down after being captured, the Versaillais general on the scene saying that Varlin was "superb in his courage." We also hear the Hungarian Jewish exile Léo Frankel, who wrote to Marx after the proclamation of the Commune that "if we succeed in radically transforming the social regime the revolution of March 18 would be the most effective revolution of those that have taken place until now," and who despite being wounded at the barricades on May 25 was able to escape Varlin's fate. And then there is Albert Theisz who, according to the Blanquist Gaston Da Costa, was "one of the rare intelligent and well-balanced workers on the general staff of the International Workingmen's Association" and who also fought on the barricades until the Commune's final moments.

Included below in these minutes are the results of the special meeting of May 20 to discuss the actions of "the minority" in rejecting the extraordinary powers granted the Committee of Public Safety by the Commune and refusing to sit any longer on that body.

Session of January 5, 1871

Chairman, Franquin; Assistant, Varlin; Secretary, H. Goullé

Frankel requests that we complete the discussion on the communication of the Eastern Section; that communication was rejected through a motion because the plenipotentiary powers admitted under the Empire were made necessary by the rigors of the circumstances. Since the founding of the republic there is no use in putting these plenipotentiary powers back in place; it is consequently irregular to accept them, especially since we have been deprived of communications with London for such a long period.

Present: Syndical Chamber of Jewelers, Cabinetmakers, Lithographers, Marble Workers, 2nd and 4th group of the Marmite [Society for Alimentation], Silversmiths, Trimmers, House Painters, Rugmakers, Weavers, Sections, Study Circle, 50 copies of the newspaper, Brantome, 50 copies for either one or three months, School of Medicine, Hospital Louis, Ternes, 100 copies, Batignolles, Poissonière, Richard-Lenoir, Combat, Couronnes, 15 copies, Roule, 20 copies.

Varlin communicates that the Batignolles section gave funds for four issues of a newspaper that it must immediately begin publishing. That section today sends two delegates who offer to place these funds at the disposal of the Federal Council if the Council can appear without delay. The results have been insufficient: only six sections have responded.

Buisson, delegated by the Batignolles section to the newspaper. The Batignolles section is able to put out a small format newspaper immediately. It has in hand the funds for four to six issues; it wants them to appear immediately; it thinks that the circumstances make it urgent to have an organ without delay. The Federal Council can be informed of the editing of the first issue and name two delegates who will confirm that the newspaper is truly in the spirit of the Association and if it can take as its subtitle this inscription: INTERNATIONAL WORKINGMEN'S ASSOCIATION, and in two lateral blocks the slogans: NO DUTIES WITHOUT RIGHTS and EMANCIPATION OF THE WORKERS BY THE WORKERS THEMSELVES. If the Federal Council later puts out an organ, the newspaper of the Batignolles section will fuse with it and will accept the title and the editorial board that the Federal Council will have chosen.

Lacord is surprised that the Federal Council has established a relationship with the newspaper that the Batignolles section wants to found when it turned down *La Lutte à Outrance* (Fight to the Finish), which sells quite well and which has conquered an important place. There is a danger in this, and that is DEMONSTRATING TO THE PUBLIC THE DISUNION WITHIN THE INTERNATIONAL WORKINGMEN'S ASSOCIATION.

Varlin: *La Lutte à Outrance* is an essentially militant and political newspaper, and the Federal Council wants a newspaper that belongs to it alone, a *propagator of the spirit of the Association and whose editorial board will be in its hands.*

Lacord: *La Lutte à Outrance* has a title appropriate to an element of struggle, aimed at the hand-to-hand fight with the forces of privilege raised up against the workers and at being a newspaper which, immediately after the war, will be exclusively dedicated to the labor question. We have offered to change the title and subtitle as you wish, reserving you first place in our columns. I fear that you are too narrowly laying out the borders for your organ's editor-in-chief. There is a danger in this that you will appreciate later. I had offered you a rapprochement between the internationals of the School of Medicine and yourselves so you could unite on this question.

Frankel: The question isn't clearly asked. We must only examine whether or not the Federal Council must have an organ that is its spokesman, and I think it's sad to see that two sections have the means to create an organ and that the International, with all of its sections combined, cannot find enough strength to create a general organ.

Buisson: The newspaper of the Batignolles section doesn't yet exist. The material question will be settled tomorrow morning at 10:00. Are you ready to appear immediately? Are you ready to appear weekly for a month without interruption? It would be an accident without consequences if the newspaper of one section alone disappeared after a few issues. Send delegates to the commission of the newspaper of the Batignolles section, which will set to work starting tomorrow.

Franquin: The number of subscriptions taken by the Federal Council is too low to ensure the existence of the newspaper.

Frankel: I hope that the siege of Paris won't last and that by sending delegates to the sections we'll find enough subscriptions.

Lacord: We can name delegates who will be charged with examining the forces of *Lutte à Outrance* and the Batignolles section so we can combine them.

Boudet: We need our own organ, one that is really ours. Let's combine our funds and not waste time. They're offering us the combined collaboration of the *Lutte à Outrance* and the Batignolles section; let's accept this and put the paper out.

Noro: It is urgent that we come to an agreement. There's no time to lose; let's unite our efforts.

Lacord: I don't have the power to settle this completely in the name of *La Lutte à Outrance*. Come see us and we'll share our views.

Camélinat: If we don't have in hand the means to fully succeed we're better off allowing a section to set out on the slippery field of journalism. It would be a very serious thing to put out a newspaper in the name of the Federal Council that risks perishing due to lack of the elements needed for it to live. Such a failure is to be feared, for it might discredit us in the eyes of public opinion.

Frankel: We need a newspaper of the Federal Council. If the associates don't understand that it is their duty to stand firmly behind it we must despair for the future of the French International Society.

Lacord: We need an organ that will stand up in the face of the big newspapers of the bourgeoisie, that will have a life of its own and that fights in our name. We need an editor with long experience in the political struggle, and who isn't of a school that would diminish the strength of our organ. The editing of *La Lutte à Outrance* offers you a trial period of three or six months so you can judge if the line you laid down will be followed. The free editing for three or six months will be for paid after this trial period, if you approve the editors. You can then change the editorial staff, even overnight if you feel it necessary.

Buisson: I don't have a mandate to ask you for a study commission; we don't want to waste time and we are determined to act tomorrow. I notice that the French International is acting weakly in so decisive a case. Our newspaper will come out Saturday; you'll judge it then.

Varlin: What puts us in an embarrassing position is that since September 4 we don't have enough money. The dues from the sections don't cover expenses and even more seriously, we still have some debts from the time of the Empire. Six sections on their own take 300 issues. This isn't much and doesn't make us feel very bold.

Frankel: The Federal Council wasn't sufficiently active in its appeal to the sections.

Franquin: Individually we each believe in success. But having mandates from our groups we can only commit ourselves proportionally to the forces we know them to have.

Election of a commission to deliberate with *La Lutte à Outrance* and with the Batginolles section. Named were: Frankel, Varlin, Noro, Boudet, Goullé.

The commission will meet Saturday, Rue Larrey 2 at the house of Citizen Molleveaux.

The Poissonière section is accepted. Address communications to Citizen Boudier, 138, Faubourg-Poissonière.

Frankel: The presence on the Federal Council of delegates from the sections is indispensable.

Varlin: We once used to send a delegate from the Federal Council every week to each section. It would be good to do this again.

The proposal is voted.

Chatel: Because of time constraints, I ask the Federal Council to accept my resignation as cashier. I'll continue to take care of taking notes.

The resignation is accepted. Goullé, Boulevard Sebastopol 78, is named cashier.

Lacord proposes that each section pay the sum of 23 centimes weekly for the costs of dispatching the minutes.

The session is adjourned.

The Secretary,

Henri Goullé

Session of January 12

Chairman, Bachruch; Assistant, Varlin

Present are: Study Circle, Ternes, School of Medicine, Couronne, Faubourg du Temple, Faubourg Antoine, Brantome, Richard-Lenoir, Hôpital Louis, Silversmiths, Clothing Trimmers, Construction Carpenters, Ceramics, Bakers, Shoemakers, Shoe Cutters.

Corrections to the Minutes

Varlin: The expression "gave funds for four to six issues of the newspaper," applied to the Batignolles section, should be replaced by "gathered funds."

The minutes are adopted minus one vote.

Communications:

The Richard-Lenoir section mandates Citizen Lambon to represent it on the Federal Council. This mandate is signed by Citizens A. Mélinat, Guénot, Mathieu, E. Rimbaut. The Federal Council adopts.

The Typographic Association of the faubourg Saint Denis requests a down payment.

Varlin: We owe that association a note.

Frankel: How many volumes of our minutes have we sold? Where are we financially?

Varlin: Franquin, who took care of the accounts, is on the front lines.

Pindy: Let Goullé, Chatel's successor, draw up a general accounting.

Laporte: I propose that the sections pay the General Council 10 centimes monthly per member.

Varlin: The workers' corporations are not active, but the existing sections should pay.

Laporte: It is understandable that the associates don't pay their 15 centimes weekly to their section, but they should and must pay the 10 centimes monthly to the Federal Council.

Pindy: Let the dues for December be provided next Thursday.

Bachruch proposes that the dues of 10 centimes monthly be paid to the Federal Council.

The proposal is voted.

Varlin: The bronze workers are dispersed among the military companies and they can't pay. We can't demand it; this is a case of *force majeure*.

Minet: In our corporation we too are dispersed. I will take steps and bring money, if possible.

André: The cabinetmakers are also dispersed.

Goullé: Report of the newspaper commission: *La Lutte à Outrance* printed 5,000 copies of its first issue, 8,000 of its second, and 12,000 of its third.

Citizen Armand Lévi proposes an agreement with the Federal Council on the political line of the newspaper and reserves for us two or three separate columns that will be so we can feel completely at home.

Armand Lévi, delegate of the Republican Association: I offer to work for your newspaper without payment until it is founded. The workers can create an indestructible newspaper by means of the forces drawn from within their own ranks. I will be your faithful echo in politics. We will fight the clergy and its encroachment and industrial feudalism; we will defend the republic, which stands above the rights of majorities.

I don't want to create a newspaper of my own or in my interests, but a newspaper that is yours. Today the worker should only want to rise with his class and not to rise on his own.

I would like the newspaper to become a weekly immediately. We can count on an average circulation of 8,000 copies. If you would like, the columns will be shared out half for you and half for the School of Medicine Club.

Laporte: I agree with Citizen Armand Lévi. I think that an exclusively worker newspaper would lack interest; I want us to add politics. Perhaps we can make an effort and come out every day.

Varlin: The newspaper *La Lutte à Outrance* is filled with the minutes from the School of Medicine. It should come out often, but the club only has funds for one issue per week. It can only come out daily if we made a very energetic effort.

Goullé: I asked sixteen sections for subscriptions. Let's try to come out three times a week.

Lacord: Citizen Laporte doesn't take account of the pecuniary difficulties to be overcome in appearing every day. We have to set up a delegation that will ask every section for subscriptions. This evening the Federal Council has only to examine the offer made by Citizen Lévi in the name of the committee of the 6th arrondissement.

Frankel: We need an organ that will clearly explain our views! How can you expect a worker who knows nothing to learn? Today we're talking to him about a COMMUNE, and the word frightens him; he doesn't know what it is. Since the establishing of the republic WE HAVE DONE NOTHING! The bourgeoisie is fighting us today. Let's answer it with a biting, independent newspaper that will proudly brandish the banner of the workers.

I don't accept the editorial board of *La Lutte à Outrance* as it is, but we can give it a program.

David: My section calls for a newspaper. Do we or don't we accept *La Lutte à Outrance*? The siege will end, and we'll need one for the provinces, which is forming sections and counts on us.

Armand Lévi: The newspaper has to contain a section called: "Tribune of the International Workingmen's Association," a section exclusively edited by us. For the political part, let's agree on a program and I'll follow it. Different clubs promised their assistance and are determined to follow along with us on the straight road of revolutionary socialism.

Varlin: We had hoped to found a daily newspaper ourselves. Our study of this showed that this was impossible. We have to accept *La Lutte à Outrance*. Perhaps we'll become a daily with the collaboration of other clubs.

Minet: In order to avoid any difficulties that might arise, it is urgent that a notice state that the International Workingmen's Association only answers for what is in its tribune.

Chalain: I am opposed to the Federal Council having a tribune in any newspaper without expressly pointing out its responsibility. In any event, an editorial committee is needed. We would do better to have our own newspaper; to this end the Batignolles section abandons its funds to us.

Bachruch: We need a worker's newspaper. *La République des Travailleurs* took the wrong path.

Frankel: Varlin and I wanted a newspaper that was ours, but we saw this was impossible. Like him, I accept *La Lutte à Outrance*. The French worker needs to have an idol; let him have one, but let us hate and fight the bourgeoisie along with him. There's no point in talking about the bourgeois republic; the *Lutte à Outrance* should talk about the social republic.

Chalain: We shouldn't have an editor in chief. *La République des Travailleurs* bears my name. I haven't written there but I accept the responsibility while declaring that the first issue was clumsily done. We ask you for copy; we don't have enough, so let's unite the two newspapers.

Minet: Let the chairman consult the Federal Council. Do we accept *La Lutte à Outrance*?

Chalons: Let's vote by section.

Bachruch: All sections should be represented; it's their duty.

Vote by sections. Fourteen sections vote "yes." The Ternes section abstains.

Voted unanimously. The newspaper *La Lutte à Outrance* will have a subtitle separated from the body of the newspaper and a section set aside for politics.

The session was adjourned at 11:30.

The Secretary,
H. Goullé
P.S. Omission from the minutes:

Lacord: It is pointless to have separate tribune, since the newspaper will belong to us. We don't want to follow the line of *La Patrie en Danger*.

Bachruch: Blanqui often has correct ideas, but we are creating a socialist newspaper, and whatever I might think of Blanqui, I don't want to stray from this line.

Editorial Commission is named: Frankel, Pindy, Minet, Bachruch, Goullé, Franquin, Varlin, Laporte, Theisz, Verdure.

Session of the Federal Council of January 19, 1871

Chairman, Rouveyrolles; Assistant, Frankel; Secretary, H. Goullé

Present: Faubourg du Temple, Batignolles, Hôpital Louis, Ternes, School of Medicine, Quarries of Montmartre, Social of the Schools, Marmite, 2nd and 4th Groups, Brantôme, Silversmiths, Weavers of all kinds, Lithographers, Mechanics, Bakers

Reading of the minutes; are adopted.

Coupry: Four delegates from the Batignolles section were designated for the Federal Council. I'm sorry that two of the four are missing. The newspaper *La République des Travailleurs* seems to want to go its own way.

This attitude is censurable.

Rouveyrolles: The working class isn't very concerned about sending us its delegates.

Mélin: The war found the corporation of lithographers disunited. Today it is getting back together and is working on the return of German lithographers to their workshops. The corporation is determined to reject those who have no international ties with them.

Reading of a statement on this subject. A communication is announced.

Tabouret: The work inflicted on bakers is oppressive. It is needlessly done at night, and this separates us from society and our families. Sleeping during the daytime, it's as if we live cut off from the world, and we also can't share in a communion of ideas with workers. The bakers request the support of the International.

A strike of bakers would have a serious influence on society.

Frankel: Varlin and I dealt with this social question. We demonstrated that in the Middle Ages bakers only worked during the day and they even celebrated the holidays of the times. There were about 100 days off a year.

Goullé: The bakers can give a report for the paper.

Varlin: Now that flour is lacking, the moment would be poorly chosen. That corporation was lacking in strength a few months ago; it would be even worse now.

I request a motion.

Chalain: I'm amazed that the Federal Council is discussing such a question at this time when the political situation is so threatening.

Varlin: Many corporations are in the same situation as the bakers. When I went to the provinces I saw entire centers emasculated by a horrible poverty. The sole remedy would be this: becoming a powerful political body so we can act ourselves.

Bachruch: I request a motion

Rouveyrolles: The bakers have been granted our assistance; the communication will be examined. I put the motion to a vote.

The motion is accepted.

Chalain: The Eastern section is fomenting discord among us. The Federal Council must carry out its mandate without taking that opposition into account. We set up vigilance councils in the arrondissements. They might once have been useful, but today it is urgent that everyone join together within the Federal Council. I request that we name delegations to go to the sections.

Frankel: This was already done and produced no results.

Balleret: The International must strive to gain ground in politics.

Goullé: Newspaper commission. It is urgent that we put out a manifesto when we take possession of *La Lutte à Outrance*.

Varlin: This is a question that must be resolved within the editorial commission. For my part, I'm convinced that there is no time to waste given the events.

Chalain: The manifesto of the International society must clearly vote the question of social liquidation. The Empire left 16 million in debt, and the war and waste have left as much. Liquidation is inevitable, and this must be told to the bourgeois.

Rouveyrolles: These proposed manifestoes must be written. It is regrettable that they haven't been.

Lacord: The International has misunderstood its role; the workers should have seized power on September 4, and it must be done today. If on the first day the International had remained on its path, everything would have turned out differently, particularly October 31. Everything is disorganized today, and the International must understand that its very existence is at stake. It could have killed the government if an organ of its own would have demonstrated the government's faults to the public as it committed them, the newspaper having been exclusively in the hands of our classes. In order to study the vital questions of the moment I propose that sessions be held daily. The International is unaware of its true strength, which is considerable. The public believes it rich and united.

Rouveyrolles: The International has always concerned itself with politics, and in criticizing it we forget that the sections are ruined, that their members are dispersed. If the public knew all this it would see how weak we are and the Association would quickly crumble.

Mélin: A manifesto not supported by effective forces would be a failure; it would be an October 31.

Frankel: Our newspaper will be a force. I have a proposed manifesto.

Reading of the proposal.

A. Lévi: The manifesto of the Federal Council is good when it comes to ideas, but it doesn't sufficiently follow our current direction. What constituted the force of the International was not limiting itself to fighting only for French workers, but rather expanding to the proletariat of the universe. In 1848 we too wanted to reform society from top to bottom. Past experience seems to prove that the surest means of becoming a fearsome power is to group workers by corporation. Each group will have its own rules and representation on a Central Council. The newspaper will be the organ of the Council and the corporations.

Varlin: Frankel's proposal, even though its ideas are excellent, is an article and not a manifesto. It is indispensable that a manifesto take possession of the newspaper in the name of the Federal Council. The International didn't want to engage in personal politics; it left this to public meetings. Personally, I don't regret this. Given the events, I think frequent sessions are indispensable.

Rouveyrolles: Citizen Lacord proposes four sessions per week and Citizen Varlin three. I'll consult the Council and then we'll vote.

Vote: There will be sessions Tuesday, Thursday, and Saturday at 8:00. Voted unanimously.

Session adjourned at 11:30.

The secretary,

Henri Goullé

Session of January 26

Chairman, Frankel; Assistant, Noro.

Present are: School of Medicine, Brantôme, Hôpital Louis, Richard-Lenoir, Faubourg Antoine, Couronnes, Ternes, Marmite 2nd Group, Shoe Cutters, Silversmiths, Mechanics, Study Circle, Cobblers, Weavers of all kinds.

Reading of the minutes—observations.

Lacord remarks that certain passages could become dangerous for us if copies were to get into the wrong hands. Rouveyrolles, according to the minutes, said that the International was weak. The judgments that the members of the Federal Council are called upon to formulate at sessions should not be known to the public. With this in mind, the secretary should judge these passages and eliminate those compromising for the Association.

Frankel: I join in with Lacord's observation. On the subject of the bakers and the support they are requesting, I used the word "difficulty" and not "impossibility."

The minutes are adopted.

Méligne: My section subscribed to the newspaper. Where are with *La Lutte à Outrance*?

Lacord: The club of the School of Medicine, which bore the costs of *La Lutte à Outrance* no longer exists. I have been busy with this newspaper these past days and, without being certain of it, I think it will continue to appear. I'll give you a definitive answer Tuesday.

Varlin: This newspaper is in danger of no longer appearing; we can no longer count on it. Misfortune has harshly struck the Ternes and Batignolles sections during the siege. The deaths of associates leave us with seven orphans in our charge.

Lacord: I wrote a manifesto. I only have enough money to publish 200 copies.

Reading of the manifesto—Approbation.

It is resolved that we will seek a means of publishing it.

A devoted man offers us 1,500 francs to start up a newspaper. I think that this proposal will be carried out and that we will have an organ which, conquering a powerful political place through our name and proudly brandishing the banner of the International, will become our spokesman and will discuss, in the name of the workers, the political questions upon which depend the fate of the country.

Starting today we want to attack the authors of those criminal undertakings that spread discord between the army, the Mobile Guards, and the National Guard.

Varlin: *La République des Travailleurs* will probably not appear next Saturday; funds are lacking. No longer having a newspaper would we could join in with some republican groups to publish a brochure that will make the truth known concerning the events of January 22. In the face of the capitulation, the International did its duty.

Lacord: *La Lutte à Outrance* can die with dignity: it can have itself suppressed by publishing an appeal to the army.

Goullé: The population is rotten. If the Federal Council wants to accept the responsibility, let's openly publish our opinion of the political situation. For my part, I don't think the people will support us.

Lacord: We shouldn't lose hope. If they abandon us let us remain the International, that is, an association of practical men, marching alone with our heads high.

Frankel: We should worry less about January 22 and more about the future.

Varlin: Currently the solid element, that is the workers, are lacking. They are happy with indemnities of 1 fr. 50 c. and .75 c . for their wives.

Goullé: If we don't remain strongly united in the face of the bourgeoisie, which is already organizing itself to reduce salaries after the war, we would be failing in our duty.

Frankel: The delegates are speaking the language of discouragement. The situation was so serious that it disoriented everyone. By making propaganda we will bring the people back to us.

The clubs, the leagues did nothing. They dropped Paris when they could have saved it. The Prussians are going to enter, the bourgeoisie will flatter them in order to maintain its power and privileges, and it will pass on to us the costs that will result from the war.

Lacord: We've talked enough; we first have to see to bringing back the workers and then have workers among those in power.

Noro: The sections must be recomposed. I request that the federal council name delegates who will go wake them up.

Varlin: *La République des Travailleurs* and *La Lutte à Outrance* will probably never reappear. Let's search for a means of starting a new newspaper. The only means we have of becoming strong is reorganizing the International.

Méligne: In this situation events could occur that will be favorable to us. We must be ready to benefit from the circumstances.

Hardy: The republic is in danger. We must unite with the republicans to defend it.

Frankel: I ask the assembly if it doesn't judge it urgent to vote, that in case of anything serious occurs all sections are to meet here.

The proposal is voted unanimously.

The session is adjourned at 11:00.

The Secretary,

Goullé

Session of February 15

Chairman, Avrial; Assistant, Frankel.

Are present: Social Studies Circle, East, Brantôme, Hôpital Louis, La Station and Bercy, Couronnes.

Reading of the minutes. They are adopted.

Communications:

Piau reads a letter from Ledoré of Brest. Resolution: Citizen Piau will publish this letter individually.

Avrial: *La Petite Presse* announces that Victor Hugo and Louis Blanc are honorary chairmen of the International and that Malon and Tolain have received a deposit of 20,000 francs of the 200,000 francs that the International allocates to them annually while they are deputies. It is urgent this be rectified.

Serailler: We must first make a rectification on the subject of the posters of the four committees. This notice in *La Petite Presse* is an affair of the same order. The only thing I see that should be corrected is the statement on our chairmen. As for the 200,000 francs, it is to our advantage to let them believe that we are rich.

Frankel: I'm satisfied to see the bourgeoisie and the newspapers pay attention to us and fear us.

Babick: *La Petite Presse* is a newspaper of little value. There's no reason to concern ourselves with what it says.

Goullé: The only response should be addressing three lines to *La Petite Presse* to declare that the International has neither chairmen nor chiefs, nothing more. If not, this newspaper will write two columns on the International in order to start a polemic with us. This would be a way of minting money.

Frankel proposes the agenda. It is adopted.
    Agenda: On the Reorganization of the Association.

Frankel: Since September 4 events have dispersed the International. It is urgent we reconstitute the sections so they can again find the strength that is necessary to them. We have a moral strength, if not in France at least in Paris. Material strength is lacking due to lack of organization. Many associates don't understand the goal of the Association. In addition, we have made up a list of socialist candidates and many members haven't understood the reasons that had us put forward obscure names instead of Louis Blanc and Victor Hugo. We want to make a few International workers deputies. It is regrettable that people haven't better understood the goal we should pursue. We need a virile organization and disciplined sections with their own regulations that participate in our labors with their own delegates and who remain dedicated to the international idea; active tireless, unflinching. Under these conditions we will be ready and mightily constituted on the day of action, however unforeseen its arrival.

Avrial: I announced in the newspapers the creation of a proletarian section in the 11th arrondissement. Here is a sample of the statutes: "Every worker is a member of the resistance society of his corporation. The proof of honorable means of existence will be demanded of every postulant."
    The council approves unanimously.

Two elements are needed in the Federal Council: the grouping of manual laborers and the thorough study of social questions. It will be difficult to reconstitute the International. The lack of work has created poverty, and we need faithfully paid dues to publish newspapers, brochures, and to go to the provincial centers.

Theisz: The International must become the social government itself in the future. The worker's societies are formed with difficulty today; the sections are constituted more easily. The worker's societies are inevitably destined for the daily struggle of the wage earners. We know how difficult this task is, encumbered with a thousand absorbing details. The sections, with a good political and social spirit, are called upon to dominate over public opinion. I thus propose to the Federal Committee to march resolutely into the future and, to open the way to it, I ask you to name a commission especially dedicated to carry out an investigation within each section and to prepare a report that will be submitted to you. The members of this commission shall be the spokesman of the Federal Commission and will develop the ideas of the Federal Commission in the sections. A split was produced in the last elections. It is deplorable to have seen a section risk approaches to the bourgeoisie.

Demay: It is urgent we have sections in every arrondissement.

Babick: We must decide if we will have sections by arrondissement or neighborhood, and if several are of the same arrondissement or neighborhood we could invite them to unify.

Hamet: For today I am against arrondissement sections. We must first reconstitute the International. Let us pass to Theisz's proposal.

Avrial: It is with reason that the statutes leave to the sections the right of creating and regulating themselves. I place Theisz's proposal under discussion.

Frankel: I support Theisz's proposal for the reconstituting of the International. I also would like us to consult on the means for having a newspaper and that we name secretaries to renew relations with France and overseas.

Serailler: We too busy ourselves with the sections and not enough with the Federal Council, which has not met its obligations.

The General Council in London has never had enough information from the Federal Council to know the situation of the French section of the International. It is urgent to reconstitute both the International and the Federal Council, and to name secretaries who will immediately correspond with overseas and the General Council.

A fusion of all dissidents is indispensable. In agreement with the Eastern section, several sections have named a new Federal Council. All offer to have it be seated here and to meld it with you, if you want to go forward.

In London the International is a political power of the first order. If a social movement breaks out THE INTERNATIONAL IS READY in England. This is not the case in France.

Goullé: The French proletarian doesn't have that atrocious and hideous English poverty as a goad. Nor does it have that patient and tenacious energy. But it also has its qualities, ardor and daring: these are the two elements we must seize. Unfortunately, since September 4 the associates have forgotten their duty, and so we haven't followed the career we should have. It is the future we must think of now. I support Theisz's proposal.

Theisz's proposal is voted unanimously. Named members of the commission are: Theisz, Frankel, Rochat, Babick, Goullé Piau, Pagnerre, Hamet, Demay, and Bernard.

The session is adjourned at 11:15.

The Secretary,

Goullé

Session of February 22

President, Varlin; Assistant, Pindy.

Present are: Study Circle, Eastern, School of Medicine, Hôpital Louis, Gobelins, Ternes, Batignolles, Couronne, Richard-Lenoir, Rècollets, Brantôme, Faubourg Antoine, Temple, Poisonnière, Designers, Bookbinders.

Reading of the Minutes.

Theisz: The phrase "the split that occurred was a scandal" etc. poorly translates what I expressed. It distorts a conciliatory idea. I request a rectification.

The Federal Council, after having voted the rectification, adopts the minutes.

Pindy reads the minutes of the session of February 11 of the Gobelins section.

Picard, in the name of the Richard-Lenoir section, proposes a peaceful demonstration on February 24 to energetically affirm the republican leanings of the people of Paris.

Combault denies the appropriateness of such a demonstration, in which the people won't follow us.

Rollet adds that a demonstration could serve as a pretext for violence against the people. This must be avoided in the current circumstances.

Ridet: A demonstration could have as a result proving that the Parisians are disposed to do anything to preserve the republic and to bring along with us that hesitant mass which at certain moments rallies to strength and number.

Frankel: While being very sympathetic to the demonstration, I contest the importance that it might have amidst current events. It is urgent to see to study and organization; what is happening before our eyes strongly demonstrates this. We must study the special questions, those of rent and general unemployment. The sections must participate in their areas in this labor and do it quickly. It is necessary to coordinate all our ideas, all our judgments, and to sum them up in a mandate to be given to Malon and Tolain, who are sitting in the Assembly and who must make heard the will of the workers. I move that we reject any discussion on the demonstration.

The assembly votes the motion. Each section will judge if it wants to take part individually in the demonstration.

Babick, Rochat, and Frankel, delegates to the sections, report on their mission:

We inform the Federal Council that our approach to the sections to propose to them the reconstitution voted by the Federal Council was well received and we have the satisfaction of seeing seated here tonight the delegates of the sections that we visited over the past few days.

Frankel: I would like to see the work of reconstruction go more quickly. We should also reconstitute the sections of the department of the Seine. I will never tire of requesting of the Federal Council the creation of an organ of the Association.

Journalism is the most powerful means of propaganda. It is urgent that dues regularly come in going forward. The Federal Council needs money to found a newspaper and to send delegates to the provinces to give immense publicity to International principles. In this way we will bring together in the Association a considerable number of workers. I request the nomination of a commission for the elaboration of new statutes fro the Federal Council.

The proposal is put to a vote and adopted.

Named members are: Pindy, Rochat, Theisz, Babaick, Lacord, Déliot, Frankel, and Varlin.

Ridet: I ask that every member of a section of the International be held to join the resistance society of his corporation and the worker's society of the union.

Malézieux: There are worker's societies that are animated by the worst political and social spirits. A citizen devoted to the principles of the International Association cannot join his corporation's society if the latter is reactionary.

Varlin: The last congress invited all workers to unite in the resistance societies of their corporation. Consequently, I am of the opinion that we should invite the members of all sections to become members of their respective unions.

Rochat: I request that we insist that Internationals join the resistance societies. This is a primordial duty for every socialist, and it is absolutely indispensable that we solidly constitute all corporative societies, for this alone is our true force for the future.

Goullé: The bourgeois and the industrial are feverishly organizing all across France, preparing themselves for the inevitable struggles in the political field and on that of wage labor. Sick of lawyers, they are seriously thinking of themselves investigating the pretentions of the working class, pretentions that are causing them much worry. In the face of the activity of the bourgeoisie, I am of the opinion that we should loudly affirm our social demands. Our sections in the provinces must be reborn, more closely united with us than ever. They each must become, in their electoral circumscriptions, a political center, respected by friends and feared by enemies, and with power over public opinion. This daring forward march seems necessary for the building of the future. A newspaper and money in our hands would be unquestionably useful to the interests of the Association. It would be good to start immediately to write to our sections in the provinces and to precisely establish our situation on each of these points.

Frankel: I propose to place on the agenda of our next session the discussion of the statutes of the Federal Commission that the Commission will have elaborated.

The motion is accepted.

Pindy gives a reading of the letter of General Cluseret.

The Federal Commission decides that this letter will be published at its expense and sold by it.

The meeting is adjourned at 11:45.

The Secretary,

Henri Goullé

P.S. Citizen Secretaries of the sections are requested to read the minutes of the Federal Commission in session

Session of March 1

Chairman, Pindy; Assistant, Varlin.

Present are: Study Circle, Couronnes, East, Gobelins, School of Medicine, Hôpital Louis, Poisonnière, Récollets, Faubourg du Temple, Social of the Schools, Station and Bercy, Vertbois, Richard-Lenoir, Marmite, 2nd group, House Painters.

Reading of the Minutes.

Rochat: The minutes don't indicate the presence of the delegates of the house painters.

The minutes are adopted with this rectification.

Frankel: The large number of National Guardsmen on service tonight explains the absence of many delegates.

Urgent Communication—Central Committee of the National Guard.

Varlin: It is urgent that the Internationals do everything possible to have themselves named delegates in their companies and be seated on the Central Committee. I request the nomination of a commission of four members who will go to this committee, who will judge if and on what subjects the International should concern itself, and which will then provide this information to the Federal Commission.

Chouteau denounces a slander that he is victim of and demands an inquiry.

Pindy: This accusation is made by Chauvière of the International. This should be taken before the members of Chouteau's section and not before the Federal Commission. I propose a vote of the Federal Commission.

The Federal Council votes that the affair will be taken before the Social Studies Circle (the section to which Chouteau belongs).

Frankel: Communication: Three weeks ago the ministry was changed in Austria, an amnesty was granted, and our brothers in these countries freed. In Hungary, in Pest, Bachruch and our friends provoke public meetings where they speak in favor of France.

Rochat: It would be good if, in agreement with the sections, the International were to put out a manifesto addressed to all workers on the occasion of the peace.

Hamet: It would be prudent to wait until the peace is concluded.

Pindy: It is useful to see to this now because of the delays in printing.

Frankel: I don't understand the hurry to put out a manifesto now. Let's give the Germans a bit of a respite so they can have the time to reflect.

Bidet: I think we must act promptly in the heat of indignation.

Varlin: I join in with Frankel's opinion. I think we must write a manifesto made of reason and cool judgment.

Theisz: We must have the Federal Chamber join with us and we'll put out this manifesto together, outside the delegations of the twenty arrondissements, this group having an activity that is strictly Parisian.

The Federal Commission votes:

A commission will be named.

It will write a manifesto in concert with the Federal Chamber.

The delegation of the twenty arrondissements will not participate in this.

Named to the commission for the Federal Council: Varlin, Frankel, and Theisz.

Central Committee of the National Guard

Varlin: Let's go there, not as Internationals but as National Guardsmen and work to gain possession of the spirit of that assembly.

Frankel: This resembles a compromise with the bourgeoisie; I want no part of it. Our road is international and we must not stray from this path.

Lacord: We must absolutely prevent the National Guard from placing itself behind reaction, as took place in the first round of voting. These people come to us thanks to the influence the International has conquered. Why should we push them away?

Hamet: The commission that we will name should gather information inside this committee and give us a report at the next session.

Clamous: In having ourselves named delegates in our companies we conquer a real force; we must use this method. We will thus know who we are marching with.

Bidet: Tonight I had the proof that Vinoy is no longer obeyed. The soldiers of the line want to avoid any conflict with the people. Vinoy sent it to get the cannons on the Place Royale. The National Guard refused to hand them over. The soldiers didn't insist.

Babick: The influence of these events is considerable. This can be of an immense advantage.

Pindy: We seem to forget that there a risk in this of compromising the International.

Frankel: No one here can commit the International before having consulted his section.

Goullé: It's not a matter of committing the International. It's a question of having Internationals among the delegates form the companies and four members on the Central Committee to act in their own name and to keep the Federal Council informed.

Clamous: It is socialists who are at the head of the affair.

Varlin: The men of this committee who we found suspect were removed and replaced by socialists who want to have among them four delegates serving as a liaison between themselves and the International. If we remain alone in the face of such a force our influence will disappear, and if we are united with this committee we will be taking an important step towards the social future.

Babick: Let's accept the elements we are offered and use them with the reservations commanded by prudence. I oppose Pindy and Frankel, but in all this I want the International to be completely protected.

Bidet: There is nothing wrong with naming four delegates with the reservations to their mandate well established, but there would be something wrong in not doing it, for if the socialists of this committee are to march forward, it would be sheer folly for the International to refuse them its tacit assistance.

Charbonneau: You say that the committee has become socialist. At its beginnings it was reactionary. I remain mistrustful. Consequently, I support the nomination of four members. They will have a specific mandate and will only involve themselves with the social struggle.

Rouveyrolles: The socialists who have gone forward in the interests of the people request support: it would constitute desertion not to give it.

Pindy: I am going to have the proposition voted in the following form, which results from the discussion:

A commission of four members is delegated to the Central Committee of the National Guard;

Its actions there will be individual and expressly reserved as concerns the International Workingmen's Association for France.

The assembly adopts. Secretariat: Goullé and Varlin are named secretaries for France.

Lacord proposes an office in the Corderie (postponed due to lack of funds). Commission for the Revision of the Statutes of the Federal Council.

The work is not yet finished. The question will be part of the agenda of the next session.

The meeting is adjourned at 11:15.

The secretary,

Henri Goullé

Minutes of the Session of the Federal Council of March 8, 1871

Chairman, Combault; Assistant, Piau.

Present are: Study Circle, Couronnes, Est, Gobelins, School of Medicine, Marmite, 1st and 2nd groups, Wood gilders, Social of the Schools, Hôpital Louis, Ternes, Batignolles, Récollets, Faubourg du Temple, Station and Bercy, Vaugirard, Pantheon, Poissonière, Brantôme, Montrouge.

Reading of the minutes: Adopted.

Introduction of communications.

Combault requests that the Ternes section's communication concerning cannons be dealt with urgently.

Franquin proposes referring the question to the Central Committee.

Lévis: The question is more than urgent; it is pressing.

Hamet: I move that we hold off on the discussion till the two groups who are to join with us tonight are here.

Buisset: I support the urgency. Perhaps tomorrow the citizens of Monmartre will be forced to surrender the cannons.

It is adopted by a large majority that this discussion will take place at the meeting of the three groups.

Agenda—Revision of the statutes.

Frankel: The condition has more or less finished its work, and the discussion can begin at the next session. If Theisz, who is the reporter of the commission, were present the introduction of statutes would take place this evening.

Combault proposes on this subject that the Federal Commission meet Saturday March 11. Adopted.

Goullé announces, in the name of the Study Circle, the state of penury in which our friends in Brest find themselves and requests that the Federal Commission vote to come to their assistance.

Franquin: There's no need to vote; it's enough to notify the sections of this fact and they will subscribe.

Lévy Lazare, a propos of the manifesto aimed at the Germans that the International should issue, doesn't want us to engage yet again in written propaganda. The time for action, he says, has come.

Combault adjourns the session for the meeting of the three groups at 10:00.

The Secretary,
Hamet

Session of the Federal Council of March 15, 1871

Chairman, Theisz; Assistant, Frankel.

Present are: Couronnes, Popincourt, Ternes, Récollets, Poissonière, Brantôme, Study Circle, East, Marmite, first three groups, Gobelins, Lithographers, Wood Gilders, Social of the Schools, Batignolles, Bronze Workers, Silversmith, Faubourg du Temple, Bercy and the Station, Pantheon, Hôpital Louis, School of Medicine, Strasbourg.

Communication:

Goullé communicates a letter from Citizen Gambon as well as a notice from Citizen Pyat. The former consults the International on the proper conduct given the attitude of the National Assembly.

Frankel: It seems to me that this consultation comes a bit late.

After discussion:

Theisz proposes inviting Pyat, Gambon, Malon, and Tolain to present themselves to us at the session of the Tuesday, the 22nd of this month in order to discuss how they should conduct themselves.

Combault proposes also inviting Millière, Ranc, Tridon, Rochefort, and Langois

The two proposals are adopted.

Babick makes mention of the part he took in the reorganization of the Combat section; he incited that section to change its name.

Avrial is of the opinion that we should reconstitute all the sections in order to expel those who made the International deviate from its goal. We need a defined program.

Buisset supports Avrial. In the name of the Social Section of the Schools he proposes to place on the agenda of the sections "On the necessity of soon holding a congress of the International in Paris."

Frankel: First we have to constitute the Federal Council and then hold a national congress.

Buisset insists on his proposal. Two members of his section have returned from Leipzig; the spirit of the Internationals there is excellent.

His proposal is adopted.

Macdonel makes, in the name of the Faubourg du Temple section, the proposal to also place on the agenda of the sections the question of rent.

After the communication of the decisions taken on this subject by that section, the assembly adopts the proposal unanimously.

Piau requests that the Federal Council grant him a mandate to found sections in the provinces, given that he will be going there in a few days.

This proposal is adopted.

Franquin requests of the Federal Council that he be authorized to advance 50 francs from the treasury for the Internationals of Brest.

This proposal, at first opposed, is unanimously adopted.

Pindy communicates a letter from Citizen Gommier requesting an audience tomorrow for Citizen Wolf, the latter having a "semi-official communication to give on the part of the English branch."

Delegated to this effect are Franquin, Pindy, and Rochat.

Frankel, corresponding secretary for overseas, communicates the results of the German elections and finds them deplorable. The progressive party had the upper hand; from the social point of view it is a reactionary party.

Combault quotes a letter from Karl Marx, reproduced in *Paris-Journal*, interpreted as a Prussian order given to us. The Federal Commission must rectify this.

Various citizens place the letter's authenticity in doubt.

Rochat: This is a police newspaper. If the letter exists it was communicated by the police. In both cases, let's leave the newspaper to the police.

Frankel: If the Federal Council authorizes me to do it, I'll officially write to Citizen Marx. If not, I'll write to him personally and I'll know what the true story is about this insertion.

It is adopted that Citizen ***Frankel*** be authorized to write.

A citizen proposes to go investigate at the offices of *Paris-Journal*. This proposal is roundly rejected. Several citizens announce the creation of new revolutionary newspapers.

Buisset announces the reappearance of *La Marseillaise*.

Bertin recalls that a commission had once been named to organize in a newspaper a separate section that would be the official section of the International.

Hamet was a member of the commission that addressed itself to *La Marseillaise* for this. He thinks that after *Le Mot d'Ordre* the editors of the previously cited newspaper will not favorably receive our proposal.

Theisz: We must spread about our communications as much as possible and place them in several newspapers, but we must also wait until we can have an organ that belongs to us.

Theisz, reporter of the commission on statutes, gives a reading of a proposal, which is annexed to these minutes by decision of the Federal Council.

Buisset requests a discussion in a fortnight.

Frankel wants it immediately.

Theisz objects to the meeting with the deputies.

Dupius supports the suspension for a fortnight, which is adopted unanimously.

The meeting is adjourned at 11:30.

The secretary,

Hamet

N.B. The minutes will only be sent to those delegates who commit to reading them in their sections. The Marmites display them.

(Note by Secretary Hamet.)

Report of Commission on the Statutes of the Federal Council

Article 1: There is established between the Parisian sections of the International Association a federation having as its goal the facilitating of relations of every nature between the various groups of workers.

This federation is represented by a Federal Council.

Organization of Sections

Article 2: The sections are organized and in the department of the Seine by arrondissement, neighborhood or commune.

Article 3: All sections belonging to another arrondissement, whatever their number, must establish relations among themselves by a delegation of two of their members in order to come to agreement on everything having to do with the interests of the arrondissement.

Article 4: Every section preserves its autonomy in questions of organization and internal regulation, as long as they are in conformity with the general spirit and statutes of the International. They also preserve their freedom of appreciation of the solution to social questions.

Article 5: The sections are to meet at least once a fortnight to cooperate in the work of the federation and to study one of the questions which the workers are interested in.

Article 6: All manual laborers, employees, and wage earners shall be accepted as members of the International Association who, after an investigation by the section which they were members of, can justify their morality.

The sections can also admit citizens who, without exercising a manual profession, have adopted and defended the principles of the International, but their admission must be ratified by the Federal Council.

Article 7: Any member wanting to found a section must make a preliminary declaration to the Federal Council, which takes note of this declaration.

Constitution of the Federal Council

Article 8: The Federal Council is composed of delegates from all the federated sections.

The number of delegates is regulated as follows:

A section with up to fifty members is represented by one delegate; from 51-100 by 2; from 101-300 by 3; from 310-600 by 4; from 601-1000 by 5; and more than 1000 by 6.

Each section will name an equal number of alternate delegates.

The delegates of each section must possess a mandate signed by the secretary and the treasurer of the section.

Article 9: Those sections formed outside of Paris, in the department of the Seine, which cannot regularly send their delegates, must correspond at least once per month with the secretary of the Federal Council.

Article 10: Each section names and changes its delegates as it deems fit; it only must communicate this to the secretary of the sessions of the Federal Council.

Article 11: At the first sessions of April and October the Federal Council will name its bureau, formed of:

A treasurer, a secretary of the session, a corresponding secretary of the department of the Seine, two correspondents for the other departments of France and two for overseas, one of whom will be specially charged with correspondence with the General Council of the International Association.

The members of the bureau are revocable at any moment by the council. Vacancies are to be immediately filled.

Article 12: The Secretary of the Department of the Seine is charged with corresponding with those communes supporting the Paris Commune. If necessary he will assist the other secretaries of France.

Article 13: The secretary charged with the minutes of sessions must give the transcript in extensor, which will be signed and sent to each section. He will put in order the correspondence addressed to the Federal Council.

Article 14: The secretaries charged with the correspondence with other departments must have permanent contact with the sections and Federal Councils of these departments so that all groups can act in concert to defend the interests of the workers.

Article 15: The corresponding secretaries for the exterior must have permanent contacts with all the Central Bureaus of other countries.

The secretary charged most specially with correspondence with the General Council must send it a report every month on the situation of the International in the department of the Seine.

Article 16: All corresponding secretaries will keep a book with copies of letters they've sent; they will give the letters received to the secretary of the sessions.

Article 17: The treasurer must inscribe in the ledger book all receipts and expenses, article by article. Every month he will submit to the delegates the balance of the accounts of the federation, and every three months he will communicate to the sections the balance sheet of the accounting during the quarter.

Article 18: In cases where one of the functionaries shall cease to be delegated by the section he is a member of the Federal Council reserves the right to maintain him in his function until the end of the term fixed by the regulations, but it cannot grant him a deliberative vote in the sessions.

Attributes of the Federal Council; relations of the Council with the federated sections.

Article 19: Only the Federal Council is authorized to represent the Parisian sections of the International Workingmen's Association.

It discusses the proposals addressed to it, decides on those of a purely administrative character, and submits all others to the discussion and vote of all the sections.

It gathers information on the new sections, investigates the reasons that determine a section to cease to be represented in the federation, and points out the negligence of delegates.

It carries out investigations of those sections that stray from the goals indicated by the general statutes of the International.

Article 20: In conformity with the Basel Resolution, the Federal Council can refuse the affiliation of a section or expel it, without being able to deprive it of its international character, the General Council alone having the right to pronounce a suspension and the congress suppression.

Article 21: The Federal Council only has the right to pronounce expulsion, to make resolutions, to formulate a program or a report of principles in the name of the Parisian sections after having consulted the majority opinion from all sections, i.e., after having consulted all of them.

The vote is settled by an absolute majority of votes counted for each section in accordance with the number of delegates that represent them.

Article 22: The sections are only responsible for resolutions adopted by the Federal Council except insofar as they adhere to them through their votes. Every resolution rendered public must relate the number and title of the sections that adopted it.

Article 23: Before publishing any resolution, manifesto, program, etc, every section must communicate it to the Federal Council. In cases where the resolution is not taken into consideration, if the section persists in rendering it public, it must mention its purely individual character and free the other contracting sections of responsibility.

Article 24: Every two months a social question shall be studied in the sections, and the reports of these discussions, followed by the conclusions adopted by each of them, shall be given to the Federal Council, which must give them the greatest publicity possible.

Article 25: The Federal Council should actively work at the creation of a newspaper aimed at the propagation of the ideas of the International. The editing of this newspaper shall be placed under its surveillance and the editors must be revocable. This newspaper should be sent to the federations of the departments and overseas. Every Parisian section shall commit to acquire at least one issue.

Article 26: In addition, the Federal Council will work at active propaganda in the departments in favor of the principles of the International. To this effect it can send delegates with a special mandate.

Article 27: If needed, the Federal Council will lend its assistance to the Federal Chamber of Workers' Societies to create societies in all corporations. The members of the Association are invited to facilitate this assistance by attaching themselves to the workers' societies of their professions or by contributing to the creation of new societies in cases where those that exist refuse to join the International.

Article 28: The Federation of Parisian sections will be represented every year by one or several delegates at the general congress of the International Association.

Article 29: For its various expenses the Federal Council disposes of the following budget: one of the delegates must pay the treasurer the sum calculated at the first assembly of the month.

After a month in arrears the suspension of the section is implemented; its delegates no longer have a vote on the Federal Council. After three months its removal is pronounced.

The Federal Council can, with supporting reasons, vote expenses greater than its budget and indicate the proportional share of each section. But in this case only the sections that voted the expenses are responsible; for the others the contribution is only recommended.

Article 30: Every month in the signed minutes and via the press, the Federal Council will publish a listing of member sections in arrondissement order.

Article 31: Any section wanted to be part of the Parisian federation must deposit two copies of its statues and its regulations, one of which is for the General Council. (General Regulations, Art. 14)

Article 32: In conformity with Resolution 5 of Basel, the General Council, before admitting or refusing the affiliation of a new sections formed in Paris, must consult the Parisian federation.

Meetings of the Federal Council, General Assemblies

Article 33: The Federal Council holds its regular sessions every Tuesday at 8:00 p.m.

Article 34: Convocations for extraordinary sessions must be signed by the secretary of the sessions and by the corresponding secretaries.

In the case where a meeting of the Federal Council and the Federal Chamber of Worker's Societies is judged necessary, the signature of the corresponding secretary should be replaced by that of one of the delegates of the Council to said chamber.

No convocation is valid without this formality.

Article 35: In case of emergency, the Federal Council, gathered without convocation, can only pass resolutions if there is as a majority of the federated Parisian sections. The members of foreign sections passing through Paris and members of sections can attend sessions.

Article 36: Every three months the sections will gather in a general assembly to strengthen the ties of solidarity among them, to determine the line of conduct of the Federation, and to discuss the management of the Council.

Relations between the Federal Council and the Worker's Societies

Article 37: The International Association being represented in Paris by the arrondissement sections and the worker's societies, those of the latter who have joined the International shall name a delegate charged with representing them on the Federal Council and to come to an agreement with the secretaries for international correspondence.

Reciprocally, it will delegate three of its members to represent it in the federal chamber.

Revision of Statutes

Article 39: The statutes can be revised by the Federal Council on the request of one or several groups, communicated at least one month in advance to all federated sections.

The revision must be accepted by the majority of the arrondissement groups represented and by the majority of delegates of all the affiliated sections, counting the votes proportionally to the number of their members.

For the commission,

The reporter,

Theisz

The present regulations are on the agenda for March 29, 1871.

Copy certified and annexed to the minutes of the session of March 15.

The secretary,

Hamet

By decision of the Federal Council taken at the session of March 15 the present proposal is submitted for study by the sections, which, where appropriate, shall modify the above articles.

The delegates are to bring the decisions of their sections concerning these articles and submit their amendments at the next session of the Federal Council.

The secretary,

Hamet

Session of the Federal Council of March 22

Chairman, Rouveyrolles; Assistant, Goullé.

Present are: Couronnes, Hôpital Louis, Brantôme, Study Circle, Gobelins, Marble workers, Silversmits, Bercy and the Station, Chateau-Rouge and Batignolles.

Reading of the two last minutes. They are adopted.

Piau didn't think it necessary to send to Brest the 50 francs voted, because of the recent events.

Goullé saw citizen Pyat; the latter acceded to our request and will attend our session.

Malon expressed the most anxious doubts on the possibility of conciliation between the municipalities and the Central Committee, as well as on the success of elections to the Commune. He fears we won't be able to avoid a bloody conflict.

Goullé: The International has only one member on the Committee: Varlin. So it is free of any responsibility.

Jacquemin: We have to know if the Committee doesn't compromise the republic.

Goullé: I propose inserting in the newspapers a summons of the Federal Council inviting the sections and worker's societies to present themselves tomorrow the 23rd at 8:00 p.m. Adopted.

Spoetler: It would be good if at tomorrow's session we were to appeal to the sections and workers' societies and that, by decision of these groups, we invited the Committee to place its powers in the hands of the municipalities.

Rouveyrolles: If the Committee were to hand over its powers it would be into the hands of the armed people, given that it emanates from them, and it would invite them to see to its immediate replacement.

The question is placed on tomorrow's agenda.

The meeting is adjourned at 11:15.

The secretary of the session,

Dupuis

Session of March 23, 1871 of the International and Federal Chambers

Chairman, Theisz; Assistant, Rouveyrolles.

Present are: Couronnes, Hôpital Louis, Wood Gilders, Gobelins, Social of the Schools, Brantôme, Study Circle, Marble workers, Silversmiths, The Station and Bercy, Château-Rouge, Batignolles, East, Marmite, 2nd group, Bronze workers, Mechanics, Ceramics, Faubourg du Temple, School of Medicine, Building carpenters, Panthéon, House painters (production), furniture carpenters, Rug makers, Toolmakers, Cabinetmakers, Tailors (syndical chamber), Marmite, 3rd group, Cooks, Weavers, Cobblers.

Bertin: This evening we must concern ourselves with the communal elections.

Frankel: The municipal council is nothing but the surveillance council of an association. This assimilation is so complete that at this time the question for all of us is no longer political, it is social. I am of the opinion that we should write a manifesto in which we will invite our people to vote the Commune.

Buisset wants the International to take an active part in the vote; he isn't a partisan of a manifesto.

Bertin: We must demand of our candidates an imperative mandate and resignations in advance.

Rouveyrolles: A number of things have been put on the back of the International. If we were to write a manifesto it would be essential to free it from these things.

Hamet: The sole question should be: what part can the International take in the elections?

Frankel: Let's write a manifesto; we'll reinforce the Central Committee with all our moral force.

Duchêne: Under the Empire the International loudly affirmed its principles; can it be mute under the republic?

Minet: We must be prudent. It isn't our persons who are in question; it's the institution and organization of the International. The latter officially named three delegates to act with the Central Committee.

Theisz wants to exculpate the International for this fact. The mandate given to the four delegates was to carry out an inquiry at that committee. If the delegates overstepped their mandate they might have done the right thing, but we can't be held responsible for this.

Rouveyrolles doesn't want us to offend those holding this or that idea. We are all in agreement on the action, but we can have different ideas concerning responsibility.

Frankel repeats that the question is purely social. Is it under the republic that the International would want to deny its goal and its past? I vote for a manifesto.

Boudet: We should give all our support to the republic when it becomes social.

Hevette: Today the International must have a militant responsibility.

Spoetler: The International, more idealistic than realistic, sees everything and makes much propaganda. I am for a manifesto, but I am against our throwing the workers' societies into this movement. An opinion was put forth yesterday that the International should be a mediator; after today's nominations idealism is no longer allowed us.

Hamet: The questions of compromise and responsibility find us all in agreement. Only the question of appropriateness divides us. We have chosen sides, so let's vote immediately. I request the closing of discussion.

Buisset would vote against cloture. We haven't discussed up to what point we could commit the responsibility of the International without having consulted our sections.

Cloture is pronounced. The question of appropriateness, placed to a vote, is adopted unanimously minus seven votes.

Bertin: In this manifesto we can only concern ourselves with the Commune.

Minet: If we were to concern ourselves with the Central Committee in our manifesto we would have to accept the responsibility for the pretended waste that reaction will accuse us of if we fail.

Theisz is not a partisan of the manifesto because the delegates are only the spokesmen for their sections, but as a citizen he is for a declaration of principles in which we will say that we want the organization of the Commune in a way different from that understood in Versailles. It is difficult to elaborate a manifesto this evening; we don't have enough time.

Frankel: We don't need to write a book; let's write a few lines to ensure the success of the elections by inviting our people to vote.

Hamet: Let's name a commission this evening charged with elaborating this manifesto that we will sign as delegates of the sections, but not in the name of our sections. Those sections not represented will adhere to the manifesto.

Spoetler would like that we make a unity list and that this list should figure at the end of the manifesto. His proposal is rejected. It is adopted that the writing of the manifesto will be done this evening and that it will be voted at the session. Named members of the commission are: Frankel, Theisz, and Demay.

The commission retires and on the proposal of Citizen Frankel the session changes form at 11:15.

Communication Hecklé and Very. Joining of the International of the rug makers and shoe cutters. These sections will take the names of their corporations.

The secretary,

Hamet

Sessions of the Federal Council of the Parisian Sections

Minutes of the session held on the night of March 23-24, 1871

Represented is The Rouennaise Federation.

Chairman, Spoetler; Assistants, Rouveyrolles, Aubry.

Relative to the adherence of the shoe cutters and rug makers, Citizen Nostag remarks that no measure was taken regarding the section and he doesn't know if it is affiliated with the Federation.

Goullé: It suffices to name two members who will carry out an inquiry on this subject.

Hamet: It is pointless to name new members; there is a commission charged with verifying the statutes of sections and ensuring their relations with the Federal Council. It is up to this commission to do the work.

Goullé: We would profit from the presence among us of Citizen Aubry to discuss the current social state of the provinces.

Nostag: It is necessary that we be able to bring true news of the movement in the provinces.

Aubry: Rouen is undecided. It is surprised to not find an intimate liaison between the Worker's Federation and the Central Committee. Nevertheless, the revolution of March 18 is entirely social and the newspapers throughout France cite the International as having seized power. We know that things are different. I think we would coordinate the movement by inviting the Central Committee to join the International.

Goullé: There is currently little we can expect from the provinces.

Hamet: The provinces are nothing but the existing power structure. The National Assembly, named to make peace, doesn't represent the sentiment of the provinces.

Rochat: I ask Citizen Goullé, who attended the Tuesday session and who was able to question Malon: why did he sign the deputies' poster?

Goullé gives a speech, closely attended to, on current events which he says could turn to our advantage. But there is little to expect from the provinces, which must have discouraged Malon. To give an example, the latest events in Roubaix, where a working class mass is summoned by its municipality in the name of honesty to return to their workshops under conditions worse than those prior to the war. And in the department of the Nord there are 700,000 workers who, rallying to this injunction, will be crushed tomorrow beneath this municipal dictatorship.

Aubry: I would say the same of the Seine-Inférieure, where 250,000 workers are in the same situation.

Rochat repeats his question.

The commission returns to session and reads the following proposed manifesto:

International Workingmen's Association

International Workingmen's Association. Federal Council of Parisian sections.

Workers,

A long series of reverses and a catastrophe that appears to be bringing about the complete ruin of our country: such is the balance sheet of the situation created in France by the governments that have dominated it.

Have we lost the qualities needed to lift ourselves from this degradation? Have we degenerated to the point that we resignedly submit to the hypocritical despotism of those who delivered us to the foreigner and only find the energy to render our ruin immediate through civil war?

The latest developments have demonstrated the strength of the people of Paris. We are convinced that a fraternal accord will soon demonstrate their wisdom.

The principle of authority is now powerless to re-establish order in the streets or to put the shop floors back to work, and this powerlessness is its negation.

The lack of solidarity of interests has created general ruin and engendered social war. It is from liberty, equality, and solidarity that we must demand the ensuring of order on new foundations, to reorganize the labor that is its primordial condition.

Workers,

The communal revolution affirms its principles; it casts aside all causes of future conflict. Will you hesitate to give it your definitive sanction?

The independence of the Commune is the guarantee of a contract whose freely debated clauses will put an end to class antagonisms and ensure social equality.

We have demanded the emancipation of the workers, and the Communal delegation is the guarantee of this. It must provide each citizen with the means to defend his rights, to effectively control the acts of his representatives charged with the management of his interests, and to determine the progressive application of social reforms.

The autonomy of each commune excludes any oppressive character from their demands and is an affirmation of the republic in its highest expression.

Workers,

We have fought; we have learned to suffer for our egalitarian principles. We cannot retreat when we can assist in placing the first stone of the social edifice.

What have we asked for? The organization of credit, of exchange, and of association, in order to ensure the worker the full value of his labor; free, secular, and integral education; the right to meetings and association; absolute freedom of the press and that of the citizen; the municipal organization of the police, the armed forces, hygiene, statistics, etc.

We were the dupes of our rulers; we allowed ourselves to be taken in by their game while they alternately caressed and repressed the factions whose antagonism ensured their existence.

Today the people of Paris are clear sighted, and they refuse the role of a child guided by his preceptor. In the municipal elections, product of a movement which they are the author of, they will recall that the principle that presides over the organization of a group or an association is the same one that should govern all of society. And just as they will reject any administrator or president imposed by a power outside them, they will reject any mayor or prefect imposed by a government foreign to its aspirations.

They will affirm their superior right to vote for an assembly that will remain master in their city and to constitute as it deems appropriate their municipal representation without pretending to impose it on others.

Sunday, March 26, we are convinced, the people of Paris will have the honor of voting for the Commune.

The delegates present at the session of the night of March 23, 1871

For the Federal Council of the Parisian Sections
of the International Association,

E. Aubry (Federation of Rouen), Boudet, Chaudesaigues, Coiffe, V. Demay, A. Duchêne, Dupuis, Léo Frankel, Henri Goullé, Laureau, Limousin, Martin Léon, Nostag, Ch. Rochat

For the Federal Chamber of Worker's Societies

Camelinat, Descamps, Evette, Galand, Haan, Jance, J. Lallemand, Lazare Lévy, Pindy, Eugène Pottier, Rouveyrolles, A. Theisz, Very

On the proposal of Rochat and Frankel it is decided that this manifesto will be published as a poster in the twenty arrondissements and every section is to pay ten francs to cover costs. Adopted unanimously.

The meeting is adjourned at 2:00 a.m.

The secretary,
Hamet

Session of Wednesday, March 29, 1871

Chairman, Sevin; Assistant, Rouveyrolles.

Present are; Study Circle, Silversmiths, Hôpital Louis, Woodgilders, Gobelins, Brantôme, Marmite, 2nd and 3rd groups, Faubourg du Temple, Panthéon, Popincourt, the Station and Bercy, Château-Rouge, Batignolles, East, Ternes, Bookbinders.

Reading of the minutes of March 22 and March 23.

Jacquemin: The minutes have me asking if the Committee doesn't compromise the Republic, while I only asked up to what point the International entered into the committee.

Spoetler: I require a rectification to the minutes of the 22nd as well. I didn't ask that there only be sent a delegation in case mediation was necessary. Also, in those of the 23rd, I didn't ask that a unity list be drawn up, but that we support those of the twenty arrondissements who are seated here.

The two minutes are adopted with these rectifications.

Rochat: Citizen Piazza requests admission to the International. It will be necessary to name an inquest committee on this subject, since he is accused of certain acts.

Bertin: A report to Napoleon III on the organization of the army is attributed to Citizen Piazza. I have doubts about his socialism.

Rochat's proposal is adopted. Named are Frankel, Combault, and Rochat.

Goullé asks that the posters of the manifesto be sent to London. Adopted.

Bertin: One of the most serious questions that should concern us is that of the social order.

REPORT OF COMMISSION ON STATUTES OF FEDERAL COUNCIL 249

Our revolution is completed; let's put down the gun and take up our tools.

Goullé is absolutely not of that opinion; we must be on our guard.

Hamet: The Guard is easy to establish; work is less so. Let's take up our tools; at the first sound of the drums we'll know how to find our rifles again.

Frankel: I support this idea. We want to found the rights of the workers, and this right can only be established through moral force and persuasion. Let despots have right—which they understand in their fashion—respected by machineguns.

I have very little time and must be at the Hôtel de Ville . If I came it's to propose the nomination of a commission that will be the intermediary between the Commune and the Federal Council.

After a few observations by Citizens Rouveyrolles and Spoetler, declaring that it is urgent that the same proposal be made to the federal chamber, and others by Citizens Goullé (Henri), Hamet, and Combault on the number of members, the assembly unanimously minus five votes adopts the proposal of Citizen Frankel and fixes at seven the number of members of the commission. Named are Serrailler, Combault, Bertin, Nostag, Goullé (Henri), Hamet, and Léger.

Hamet proposes two meetings weekly, one of which will be on Sundays. Adopted.

The hour of the sessions is under discussion.

Combault: We must choose 9:00 a.m. Obviously each will make sacrifices and will leave aside his family interests. But we shouldn't count too much on everyone's dedication, for we will expose ourselves to having few people at the sessions.

9:00 is adopted. Three votes are cast for 3:00.

Rochat: I repeat a question I posed at the last session. Why has Malon linked up in common cause with the mayors and deputies against the committee? He must be heard here.

This proposal is adopted. Citizen Malon will be summoned for Sunday.

Rouveyrolles insists that the summons state: Citizen Malon *must* present himself, etc. Adopted.

Nostag announces the creation of a newspaper with the title *La Révolution*, and subtitled *International Workingmen's Association, Bercy Section*. I request the opinion of the Federal Council on this subject.

After opposition from Citizen Jacquemin concerning the subtitle, and defense by Citizens Combault and Sevin, the Federal Council declares it has taken note of Citizen Nostag's declaration.

Agenda: Revision of the Statutes.

Hamet: The printed report is submitted to the sections for their information. Each should send in its amendments, and when all the sections have done this we can discuss it. Adopted.

Goullé proposes that the Federal Council withdraw funds from its publicity fund, given that a sum was placed at the disposal of the arrondissements for electoral propaganda. His proposal is adopted.

Combault proposes asking the General Council in London to schedule the next international congress for Paris on May 15. (The proposal had already been submitted by the Social section of the Schools) This proposal, enthusiastically received, is unanimously adopted.

Rouveyrolles requests an investigation into an electoral split that took place in the 19th arrondissement. This question is postponed.

The meeting is adjourned at 11:30.

The secretary,

Hamet

Federal Council of Parisian Sections, Session of April 12, 1871

The Federal Council unanimously adopts the following resolution:

> "Considering that M. Tolain, named to the National Assembly to represent the working class, has deserted his cause in the most cowardly manner, the Parisian Federal Council of the International casts him out and proposes that the General Council in London consecrate this expulsion."

The Federal Council

Sections of the Gare d'Ivry Station and Bercy Assembled Together, Session of April 28

On the proposal of Citizens Nostag, Chaudesaigue, Artru and others;

The assembly decrees:

The Gare d'Ivry and Bercy sections together adopt the children of Citizen Simonot, murdered by the Versaillais.

A family council, composed of citizens Carville, Chollet, and Rossignol, is charged with executing the present decree.

On the proposal of various members:

> Considering that Citizen Persico (Joseph), member of the group, has not presented himself for more than two months at meetings of the group;
>
> Considering that he officially took part in the electoral struggle relative to the Communal elections in a direction contrary to the vote of the groups;

Decrees:

> Citizen Persico (Joseph), professor of music, 24, passage Tocanier, is expelled from the International Association (Station d'Ivry and Bercy sections together);

Notification of the present decree will be sent to the Federal Council.

The secretary,

Nostag

Minutes of the Session of the Federal Council May 3

Chairman, Goullé; Assistant, Nostag.

Present are: Gobelins, Montrouge, Gare d'Ivry and Bercy, Quarries of Monmartre, Batignolles, Richard-Lenoir, Pantheon, Shoe cutters, Rug makers, Malesherbes.

After a discussion, in which Citizens Goullé, Hamet, Nostag, Beauchery, Compas, Beauchart, Féron, and Bonnafaut took part, the following resolution is adopted:

The Federal Council of the International Workingmen's Association delegates Citizens Hamet, Martin, Nostag, Goullé, and Compas to constitute an initiative commission charged with presenting the results of the work of the Parisian sections for the discussion and approval of the Commune.

The commission will have its seat in the Hôtel de Ville and will serve as intermediary between the Federal Council and the Commune.

The members of this commission will report at each session on the results of their work.

They shall be revocable by the Federal Council.

The Federal Council revokes all other commissions acting in its name, named by it for the above mentioned task.

Communication: the Federal Council has received the membership of two new sections.

The secretary of the sessions,

Hamet

Quarries and Paris-Montmartre Sections, Session of May 9, 1871

The following motion was unanimously voted:

> Considering that the Paris Commune has honestly entered the road of the political and social reforms that are noted at the head of our statutes;
>
> The Quarries section of the International Workingmen's Association expresses the wish:
>
> That the Paris Commune, in order to persevere on the road of the progress of the human spirit, decree:
>
> Secular, primary, and professional education, mandatory and free at all levels.

Session of May 10, 1871

Chairman, Compas; Assistant, Nostag.

The three following resolutions are unanimously voted:

Added to the commission already named at the previous session, and formed of citizens Goullé, Nostag, Martin, and Compas, are Citizens Armand Lévy and Beauchard.

Until such time as it is established provisionally and definitively at the Hôtel de Ville , it will hold its sessions and the ministry of Public Works, 2 rue Dominique-Germain, every day at 2:00.

It is charged with the writing of a manifesto to the Internationals of the provinces.

The Federal Council has also received the announcement of the foundation of two new sections.

Present are: Gobelins, Poissonière, Montrouge, Chateau-Rouge, Stephenson, Malesherbes, The Station and Bercy, School of Medicine, Great Quarries, Shoe cutters.

The secretary of the sessions,

Hamet

Quarries Section, Session of May 16, 1871

At its session of May 16, 1871, the Quarries section adopted the following resolution:

The Quarries section declares that it energetically protests against the article inserted in *Le Rappel* of the 22nd and conceived in these terms:

> "We have been assured that Piétri and Bazaine, at this moment in Geneva, attempted to involve the Swiss International in a Bonapartist conspiracy.
>
> "Overtures in this direction were also made to the International of Paris."

Le Rappel before inserting this malevolent attack should have remembered that the International Association, founded in London September 26, 1864 to demand the rights of the workers and assure their emancipation, has never ceased fighting courageously against the Empire.

We are all aware of how many condemnations and persecutions this has earned it. It is as unjust as it is perfidious to lead people to believe, by the ambiguity of the above quoted writing, that the very people who voted the declaration of the Basel congress, signed the two manifestoes during the siege of Paris, and took an active part in the revolution of March 18, can in any shape or form, come to an agreement with a dynastic party to re-establish the monopolies and privileges they want to abolish definitively.

Parisian Federal Council

The following resolution was adopted at the Session of May 17, 1871:

An extraordinary meeting of the Federal Council will take place Saturday the 20th of this month, at a precise hour, to judge the current situation.

The members of the Commune who form part of the International are summoned to that session.

They will have to answer for their conduct at the Hôtel de Ville and will be interrogated concerning the reasons for the split that has occurred within the Commune.

Upon presentation of their booklets, the members will be able to attend this meeting.

Citizens Frankel and Serailler, delegates of the sections and present at the session, voted.

Federal Council of the Parisian Sections, Extraordinary Session of May 20, 1871

Chairmanship of Bastelica.

The Federal Council adopted the following resolutions:

Having heard the explanations of the citizens of the International who are members of the Commune; appreciating the perfect honesty of motive that ruled over their actions, invites them, while safeguarding the cause of the workers, to do all they can to maintain the unity of the Commune, so necessary for victory in the struggle against the government of Versailles.

The Federal Council approves their having called for the openness of their sessions and the modification of Article 3, which establishes the Committee of Public Safety and renders impossible any control over the acts of the executive power, in other words, of this Committee of Public Safety and the delegations.

Present are: Stephenson, Gobelins, Recollets, School of Medicine, Vaugirard, Chateau-Rouge, Batignolles, Hôpital Louis, Popincourt, Vertbois, Couronnes, Ternes, Montrouge, The Gare and Bercy, Marmite,

1st, 2nd, and 3rd groups, Ceramics, Great Quarries of Montmartre, La Villette, Richard-Lenoir, 13th Arrondissement, Poissonière, Acacias, Social Studies Circle, Duval, Bookbinders, Opticians, Faubourg du Temple.

Attending the session: Avrial, Theisz, Serailler, Jacques Durand, Léo Frankel, and Ostyn, members of the Commune.

The secretary of the sessions,

Hamet

Annex 1

To Citizen Gambon, people's representative to the National Assembly at Bordeaux

>Paris, March 17, 1871
>Citizen Gambon:

We have received your good letter and thank you for it. Like you, the Federal Council of the International Workingmen's Association is embarrassed by the obscurity of the political situation. What is to be done? What do the people think in the depths of their consciences?

The delegates unanimously resolved to write to you, as well as Citizens Félix Pyat, Malon, Tolain, Tridon, Langlois, Ranc, Millière, and Rochefort, friends in various ways of the International, to ask if it is at all possible that you attend the session next Wednesday, March 22, Place de la Corderie, at 9:00 p.m. We would be happy to hear you speak, to learn what you think it is practical to do, and finally, how you judge the current events.

The delegates of the Federal Council send you their fraternal greetings.

One of the secretaries for France,

Henre Goullé

78 Boulevard Sébastopol

Annex 2

To Citizen Pindy, or, he not being available, Citizen delegate sitting in the name of the International

>Citizen:

I have the honor and pleasure of presenting you Citizen Wolf of London, my close friend and my former chief in the Garibaldian army. Citizen Wolf, one of the founders of the International in London, wants to carry out a semi-official commission on behalf of the English branch at the Parisian branch of the International.

Greetings and brotherhood,

M.-A. Gromier

2 rue des Martyrs

Annex 3
Fatherland—Humanity!

The fatherland: a word, an error! Humanity: a fact, a truth!

Invented by priests and kings, like the "god" myth, the fatherland has only ever served to establish human bestiality within narrow, distinct limits where it was sheared by the hands of the masters and bled for the greater profit of the latter in the name of the foul fetish.

When the rotten wood of the throne cracked and ruin threatened, the shepherd or, to phrase it better, the butcher, came to an agreement with his neighboring dear brother or cousin. The two crowned wretches then sent out against each other the stupid multitudes who, while the masters laughed behind their backs, went out—these frightened hordes—to kill each other, crying out: "Long Live Glory! Long Live the Fatherland!"

The bloodletting was done! Caesar stopped the killing, embraced his dearly beloved enemy, and had his decimated herd return home, incapable for long months to cause him any problems.

The trick had succeeded.

Today we've had enough! The peoples are brothers and the kings and their lackeys are their only enemies.

Enough blood, enough imbecility. People: fatherlands are no longer anything but words. France is dead! Humanity is here.

Be men and prove it!

Anacharsis Cloots' utopia is coming true. Nationality, an error, a result of birth, is an evil: let us destroy it.

To be born here or there is an act of chance, of circumstances; changing our nationality makes us friends or enemies. Let us repudiate this stupid lottery, a farce of which we have always been the victims.

The fatherland should no longer be anything but a vain word, an administrative classification of no value. Our country is wherever we live free, wherever we work.

Peoples, workers: the light is bursting forth. Let our blindness end. Down with despots; no more tyrants.

France is dead. Long Live Humanity!

Jules Nostag.
From *La République Politique et Sociale*, April 16, 1871.

Annex 4
To the Commune

The Paris Commune is today the only guiding light that shows the workers their path.

Your labor is sacred. You must all work together, you representatives of the oppressed and disinherited, in a word, of all you who have suffered in Paris as long as it has existed.

You must save us! Outside of you we have no hope.

Go forward then, heart high and hand firm: forward! Smash the enemy, march on everything that stands in the way of the people. Don't turn your head before reaching the goal. Bloodshed, screams, weaknesses: may none of this exist for you. The people aren't asking accounts of you: whatever is not us does not exist in the world.

March on your road with a cold, implacable conviction. Destroy the past, both men and things. All means are good. Act, and we'll talk later.

Your right, your virtue is your goal, and success is your duty.

It's a matter of life or death. They want to kill the people, and the people want to live.

It's no longer time to think about philosophers and scholars. They are all are foolish and chatter while the cannons speak.

All Frenchmen are covered in the blood of the French. Today, the assassins are those who refuse combat.

Those who kill the largest number of the enemy are the most humane.

This is no longer a foolish war against a foreigner who we don't know from Adam and Eve; it's the past that wants to kill the future. They want to kill the poor, and the poor want to live.

Listen, representatives of Paris, here is the people's verdict:

In all periods, reaction's sole force was the guarantee of impunity. When it has us in its grips it assassinates us, some of us in public, and the rest in secret. The next day it says that this isn't true, and its police having arranged things the victims become the murderers, and the whole world believes it.

Let anger carry out its task. It alone has conquered in the past; since societies have begun, it alone has ever founded anything.

Stand up proud and avenging! You preside over a holy war! You will save humanity!

>Henri Goullé
>From *La Révolution Politique et Sociale*, organ of the Gare d'Ivry and Bercy sections, issue of April 23, 1871.

Annex 5
Tolain, Langlois, and Versailles

We saw the German and French bourgeoisies acclaim their monarchs last July 12 when war was declared.

In pushing these two proletariats on each other, the most lively and intelligent on earth, they hoped to crush them in a human hecatomb and then divide them through the awakening of international hatred.

That done, they would have fifty years to sleep peacefully, ensured of the maintaining of their privileges, of the growth of their supremacy.

Their calculations were incorrect. They were certainly clever, but the bourgeoisie, emasculated by its morals, by the flabbiness of luxury, and above all by its newspapers, no longer had the energy required to carry out its work among the unforeseen events that could not help but to occur.

Today the bourgeoisie is at Versailles, prostrated before those it adores as its protecting gods: Thiers, Favre, Picard.

Deep down in its conscience, the bourgeoisie tells itself that Thiers is a skillful man. It counts on division in our camp. It has won over Langlois and a renegade, Tolain. This Tolain, this so-called socialist, who it believes has a high position in the General Council in London.

We who understand nothing of the political finesse of Thiers, understand that they place hope in Tolain as a powerful element of discord, destined to lead the proletariat astray into a Caesarite socialism that he will be at the head of.

He is a chief devoted to and forever in the hands of the bourgeoisie. It is true that the bourgeoisie doesn't know that we recognize no chief and that our sole force consists of our never having had one.

Neither Tolain, nor Langlois, or Hugelmann will succeed in creating a Caesarite socialism.

The people are thirsty for probity, dedication, and shining honor. The fire of their anger is never extinguished in their soul.

The people are inextinguishably attached to their noble sentiments during periods of calm.

They judge without malice, but they judge clearly.

Tolain and Langlois, courtiers of the wealthy class, have denied the poor class.

The decree is pronounced: we no longer know them. Under the Empire we believed in their weakness; today, we see them in Versailles accepting our blood as their wages.

It will be up to the Council General in London to pronounce on Tolain for the other branches in the two worlds. It will judge in this case, as is its role.

 Henri Goullé
 La Révolution Politique et Sociale, issue of April 16, 1871

*

Rejected by all parties, this is M. Tolain's current political situation.

It is he who wanted this. He committed suicide with his own hands and has no right to complain.

Fate harshly punishes the guilty.

A worker renegade to his class, he fled his duty. We sent him to the Chamber to demand the rights of the workers.

As it developed, the bourgeoisie of 1789 reduced the working class to the state of flesh crushed in the gears of the social machine. There does not exist a law, an act where the workers have not left a shred of their flesh. We are reduced to degree of poverty previously unknown in universal history. It was Tolain's mission to denounce this to the whole world from the height of the French tribune.

He had the right to say he was the sole representative of the people, since Malon's retirement.

Deserting his post, fleeing his duty as an International, abandoning the workers' cause, he has reached the point where he is selling himself to the rich who, in their turn, reject him.

La Révolution politique et Sociale, issue of May 8, 1871.

Annex 6
Arise, France!

Enough is enough! An end must be put to this!

These fools no longer even have the decency to save appearances.

Versailles, which was no longer anything but an immense bordello where the girls driven out of Paris dragged their shame between Prussians and royalists; where orgies and debauchery were displayed with impunity; where the refuse of the farmyards of the past: Thiers, Dufaure, Favre, Simon, Picard and the other rascals party with your money, France! Versailles has become worse than Coblenz; Versailles mimics Cayenne.

The penal colonies have set loose their prey. The Empire has vomited up its henchmen, Canrobert, MacMahon, Gallifet, Devienne. Excuse me, people, these ruffians have returned. Laughing, they kiss the ham actor Thiers, and we see in a corner the cop Cassagnac cry while wearing Simon's vest.

Look then: it's the Empire. It's the Empire with all its shame, its parade of swindlers, thieves, assassins, and pimps. It's the Empire, manure and blood, that is returning.

Will you finally understand this, France?

And while all is calm and peaceful in Paris, while the woman goes out in the springtime sun to stroll with her children along the boulevards, which the girls and their pimps no longer sully, and the man, down there in the trenches, behind the barricades, is on the alert with his eye on the trigger, for the figure of a Corsican, you wait, people. You wait, provinces. You wait.

France, your freedom is at risk at this moment. That man, that unknown scout who will soon fall from a Versaillais bullet, fights for you, for your salvation, for your independence.

Paris, prodigal child, sheds its blood in torrents to save you.

You always accused it of dictating laws to you, of depriving you of your right to initiative. Despite its heroic defense against Prussia, all you had for it were reproaches, insults, and calumnies.

You held against it the fact that in 1848 it gave you the signal for deliverance, this city that had almost forgiven you for the twenty years of Imperial shame.

And today you allow Versailles to bombard Paris.

Arise, France! Lyon, Marseilles, Toulouse, Lille, Bordeaux. You, the intelligence, the labor, the wealth—the true wealth—arise! Enough of shame, of poverty, of degradation.

Arise, arise you all, you in whose hearts there still remains a spark; you who still have faith, hope, and confidence in the idea. Arise, and crush this mass grave with your contempt, this hideous Monfaucon where from Vinoy the *décembriseur* to the grotesque Aumale, everything that is covered with mud on its face, blood on its fingers, and hatred in the heart, swarms and awaits its moment.

They are all there, all of them. Not a single one is missing.

The occasion is unique; will you allow it to escape you?

No!

Toulouse is armed, Lyon has its red flag, and Marseilles, despite the assassin Espivent, is still active under the blade of the butcher.

The revolution has rent the clouds and awakened the sleeping.

Lazaruses, rise up from your graves; the hour has sounded!

France, arise!

>Jules Nostag
>*La Révolution Politique et Sociale*, April 13, 1871.

The Dawn

The old world is collapsing. The shroud of the deep night that covered the earth is being torn. The dawn appears.

Greetings liberty! Greetings, blessed revolution!

The proletarian, slave of the ancient world, serf of the world prior to '89—different words, same meaning—the proletarian is straightening his body crushed by labor.

Martyr of wage labor, stop suffering; you will win.

You will win, if you want to, and your triumph, watered with your blood, will be that of your brothers around the world who are watching you.

O, sublime worker, yesterday's beast of burden, today's hero, you finally understand that you are the majority, that is, strength, right, and justice. You finally see that your emancipation can only be your own labor; that in a word, you are your savior. Your Christ is you!

Blind, you no longer deny the light. You see, you understand. All is saved!

Dawn rises on the horizon; freedom appears in a blaze. The day has arrived.

O proletarians, O the starving of the world, you thought them dead, and well dead, this old people of Paris, who once gave the world the signal to awaken.

It suffered without a complaint. It had put up with so many chains, its blood had so often flowed without any results that, turning your eyes from the immortal cradle of your own independence, stifling a sigh, you had denied this saving corner of the earth.

Well, you were wrong. This people lived, suffered, waited. The day has come, the hour for combat has sounded. It is there, upright and uncountable, and cries out: "Here I am!"

O old world, you jumble of imposters, corrupted idlers, insolent parasites, all of you who live off the labor of others: do you finally understand that your reign is over and that today, with the people's triumph, labor's era begins?

Will you finally understand that you can no longer squeeze human matter to make it render gold without that bleeding flesh one day resisting?

That day has come! Dare to deny it now.

And we, the *sharers,* finally tired of working while you are idle, we will *share* with you. But not your useless gold—that eternal calumny—but rather our indispensable labor.

Brothers of the whole world, our blood flows for your freedom; our triumph is yours. Arise all!

The dawn has arrived!

Annex 8

General listing of Parisian sections during the Commune.

Indication of their secretaries and their meeting places.

Federal Council of Parisian Sections

6, Place de la Corderie. Meetings every Wednesday at exactly 8:30 p.m.

Secretaries:

For France: Varlin, 8 rue Larrey; Goullé, 78 Boulevard Sébastopol

For overseas: Theisz, 12 rue Gessin; Frankel, 6 Impasse Saint-Sébastien

Of Sessions: Hamet, 41 rue de Jussieu

Treasurer:

Franquin, 40 rue des Blancs-Manteaux, at the Marmite.

Social Studies Circle

Meetings every Monday at 8:00 p.m., Place de la Corderie. Secretary; Ch. Rochat, 380 rue Saint Denis.

Gobelins

Meetings Tuesday 8:00 p.m., 11 rue des Fossés-Saint-Jacques. Secretary: Hamet, 41 rue de Jussieu. Corresponding secretary: Bestetti, 46 rue des Boulangers.

Social of the Schools

Meetings Monday at 8:00 p.m., 3 rue d'Arras, third floor. Delegate to the Federal Council: Buisset, 20 rue des Boulangers.

Brantôme

Wednesday 8:00 p.m., 8 rue Poultier. Secretary: Gandinière, 65 Faubourg Saint-Denis.

Montrouge

Meetings Thursday 8:00 p.m., 110 rue de la Procession. Secretary: Miard, 15 Passage Saint-Victor.

Vertbois

12 rue Phélippeaux, Wednesday at 8:00 p.m., Secretary: Aubert, 8 rue du Fer-à-Moulin.

Gare d'Ivry and Bercy

Friday at 8:00 p.m., 13 Quai de Bercy. General Corresponding Secretary: J. Nostag, same address.

Récollets

Information and meetings, chez Citizen Lévy, 91 Quai Valmy.

Poissonière

Meetings and information, at Boudier's, 138 Faubourg Poissonière.

Combat

Secretary: Delaut, 207 rue de la Chopinette.

Faubourg du Temple

Meetings every Sunday at 2:00 p.m., 108 rue Saint-Maur. Secretary: David, 37 rue Servant.

Great Quarries of Montmartre

Information: Kumenmann, 83 rue Lafayette.

Ternes

Information: Davoust, 29 rue Ponselet.

Couronnes

Folichon, secretary, 34 rue des Couronnes.

Belleville

Meetings 4 rue des Partants. Secretary: Préault, 117 rue Saint-Maur.

Hôpital Louis

Meetings 9 Passage Saint-Joseph Tuesday and Fridays at 8:00 p.m., Minet, Secretary, 14 Passage des Trois-Couronnes.

Marmite, First, Second, and Third Groups

Civil Alimentation Society:

First Group: 8 rue Larrey

Second Group: 40 rue des Blancs-Manteaux

Third Group, 42 rue du Château (Plaisance).

Batignolles

Meetings every Saturday, 3 rue des Dames, Secretary: Combault.

Stéphenson Section

Secretary: Albrand, 45 rue Stéphenson.

Grenelle and Vaugirard

Meetings every Wednesday, 10 rue de Théatre, in Grenelle.

Richard-Lenoir

Meetings every Wednesday at 8:00 p.m., 1 ruelle des Lilas.

La Glacière

Meetings every Monday at 8:00 p.m., 53 Boulevard d'Italie.

Popincourt

Meetings every Monday at 8:00 p.m., Cour Darmoyé, 12 Place de la Bastille.

13th Arrondissement

Secretary: Tardif Martial, 18 Avenue d'Italie, meeting Tuesday at 2:00 p.m. at 5 of the same avenue.

Duval Section

Secretary: Hamet. Meeting Sunday at 3:00 p.m., salle de Juin, 76 Avenue d'Italie. Contact Citizen Pouillet 203 Boulevard de la Station for all information.

Malesherbes Section

The meetings take place Monday and Thursday at 8:00 p.m., 24 rue Malesherbes. Secretary: Bonnefont.

East

Meeting every Sunday at noon, Cour de Miracles. Secretary: Dumontel.

Flourens Section (2nd Arrondissement)

Membership, meetings and information at Citizen L. Laverine, 53 rue Montmartre.

Ivry Section

Membership at Citizen Alexandre at Ivry City Hall; Delaville, 48 rue de Paris in Petit Ivry. Information at Citizen Hamet, 48 rue de Paris in Ivry.

Eugène Vermersch:
The Incendiaries

Eugène Vermersch's *Les Incendiaires*, (The Incendiaries), is sui generis in the canon of Communard writings. Uncompromising in its call for revolutionary violence, it does so in the form of a poem in four sections, each section written in a different classical French verse form. Despite its classical form, its message is purely revolutionary. The flames that dominate the poem and the incendiaries of the title, were the fires and the arsonists who burned down many of Paris's great buildings (most notably the Hôtel de Ville) in the final days of the Commune. While pro-Commune writers have usually explained, apologized for, or denied the intentionality of the fires, Vermersch takes a different tack: the fires were good and right, and were a first step toward the true working-class revolutionary principle of "no more reconciliation." This idea was a constant in Vermersch's thought. He would later write that, "It is more useful to teach a proletarian how to construct or command a battery, to organize a battalion, how to carry out reconnaissance or a retreat than to write a thousand volumes on capital or give a speech in three provincial cities."

Vermersch, like so many Communard journalists, began his career writing against the Empire, activities that earned him two stays in prison. During the siege he served as an ambulance driver while continuing to write, including a sonnet cycle on the bizarre diet (which included rat salami) to which Parisians were reduced.

After a period writing for Vallès's journal *Le Cri du Peuple*, Vermersch became one of the founders, along with Alphonse Humbert and Maxime Vuillaume, of *Père Duchêne*. He fled France with the fall of the Commune and was sentenced to death in absentia in November 1871, by which time he was living in London. He continued to work as a journalist, and while in England he wrote a biographical article on Karl Marx, based on notes dictated by Marx to his daughters, who furnished these notes to Vermersch. The article was published in the French review *L'Illustration*.

As was so often the case with French revolutionary journalists, he continued to found newspapers, and it was in his paper *Qui Vive* that *The Incendiaries* first appeared in 1873.

Vermersch was in many ways a troubled individual, and if he wasn't shy about taking on those in power, he also attacked former comrades. Francis Jourde, Commune member and former delegate for Finance, publicly slapped Vermersch after the latter wrote an article accusing him of being a police informant, and Vermersch fought a duel with Gustave Lefrançais in 1876 when Lefrançais defended Jourde. Sign of his troubled nature can be found in the excerpt here from his pamphlet *Un Mot au Public* (A Word to the Public), in which he delivers an unbridled attack against his unnamed—but omnipresent—foes in the exile community.

Vermersch died in 1878 in a lunatic asylum.

Author's note: It's been about fifteen months since *The Incendiaries* first appeared. In France it caused a great sensation, and when I heard the clamor it caused, both in the Tartuffian newspapers of the conservative republic and in the papers whose ties to the police are well known, I knew that my aim had been true. And, in fact, in saying that the slogan of the coming revolution must be "no more reconciliation" I could not but exasperate anyone who wasn't of the people, everything that would long since have ceased to exist if in every one of their insurrectionary movements the crowd's pity hadn't held back the arm of their justice. Foolish mercy! In order for the goal of the revolution to be reached, for the old society to be liquidated, and for equality to be definitively established, it is enough that on the day when they smash tyranny the people model their conduct on that of their eternal enemies and that they finally take their vengeance. But instead of listening to the counsels of logic they preferred to stupidly smile at the hope of an impossible brotherhood. And yet, how many times were they the master between the night of July 14, 1789 and the morning of March 18, 1871? And is it possible that they have so quickly forgotten how many corpses they've paid with each time they've made the mistake of pardoning reaction? They had barely finished demolishing the Bastille and already the royalists were executing and sending to the penal colonies the patriotic soldiers of Chateau Vieux, had already begun in Nîmes their massacres in the south, and the Parisian bourgeoisie, unfurling the red flag of martial law and under the orders of Lafayette and Bailly, had already trampled on the blood of the poor. Read the tales of the Companions of Jéhu in 1796 and you have to hold your sides from laughing at the ridiculous scaffolds of 1793, which barely deserve to be taken seriously. And the white terror! And the Louis-Philippe riots! And the Rue Transnonain! And the Croix Rousse! And the June days! And the May days! Does anyone find in these events pressing reasons for reconciliation? Experience shows it: the people always grant grace and they are never granted mercy. It is certain that the proletariat and the bourgeoisie are in a state of inevitable war and that one or the other must perish in the battle. It remains to be seen if the 35,000,000 proletarians will always be so resigned as to allow themselves to be decimated by 200,00 families of do-nothings. But at least let them know this: there will never ever be sincere reconciliation between them and the bourgeoisie. The most ardent protests of the privileged are nothing but bald-faced lies dictated by fright, and a people who allow themselves to be taken in are nothing but a people of dupes. Marat already said it in issue 29 of *L'Ami du Peuple*: "Fools that we are, our enemies treat us like imbeciles, and are they wrong? In their eyes we are nothing but ferocious animals whose first snout blow must be avoided, but who can afterwards be led by the nose." The times haven't changed. Now as in the past, the people know how to win, but no more than then do they know how to profit by their victory. And this is why I wanted to again say what I have often repeated elsewhere: "Hit them with your snout!"

London, January 1, 1873

I

Through the dark and ferocious night
Paris burns.
The heavens are blood filled and
history, theater, the convents, homes, chateaus, palaces
which, after the Tiboulets, saw struggle the Fleurys,
all burn
in the whirlwind of flame
that floats over Paris like the banners of a people who
take vengeance with their dying breaths.
Like a sigh the flames of purple and gold rise
toward the secret rooms of the Tuileries,
lick the painted ceilings, the flowered chambers
and devour,
deep within the starry boudoirs,
the precious appointments, the finely fashioned furnishings
the lacquer ware, the paintings, the white statues
whose bare breasts are swollen with virginal pride
shows a horrified world how,
draped in its pride,
Paris falls.
These heavy piles are the proof of solemn facts:
the Louvre too burns and buckles into ruin

with its marbled walls and its gates of steel,
the lair where Mazarin's shade roams
and which trembled the day Camille's voice
told the people to take the Bastille.
Philippe-Egalité's palace is no more;
these blackened walls, this unknown debris
these stones that cover the ground: this was Finance!
This weightless edifice where,
To the sound of the dance, of cups and lovers' kisses,
the traitor Salm sold France to the Germans
and which later consecrated Corinne's breath,
The Legion of Honor is naught but a ruin.
The Palace of Justice, Petri's palace
and the Conciergierie where
the tortured Damiens
Robespierre
Vergniaud
and those from La Rochelle
appear, like three superhuman and sacred flames around
the Sainte Chapelle
And burn together in the eyes of the frightened killers.
That torch over there, yellow and violet
were the docks of La Villette.
Here at hand it's the Cour des Comptes that twists
in the ferocious blaze that bites and smashes as it runs,
its pillars and roof and its library where impure larvae slept
in the files of the imperial world.
Farther away the avenging winds of Prairial
have unleashed their storm on the Gobelins:
the finished silk on the looms
curlingly melts like a child's tress.
The fire is everywhere: immense, triumphant.
It dances on the roof
it crawls in the cellar.
Lead flows like lava,
and on the black streets spreads in silver streams.
Suddenly,
an immense flame emerging from
the frightening city:

The grandiose horror of the cannon, of mines,
dazzling as they destroy a quarter.
And from the trembling and fallen wall,
like the prolonged rumbling of thunder:
the voices the sobs the war cries.
And we see, soaring toward the stars in their surprise
The great soul of the city
That was Paris.
The pitiless flame embraces the Hôtel de Ville
O memories, O history heroic and servile,
O Maison-aux-Piliers! O Etienne Marcel!
Council of the Sixteen! O League! O silence cruel
that gagged Paris for two hundred years.
Commune where, to punish princes,
like the sound of a wind unleashed o'er the sea
Danton's daring covered over Hebert's voice;
balcony that thrice saw
France insulted and sold,
acclaim reclaimed freedom!
Once, in '89 with its ribbons green
on a gentle July night
your word reached out to the old world, O Republic.
It was from there that the epic people
saw on the horizon full of laughter and voices,
the past in flight in the king's carriage.
It was there that it smashed its imperial chains.
It is there that it affirmed Communal might!
O devotion, pride, glory, collapses!
O blood of the people, of our ancestors! O sleeping centuries!
Paris is dead.
And its consciousness in ruins
Floats forever away in the smoke.

When the horrifying flame won the day
A voice within my heart said:
Well done.

II

And yet I love roses
and kiss their closed lips
through the morning's tears.
And the bees, who trail
butterflies through
vermilion buds
know me well.

All my dreams fly
towards the swallows' return,
and glide in the heavens' blue.
A white legion,
They travel through the light
Spread by the dawn,
and through sweet oblivion.

When July comes
I must go to the woods where
quail wander through perfume
and song.
I lose my way, and
the song of the bird hidden in the branches
guides me home.

Lost in the peaceful ravine
I am happy beyond dreams,
no longer knowing where I am.
The wild odor of heather
ravishes me, and
many are the nights when
I slept in clearings

Nothing in my soul
murmurs against the burrs where
the berries bleed, or the lily's pride.
I forgive the blackbirds
their chatter
in the buried leaves.

I love the roses' garb,
the amethyst of violets,
the topaz of fireflies,
the strange luxuriousness of the golden pheasant,
and the orange silk of the oriole
burning on their breasts.

I say not a word against
the spring that streams babbling
over the rocks,
Reflecting the splendor of the skies
like the eyes of the woman,
into which my soul once plunged.

As day dies on Autumn eves,
when I see the purple grapes
that a moon ray pursues,
I forgive the greedy thrushes
who chatter like Flemish women
at midnight at the kermesse.

I hide my serene soul
when eyes sparkle with
triumphant hatred and,
and my lost illusions
appease their saddened lips
on the chaste foreheads of children.

Oh how often have birds of prey,
croaking their cries of joy,
torn my heart with their beaks.
But I purified my soul
with the gentleness of a woman,
and the humility of a sinner.

Despite the storm
I sought
the blue dahlia,

the flower that sings far
from the jealous and the wicked.
I wanted to make a life for myself
pure as a symphony,
white as the whitest wood dove.

During the battle,
during the machine gun's rattle
I aspire
to gentle peace, the dawn, the day,
with no more ferocious ambition
than to kiss the lips on which
will be born
words of love.

I hate war,
and I dream of distant centuries where
the sword will be a scythe;
where glory will go
to heroes strong and calm
who will have offered souls their balm.

And I hope for the blessed hour
when men, that sacred troop,
with milk and with honey,
garbed in white,
will celebrate
universal peace.

III

The victors cried:
Silence the clamor of these malcontents!
To be happy we must purge the earth
of these rascals, these brigands!
Has their like ever been seen?
They cry, scream and carry on
because they're a little bit starved.
They balk, they complain

that we stuff ourselves on cake
when they don't even have bread!

Their words are intolerable;
put down these bitter rebels.
Between us and these rebels
let us put the immensity of the sea.
Their voices at times awaken us
and climb into the rosy dawn,
driving our dreams away.
May the hulks be covered in fog,
and may the desperate lose their way
and drown in the foam.

We want to be rid
of this jealous mob;
this race must be destroyed
that wants to live as we do.
Cut off their hands, sew shut their mouths,
banish these madmen who,
at the moment of their death
still dream of revenge,
and let the seagulls
see to their burial.

Didn't they take it
into their heads that—
like our sons—
they had the right to ripened fruit, to new blossoms?
And didn't they dare proclaim
that work is noble,
speculation vile,
rent unjust?
Didn't these brutes'
doctrines
want us to harden our hands
by handling their tools?

No pity!

The God we rely on
sees to it that when he passes
the rich man
is followed by perfume and rays.
God wanted this, and his creature,
tomorrow dust and rot,
Can't but adore his decrees.
And we owe it to ourselves
to stifle the daring blasphemies
that are their wishes.

We are the chosen, the masters.
We are the predestined ones,
and God subjected all to us
Before we were even born.
Men and things: ours.
The golden sky, the rose's scent: ours.
The woods where play the winds: ours.
A woman's gentle gaze full of fire
and her soft kiss in the tenderness of spring:
ours.

We are fine as we are.
Glory to the young fools
who will kill a hundred thousand
to give us order and peace.
Sound the bugle! Crash the cymbals!
Long live the logic of the bullet!
Nothing is more certain to convince the
mutineer.
Call out the pope's soldiers
and raise the squealers
from the trap doors.

And don't spare the women,
no pity for children.
Sometimes there's a hero in the soul
of a child twelve years old.
Massacre them

as Bonaparte dreamed to do.
Smash this band of scoundrels,
and if a few democrats survive
we can bury them alive
in a penal colony.

IV

O revolution! We had forgotten you and
now you justly punish us for it.
For the vanquished people,
for France chained to the German cart;
for the human brains smashed and smoking on the rue
Transnonain,
for April and
for June,
for the dead who trouble forgetfulness under the African skies,
for reaction and
for the hecatombs;
for our rights sentenced to death,
For December dancing gaily on
                          The graves of our murdered brothers.
For Blidah
for Cayenne and the
               unspeakable horror of
                            prisons on the waters.
We owe these bastards justice:
               the guillotine and the executioner.
O revolution!
I saw your austere visage where
               indignation burned.
You shouted:
Strike the earth with your feet!
               Make it cough up the scaffold.
Between you and these rats
             war is eternal;
                      haven't you learned this?
It's not enough to brand their shoulders:
                        no penal colony and

                                        no more
                                        contempt:
                    Death!

When the prisoner escapes and
                    returns to crime
                                        pity no longer has a
                                        place.
Ask the past what clemency brought it.

O People:
Listen to reason.
Go to the cemetery where your
                    fathers are buried
                                        bullets in their
                                        hearts.
Listen to these words
            and be the avenger of these dead.

But sentimentality has
                    destroyed this race;
                                        In this century,
                                        everyone is innocent.
None of them remember that the bandits
                                        want to kiss them,
                                            their hands red
                                            with blood.
They were spared,
            Indulgence was preached,
                                        the bastards are told
As they retire to their corner:
                    "We forgive you your sins;
                                        rest easy,
                                        brigands that
                                        you are.
You are no longer anything
                    but the defeated;
we won't take a hair of your heads,
                    a penny from your fortune."

And so it was.

The murderers
                traitors
                              highway robbers
                                              all breathe easy.
Bourgeois
        investors
                nobles
                        priests
                              slyly wink.
Today these scoundrels
                          covered in blood to their elbows
                                                    laugh like
                                                           fools,
and mock their past fears with
                          wine and the
                                        kisses of whores.
In Paris,
    on our streets
                      hey trample on our dead:
the gunned down fathers,
the murdered mothers,
the orphans whose cradles were soiled with blood
their hands raised,
                    beg for pity from
                                      the triumphant murderers.
What the future holds of threatening:
                                    the hands of these children;
what the bloody corpses
                will one day say:
the marching orders from
            the mass graves,
the somber call of the
                deportees:

            No!
Triumphant butchers

                No!
Wretches
                No!
You have no idea.

The day will soon come when
                      Children,
            women,
                                  frail hands,
                                      thin arms
                                      will take
                                      up the
                                      gun,
                fearing not your fire,
                          respecting not your
                          cannons.
The weak
        Feeling no fear
                will go to the barricades, and
                              the children
                              will
be our clarion.
On the frightful battlefront
                      the masses will stand erect.
And, rising from the cobblestones
                      to sound the charge
                              The ghost of
May will speak.
It will no longer be a matter of
                      killing in the dark a few squealers,
                              a few
hastily canonized Jesuits.
It will no longer be a matter of
burning three huts to defend a quarter.
No more hesitation!
        No more doubts!
Bourgeois: you will all die,
You killed reconciliation.
Your cries won't save you.

                    You'll vomit up your criminal soul,

invoking Thiers and Judas.
We brought you peace and
                              you wanted war.
Well, this is just how we want it.
This insurrection will
                be the last.
We will found our order too.
Nothing will remain of those famed rascals.
                              Their world will fade
                              away.

And you
        Marat,
             whose eye follows us
                         in our darkness,
                                      we invoke you.
You alone were right:
For the people to reach
                    Its ever fleeing goal
                                 we need,
                                       in broad
                                       daylight,
                         ferocious justice.
With neither hatred
                nor love
its voice, louder than the storm

serenely speaks,
and its calm hand
              raises to the heavens
                              the bourgeois'
                                       severed head.

A Word to the Public

The slanders cast against me recently with a touching unity by the police's newspapers of Paris, as well as by a band of individuals calling themselves revolutionaries who reside in London, force me to provide the public with a few explanations. I ask a thousand pardons for them, but they have become necessary. But let the public be reassured: I will only speak of myself because I must speak of others. The combined insults and lies of the scoundrels on both sides of the straits don't have the talent to impress me, and two and a half years ago I wrote, "It no more matters to me that I be esteemed while alive than that I be rehabilitated after my death." (*Qui Vive!* No. 47) In any case, Proudhon was called a Bonapartist; Marat was accused of selling out to the house of Orleans; Blanqui was publicly called a police informer, with supposed proofs in hand; and Cloots and Hébert were called Prussian agents. I'm not in bad company, and I would rather be with this group than with those who accuse me. But make no mistake: what you are going to read is thus not a justification, but an accusation.

I will lay out the facts as calmly as possible, with neither passion nor anger; for in truth I feel that these people don't deserve the honor of indignation and that it is enough to calmly parade these little comrades before the public.

But, it is said, you attacked the Commune.

The Commune? Not precisely. A certain number of members of the Commune and high civil and military functionaries of March 18, to be sure. I attacked them and I'm proud of it. I didn't wait till we were in London to do this, and *Le Père Duchêne* didn't hesitate to say what it thought of them when they were in government. I said what had to be said to certain people, and this was my right. We are here, and 6,000-7,000 men of the people are in Noumea and the Isle of Pines only because of those who solicited leadership posts in the government without having any of the qualities needed to fulfill them. We are all paying for their stupidity, and the blood of the 30,000 executed during those days in May will forever be on their heads. And we're supposed to fall on our knees before these mighty geniuses. We're supposed to light incense to them. We should sing them hymns and build alters to them. Surely they jest!

I would have failed in my duties as a revolutionary publicist if I hadn't used my independence to speak the truth and hadn't carried out the task incumbent on me in the interests of the people, however slight that task might have been.

Note should be taken of this:

Under the Commune I had neither rank, position, honor, nor favor of any kind. I didn't stick plumes in my hat or embroider flowerpots on my back. I didn't grant myself a daily allocation of 15 francs of the people's money when it was felt that 30 sous sufficed for a National Guardsman. I didn't have myself housed in a palace, myself, my mistress, my kitchen help, my courtiers, and my lackeys. I didn't take advantage of my friendships in order to have the nuns, priests, and squealers released who were arrested by the patriots. I wasn't honest and moderate. I didn't request pardons for traitors and spies. I didn't protest against the executions of Lecomte and Clément Thomas. I didn't make my body a rampart in front of the Bank of France. I didn't decree that they only return those objects in the National Pawn Shop with a value of less than 20 francs to the unfortunates worn out by eight months of incessant war. I didn't fix the daily wage of a Parisian worker at 3 francs 50. I didn't protect property against the proletariat. I didn't think it was better to leave the homes on the Champs Elysées and the noble faubourgs empty rather than house in them the wives and children of those who fought for the triumph of the revolution. I didn't give myself 10,000 francs in order to save myself while on the barricades the people lacked provisions. And I didn't take any strongboxes along with me into exile.

This is why I have the right to speak, and it's why I do speak. This is why I have the right to say that there were imbeciles among the members of the Commune. This is why I said it and why I repeat it.

Nevertheless I must declare that I would have offered no recriminations; I wouldn't have brought up the burning question of responsibility; in a word, I would have remained silent if certain of these men, to whose insufficiencies the people's defeat must be attributed, had sought to have themselves forgotten and assumed the modest attitude that was appropriate after those sad days. If they had given the appearance of wanting to retire and abandon the political scene no one would have attacked them and disturbed them in their solitude. But since far from remaining on the sidelines and having themselves forgotten they proclaim their pretention to one day again take power and confiscate the revolution, it became the duty of all those who have a voice or pen to remind them that they don't exactly deserve floral crowns or triumphal arches. And doing this didn't mean doing carrying out a wicked act, on the contrary, it was doing the work of a revolutionary. Saint Just said "The revolution is in the people and not in the reputation of a few individuals." Indeed! May the individuals disappear and may the revolution be saved!

Such was my conviction, such it still is, and this is what has guided my conduct. And so I have never dug into the past of those I combated. I didn't attack their private lives, which with I didn't even concern myself. I have never reproached them a single one of their acts dating from prior to or after the Commune: I have only concerned myself with their conduct and their political conduct during the insurrection. Why then are they angry? They should have done better and then everyone would have praised them. But what I said history will say, and doubtless more severely. And it is with difficulty that they will persuade posterity that they defeated the regular troops and executed M. Thiers and his ministers in Satory.

*

Deep down my enemies know perfectly well that I am the agent of no party and that I have fewer relations than they with reactionary newspapers, for I never asked them to insert anything at all and they were able to insult and slander me at will without my ever deigning to write them: "You are imposters!"

Since 1871 I've been reviled, ridiculed, caricatured, scorned, and dragged in the mud by reaction. Pen, pencil, newspaper, book, and pamphlet: everything has been used against me by all parties with a relentlessness the like of which you have to go back to the filth spread about Marat to find. And about all this I cared not a fig, and rightly so. All that was needed to complete this was for a so-called revolutionary group to join in with the wretches of the French press and to try to outdo them.

Yes, in London there is a so-called political society that proudly calls itself the "Revolutionary Commune" and which, originally founded by a certain number of serious elements who progressively left the group, became the receptacle of all that is most tarnished among the outlaws. We find there no political ideas, no overall view of things; nothing but vanity, appetites, and fears, and as a principle that of the Jesuits: "By all roads towards one sole goal and we can succeed in everything." Unfortunately they do everything, they dare everything, but even so they don't succeed, and they limit themselves to trying to ridiculously remake a kind of Catiline conspiracy in a hothouse. Their goal is to arrive. They want to pierce, and they do pierce, like an abscess. In order to ruin the man they are angry with all methods are good: lies, calumnies, insinuations, demonstrations. There is no infamy, no turpitude, no ignominy that doesn't find its enthusiastic propagator. Leaders, who seem to be all the more authorized as they are rotten, point out the road and the herd follows. These people are like men who hide in ambush in their dozens, like thieves, and who throw themselves on the man they think they might one day have to fear. We saw them the day when the two individuals I brought before the police went before the tribunal of Bow Street. Forty of them came, and all that was missing was Ali Baba.

These are the people who attack me and who rival the *Figaro*, the *Paris-Journal* and the *Patrie* in invective against me. It's true that I called this gang a "mutual protection society of armed robbers" and that in doing so I was the echo of the revolted public conscience. I knew that this could cost me. But as long as I have the nub of a pencil in my fingers they will not prevent me from saying what I have to say. The political acts of politicians can and must be discussed, even if by the humblest and smallest of those whose representatives they were. And everyone has the right to judge a government that fell after losing a revolution, especially when it pretends to still be the government of the future.

The government of the future!

Yes it would be a lovely spectacle to see these men, covered in the blood of the people, and their hands full of the gold they took from the people's pockets again running their business in the Hôtel de Ville , hiding their faces before the rue Haxo, and then saving themselves by hastily wrapping the wages of the murdered starving in a shred of the red flag.

Rather than see these things may we all die in an endless exile and never set foot again on the soil of the fatherland.

Epilogue

Eugène Pottier: It Isn't Dead

For the survivors of the Bloody Week

They killed it with rifle shots,
with machine gun shots
and rolled it in its flag
into the clay-like earth.
And the mob of fat executioners
thought themselves the stronger,
but none of this changes anything,
Nicolas,
for the Commune isn't dead!

Just as harvesters clear a field,
just as apples are brought to earth
the Versaillais massacred
at least a hundred thousand men.
And these hundred thousand murders,
See what they bring.
But none of this changes anything,
Nicolas,
for the Commune isn't dead!

Though they killed Varlin,
Flourens, Duval, Millière,
Ferré, Rigault, Tony Moilin,
filling the cemeteries.
They thought they cut off its arms,
emptied its aorta.
But none of this changes anything,
Nicolas,
for the Commune isn't dead!

They acted like bandits,
counting on silence.

They killed the wounded in their hospital beds,
and the blood,
flooding the sheets
flowed under the door.
But none of this changes anything,
Nicolas,
For the Commune isn't dead!

Bought-off journalists,
merchants of slander
spread over our mass graves
their flood of ignominies.
Maxim Ducamp, Dumas
vomited up their booze.
but none of this changes anything,
Nicolas,
for the Commune isn't dead!

It's Damocles's sword
That floats over their heads.
At Vallès's funeral
they were made mute.
The fact is there were many of us
who served as his escort;
which proves in any case,
Nicolas,
that the Commune isn't dead!

And so, all this proves to the fighters,
that Marianne's skin is brown;
she's ready to fight and it's time to cry out:
Long Live the Commune!
And this proves to all the Judases
that this is how things are,
and in a short while they'll know,
God damn!
That the Commune isn't dead!

Paris, May 1886

Biographical Index of Names of Communards Mentioned in Texts

Allemane, Jean (1843-1920)—Republican under the Empire and active as an administrator under the Commune. Deported to New Caledonia for his activities, he returned and was an important figure in French socialism in later years, serving as a deputy.

Amouroux, Charles (1847-1885)—Hatmaker. Freemason. Member of the International. Member Commune representing the 4th arrondissement. Member of the external relations commission. Captured during the Bloody Week, he received three sentences to deportation. In New Caledonia volunteered to serve in the French forces fighting the native rebels.

Arnold, Georges (1837-1912)—Architect, member of the Central Committee of the National Guard, member of the Commune for the 18th arrondissement. Sentenced to deportation to New Caledonia, he designed buildings there and was an architect for the city of Paris upon his return from deportation.

Arnould, Arthur (1837-1895)—Employee at the ministry of public instruction. Member of the International. Member of the Commune for the 4th arrondissement. Friend and ally of Bakunin while in exile. Embraced theosophy in his final years.

Aubry, Emile (1829-1900)—Lithographer. Corresponding secretary of the Rouen section of the International. Postal administrator under the Commune. Later an active supporter of General Boulanger.

Avrial, Augustin (1840-1904)—Mechanic. Member of the International. Member of the Commune, representing the 11th arrondissement. Distinguished himself on the barricades during the Bloody Week. Sentenced to death in absentia. Patented a sewing machine of his invention in 1892. Socialist militant until his death.

Babick, Jules (1820-1902)—Freemason, member of the International. Member of the Commune representing the 10th arrondissement. Considered an extreme eccentric, if not a madman, he wore so many medals, along with his Commune and Masonic sashes, that "he jingled as he walked." Later worked as a theater prompter.

Bachruch, Henri (?-?)—Secretary of the German section of the International. Lived for a time in Paris and was a member of the editorial committee of *La Lutte à Outrance*.

Bastelica, André (1845-1884)—Typographer and one of the most influential leaders of the International, for which he was an active propagandist in the south of France. Director of indirect taxation under the Commune. Rallied to Bonapartism after the fall of the Commune.

Beslay, Charles (1795-??)—Engineer. Close friend of and follower of Proudhon. Member of the International. Elder of the Commune, elected by the 6th arrondissement. On the finance commission he ensured that the money held by the Bank of France wasn't touched: "I went to the bank with the intention of protecting it from violence on the part of the extremist party of the Commune." Acquitted of all charges against him after the fall of the Commune. In later years adopted a "liberal socialism."

Billioray, Alfred (1841-1877)—Artist. Member of the Commune and the Committee of Public Safety. Died in deportation in New Caledonia.

Brunel, Antoine (1830-?)—Career officer. Member of the Commune representing the 7th arrondissement. General of the National Guard. Participated in the final defense of Paris.

Camélinat, Zéphirin (1840-1932)—Bronzeworker. Founding member of the International. Director of the Mint under the Commune. The motto on the five-franc piece he struck was "Labor: National Guarantee." Treasurer of the SFIO before World War I. Founding member of the French Communist Party.

Chalain, Louis (1845-?)—Bronze turner. Freemason. Member of the International and the Commune, representing the 17th arrondissement. Served as a police informant in Switzerland while in exile after the fall of the Commune.

Charbonneau, Pierre (1830-1905)—Carpenter. Member of the International. Captain of the National Guard. Deported to New Caledonia.

Chouteau, Henri (1834-?)—Blanquist dissident and member of the International. Joined the revolutionary Masonic Lodge "The Federation" in London in 1872.

Clément, Jean-Baptiste (1836-1903)—Writer. Elected to the Commune for the 18th arrondissement. Served on numerous commissions of the

Commune. Tireless socialist militant until his death. Author of the song "Le Temps des Cerises." Buried near the Mur des Fédérés at Père Lachaise cemetery.

Clément, Victor (1824-?)—Mutualist. Member of the Commune for the 15th arrondissement. Sentenced to three years imprisonment for his role on the Commune.

Combault, Amedée (1837-after 1884)—Jewelry worker. Freemason. Founding member of the International. Defeated in election to the Commune. Continued his International activities after the Commune.

Courbet, Gustave (1819-1877)—One of the greatest of French painters. Member of the Commune for the 6th arrondissement. In charge of the demolition of the Vendôme Column, in payment for which his works were seized after the Commune. Sentenced to prison, he fled to Switzerland.

Demay, Antoine (1822-1884)—Member of the International and the Commune, representing the 3rd arrondissement. Sentenced to death in absentia. After exile in England he returned to France and joined the Parti Ouvrier.

Dereure, Simon (1838-1900)—Cobbler. Member of the International. Member of the Commune for the 18th arrondissement. Sentenced to death in absentia. After a period in exile in New York joined the utopian community in Corning, Iowa.

Ferré, Théophile (1846-1871)—Militant Blanquist and accountant. Member of the Commune elected by the 18th arrondissement. Assistant procurator of the Commune. Tried and sentenced to death he told his judges "I lived free and I intend to die the same way." Executed November 28, 1871.

Frankel, Léo (1844-1896)—Silversmith. Born in Hungary. Member of the International and the Commune, representing the 13th arrondissement. Responsible for many of the Commune's socialist measures, including the abolition of night work for bakers. At the Commune he said, "The revolution of March 18 was exclusively made by the workers. If we do nothing for this class...I don't see what the Commune's reason for being is." Wounded on the barricades during the Bloody Week he fled France and lived in various countries, fighting for socialism wherever he lived.

Franquin, Jules (né Colmia) (1838-?)—Printer, lithographer. Member of the International.

Gambon, Ferdinand (1820-1887)—Lawyer and magistrate. People's representative in 1848 in the Jacobin faction. Member of the Commune, elected by the 10th arrondissement. Fought until the final moments of the Commune and fled to Switzerland, where he joined the International.

Goullé, Albert (1844-1918?)—Journalist and writer. Blanquist and member of the International. Wrote for Jules Vallès's *Le Cri du Peuple*.

Grave, Jean (1854-1939)—One of the central figures of French anarchism in the period after the Commune. Editor for *Le Révolté*, *La Révolte*, and *Les Temps Nouveaux*.

Grousset, Paschal (1844-1893)—Journalist, opponent of the Bonapartist regime. Victor Noir was murdered while acting as Grousset's second in a duel with Pierre Bonaparte, setting off massive anti-government demonstrations. Member of the Commune for the 18th arrondissement. Member of the external affairs commission. Sentenced to deportation to New Caledonia. Escaped along with Henri Rochefort and Francis Jourde. Later an independent socialist deputy.

Hamet, Jules (1848-after 1879)—Wood gilder. Member of the International. Signatory in 1870 of the anti-war manifesto addressed to the workers of all nations.

Humbert, Alphonse (1844-1922)—Militant Blanquist. Journalist at *Le Père Duchêne*. After his return from exile was a Radical Socialist deputy and municipal councilor.

Jourde, Francis (1843-1893)—Accountant. Freemason. Member of the Commune for the 5th arrondissement. Member of the finance commission. Author of the decree on the postponing of payments due, the National Pawn Shop, and pensions for widows of fallen National Guardsmen. Attacked for being too respectful of the money held in the Bank of France. Sentenced to deportation in New Caledonia, escaped with Grousset and Rochefort.

Lacord, Emile (1838-?)—Chef. One of the International's most active members. Failed in his election to the Commune. Continued his socialist activities in exile. Died in Paris in extreme poverty, selling fried potatoes on the streets.

Langevin, Camille (1843-1913)—Metal turner. Member of the Commune for the 15th arrondissement. Sentenced to deportation, but had already fled France. Active in the cooperative movement after the amnesty.

Lefrançais, Gustave (1826-1901)—Schoolteacher and accountant. Member of the International. Member of the Commune, representing the 4th arrondissement. Member of the Commune's executive and labor commissions. Fought on the barricades at the Bastille and the Arsenal during Bloody Week. In exile in Switzerland sided with the Bakuninists in their fight with the Marxists in the International. Eugène Pottier dedicated "The Internationale" to Lefrançais.

Lévy, Armand (1827-1891)—Journalist. Freemason. Advocate of "imperialist democracy" and defender of oppressed nations and the working class. Failed candidate for the Commune.

Levy, Lazare (1844-?)—Optician. Member of the International. Secretary at the ministry of public works during the Commune. Sentenced in absentia to deportation, later deported to Germany after conviction for fraudulent bankruptcy.

Lissagaray, Prosper Olivier (1838-1901)—Journalist and writer. Fought at the barricades and edited two newspapers under the Commune. In exile grew close to Eleanor Marx, who translated his *History of the Paris Commune of 1871*. Later active in the fight against Boulanger and in support of Dreyfus.

Macdonel, Paul (1832-?)—Carpenter. Member of the International. Sentenced to death in absentia. Politically active in England while in exile and member of the Masonic lodge "The Revolution."

Meillet, Léo (1843-1909)—Law clerk. Freemason. Member of the International. Member of the Commune, elected by the 13th arrondissement. Member of the justice and external relations commissions and the first Committee of Public Safety. Sentenced to death in absentia. Elected deputy in 1898 as an independent socialist.

Michel, Louise (1830-1905)—Central figure of French anarchism. Held no position on the Commune but fought actively at the barricades. Deported to New Caledonia she never ceased her anarchist activities. An historian of the Commune wrote of her: "She was always adored by those who knew her, esteemed by those she fought, venerated by those who esteemed her big heart and admired her valor."

Minet, Jules (1835-?)—Porcelain painter. Member of the International. Delegate to the ministry of public works under the Commune. Sentenced to deportation in absentia, he died in poverty in exile.

Miot, Jules (1809-1883)—Pharmacist. Democratic socialist representative in 1848. Member of the International and the Commune, representing the 19th arrondissement. Member of the commission that proposed the establishing of the Committee of Public Safety. Sentenced to death in absentia. Politically active in exile, though he withdrew from politics upon his return to France after his pardon.

Mortier, Henri (1843-1894)—Jigsaw operator. Blanquist. Member of the International. Member of the Commune for the 11th arrondissement. Presided over committee for pensions and indemnities of widows and orphans. Sentenced to death in absentia. Lived most of his remaining years in exile, continuing his Blanquist activities.

Noro, Jean-Baptiste (1842-?)—Painter. Commander of a National Guard battalion. Sentenced to deportation in absentia. Joined the Section for Propaganda and Revolutionary and Socialist Action in Geneva.

Nostag, Gaston (né Buffier) (1845-?)—Writer and wine merchant. Member of the International. Edited the newspaper *Révolution sociale et politque* during the Commune. Sentenced to deportation in absentia. Raised poultry while in exile.

Ostyn, Charles (also Hosteins, Francois) (1823-1912)—Turner. Member of the International. Member of the Commune for the 19th arrondissement. Sat on the subsistence and public services commissions. Sentenced to death in absentia. While in exile allied himself with the anarchists. In 1971 his hometown of Colombes renamed the rue Thiers the rue Ostyn.

Parizel, François (1841-1877)—Physician. Member of the Commune, representing the 7th arrondissement. Exiled to the U.S., where he was active in the socialist movement, dying in Newark, New Jersey.

Pillot, Jean-Jacques (1808-1877)—Ordained priest, though he never practiced. Neo-Babouvist communist member of the International. Member of the Commune for the 1st arrondissement. Accused of having set the fires at the Louvre and the Tuileries. Sentenced to life imprisonment, he died in jail.

Pindy, Jean-Louis (1840-1917)—Carpenter. Member of the International. Member of the Commune for the 3rd arrondissement. Ordered the fire at the Hôtel de Ville . Sentenced to death in absentia. Lived in Switzerland and was an active anarchist.

BIOGRAPHICAL INDEX   293

Protot, Eugène (1839-1921)—Lawyer. Member of the Commune, representing the 17th arrondissement, though also elected by the 2nd arrondissement. Delegate for justice, he proposed that judges be elected by the National Guard. Sentenced to death in absentia. Of Blanquist tendencies, he was a fierce opponent of Marx.

Reclus, Elisée (1830-1905)—World renowned geographer and early follower of Bakunin. Member of the National Guard, he was captured during the failed sortie of April 3. Sentenced to ten years banishment by a military tribunal. Returned to France in 1890 and was a tireless propagandist for anarchy till his death.

Regère, Dominique (1816-1893)—Veterinarian. Member of the International. Member of the Commune for the 5th arrondissement. Member of the finance commission. Arrested after the fall of the Commune, claimed he only acted under pressure from his voters and attacked the Commune. Sentenced to deportation.

Rigault, Raoul (1846-1871)—Student, journalist. Procurator and member of the Commune for the 8th arrondissement. Intimately involved in the hostage question, he ordered the execution of at least nine men during the Bloody Week. Accused of the setting of several fires. Arrested May 24 he was executed immediately. Also sentenced to death in absentia in June 1872.

Rochat, Charles (1844-?)—Accountant. Member of the International. Secretary of the Commune's executive commission. Commanded a battery of five artillery pieces during the final days of the Commune. Sentenced to deportation. Continued as a militant of the International upon his return to France.

Rochefort, Henri (1831-19130—Indefatigable propagandist. Exiled under Napoleon III for his writings in *La Lanterne*, upon returning to France he led Victor Noir's funeral cortège. Refused to be a candidate for the Commune. Arrested by the Prussians he was sentenced by the Versaillais to deportation, from which he escaped. Main propagandist for the Boulangist movement, and later a virulent anti-Semite and opponent of Dreyfus.

Serraillier, Auguste (1840-?)—Bootmaker. Member of the International. Member of the Commune for the 2nd arrondissement. Member of the labor and exchange commission. Sentenced to death in absentia. Befriended by the Marx family while in exile; relations that ended after a financial disagreement with Marx's son-in-law Paul Lafargue.

Sicard, Auguste (1839-after 1911)—Crinoline maker. Member of the Commune for the 7th arrondissement. Said to be "the soul of the administration of the 7th arrondissement." At the barricades on March 18. Supporter of the Committee of Public Safety. Sentenced to deportation. Lived in exile in London.

Spoetler, Jean (1834-?)—Chair maker. Captain of the National Guard. Denied his support for the International. Sentenced to five years banishment.

Theisz, Albert (1839-1881)—Bronze carver. Member of the International. Member of the Commune for the 18th arrondissement (also elected by the 12th). Member of the labor commission. Fought on the barricades during the Bloody Week. Sentenced to death in absentia. Participated in the International's activities in London while in exile. Worked at Rochefort's *L'Intransigeant* upon his return to France in 1880.

Tolain, Henri (1828-1897)—Bronze carver. Freemason. Proudhonian. Founding member of the International. Hostile to the Commune and supported the Versailles government. Expelled from the International.

Urbain, Raoul (1851-1902)—Schoolteacher. Member of the Commune for the 17th arrondissement. Member of the education commission. Opponent of religious schools and supporter of the execution of the hostages. Captured after the fall of the Commune and sentenced to forced labor for life in a penal colony. Later active in the cooperative movement.

Vaillant, Edouard (1840-1915)—Engineer. Blanquist. Member of the International. Member of the Commune for the 8th arrondissement. Member of the executive commission. Proposed worker control of abandoned workshops and oversaw the reopening of Paris' museums. Fought on the barricades till the final moments. Sentenced to death in absentia. In London became a friend and ally of Marx in the fight with Bakunin.

Vallès, Jules (1832-1885)—Revolutionary journalist and writer. Member of the Commune for the 11th arrondissement. His *Le Cri du Peuple* was the most successful of Communard newspapers. Sentenced to death in absentia. His novel *Le Révolté* tells of his experiences during the period. 60,000 people accompanied his coffin to Père Lachaise cemetery.

Varlin, Eugène (1839-1871)—Bookbinder. Leader of the International. Member of the Commune, elected by three arrondissements, serving for the 6th. Member of several commissions. Served on the barricades during the Bloody Week and attempted to prevent the execution of the hostages on the rue Haxo. Captured on May 28 and summarily executed, shouting "Vive la République! Vive la Commune!"

Vésinier, Pierre (1824-1902)—Journalist. Member of the International. Member of the Commune for the 1st arrondissement. Editor in chief of *Paris Libre* and directed the *Journal Officiel* during the Commune's final weeks. Sentenced to death in absentia. Described by a contemporary as "one of the least sympathetic personalities of the Commune."

Viard, Pompée (1836-1892)—Paint merchant. Member of the Commune for the 20th arrondissement. Delegate for subsistence and security. Sentenced to death in absentia. In exile grew close to the Blanquists and died an anarchist.

www.ingramcontent.com/pod-product-compliance
Lightning Source LLC
Chambersburg PA
CBHW022052160426
43198CB00008B/205